FIRSTLIVE

MESSAGE FROM THE PUBLISHER

FirstLive guide is for the fan and the musician. If you work in the music industry, you are likely one or the other, or both. In the guide, there are more than 100 detailed profiles of full-time music venues plus a list of additional noteworthy venues. The venues are listed in alphabetical order by neighborhood, and provide the music genre(s), venue type, admission and drink price ranges, cross-streets, tech specs, and more.

Live music is a way of life. The venues profiled in this guide will be around for years to come. It's taken 18 months to make FirstLive a reality. In the process, we wondered how many venues would come and go. We lost one Brooklyn venue, due to closure. Amusingly, there were more subway line changes than venue changes. We extend our gratitude to the incredibly dedicated people that make New York City the best city in the world for live music — venue owners, managers, bookers, sound engineers, bands, friendly door and security staff; and FirstLive contributors — writers, editors, photographers, and the multimedia team.

Community is important to us. New York City is a better place as a result of organizations such as The Jazz Foundation, Music Unites, Road Recovery, Sickday House Calls, and the Staten Island Creative Community. We are committed to donating 10% of the proceeds from the sale of FirstLive guide to these organizations. Go to page 172 for more information.

We want your feedback! As cool and informative as we think this guide is, we look forward to making it better. For dynamic and interactive content visit our website, or download a mobile media application.

Whether you are a local or from abroad, FirstLive looks forward to being your guide to live music venues in New York City!

Danny Garcia,
Publisher and Founder
danny@firstliveguide.com
347-531-6372

www.firstliveguide.com
twitter.com/firstlive
facebook.com/firstlive

DANNY GARCIA, PUBLISHER
EMILY NIEWENDORP, SENIOR EDITOR

CONTRIBUTORS:
Stephanie Summerville, Editor
Monica U. Garcia, Writer/Editor
Daniel Morrow, Writer/Editor
Bill Nevins, Writer/Editor
Mark Osborne, Writer/Editor
Nick D'Amore, Writer/Editor
Jasmine Lovell-Smith, Writer/Editor
Jason Siegel, Writer/Editor
Rachel Antonio, Writer
Allie Arias, Writer
Kyle Benson, Writer
Ruth-Anne Damm, Writer
Robbie Gonzalez, Writer
Sari Henry, Writer
Aidan Levy, Writer
Dmitry Iyudin, Writer
Heather McCown, Writer
Jen Meola, Writer
Erika Omundson, Writer
Sarah Oramas, Writer
Paula Pahnke, Writer
Benjamin Ramos, Writer
Laura Sherman, Writer
Brian Thunders, Writer

ONLINE CONTENT CONTRIBUTORS:
Videographers: Kelly Nesper, Jason Siegel, Jen Meola, Ariel Zino, Mikey Burgoyne, Todd Bryant, Heather McCown
Audio Engineers: Victor Munoz, Mikey Burgoyne, Lenny Bernardez

All Photographs by Danny Garcia
*except where noted
FirstLive Contributing Photographers:
Jasna Boudard, Rupert Hitchcox, Eric Reichbaum
Layout & Design: Danny Garcia
Creative Assistant: Daniel Morrow
Cover & Logo Design: John Bergdahl
www.johnbergdahl.com
Maps: Ben Ramos
Venue Coordinator: Rachel Martinez

ADVERTISING & DISTRIBUTION:
danny@firstliveguide.com

1st Edition Print: 2011-12

Copyright © 2011 FirstLive™
All rights reserved. No part of this book may be reproduced or transmitted in any form or by any means, electronic or mechanical, including photocopying, recording, or by any information storage or retrieval system, without permission in writing from the Publisher.

Contents

MANHATTAN DOWNTOWN

	5

TRIBECA
92YTribeca	7
Canal Room	8

SOHO
City Winery	10
Don Hill's	12
Jazz Gallery	13
SOB's	14

NOHO
Ace of Clubs	15
Bowery Poetry Club	16

CHINATOWN
Fontana's	18
Santos Party House	20

LOWER EAST SIDE (LES)
Arlene's Grocery	22
The Bowery Ballroom	24
Cakeshop	25
The Delancey	26
Fat Baby	27
The Living Room	28
The Local 269	29
Mehanata	30
Mercury Lounge	31
National Underground	32
Parkside Lounge	33
Pianos	34
Rockwood Music Hall	36

EAST VILLAGE
Banjo Jim's	37
The Bowery Electric	38
Dominion	40
Lakeside Lounge	41
Lit Lounge	42
Joe's Pub	43

Jules	44
Nublu	45
Nuyorican Poets Cafe	46
Sidewalk Cafe	47
Webster Hall	48
The Studio at Webster Hall	49

GREENWICH VILLAGE
Bar Next Door	50
The Bitter End	51
Blue Note	52
Cafe Wha?	54
Groove	55
Kenny's Castaways	56
Le Poisson Rouge	58
Sullivan Hall	60
Red Lion	62
Terra Blues	63
Village Underground	64
Village Vanguard	65
Zinc Bar	66

WEST VILLAGE
55 Bar	68
Caffe Vivaldi	69
Cornelia St. Cafe	70
Fat Cat	72
Garage	73
Smalls	74

ADDITIONAL VENUES 76-77
169 Bar (Chinatown)
ABC No Rio (LES)
Arthur's Tavern (West Village)
B Flat (Tribeca)
Crash Mansion (LES)
The Duplex (Greenwich Village)
Marie's Crisis (West Village)
Otto's Shrunken Head (East Village)
R Bar (SoHo)
Tammany Hall (LES)

Contents

MANHATTAN MIDTOWN 79

GRAMERCY
Jazz Standard	80
Rodeo Bar	82

MURRAY HILL
The Kitano	84

CHELSEA
Highline Ballroom	85
Hill Country	86

GARMENT DISTRICT
Madison Square Garden	88
Manhattan Center	89

MIDTOWN
Carnegie Hall	90
Miles' Cafe	91
Radio City Music Hall	92
Terminal 5	93
Tutuma Social Club	94

THEATER DISTRICT
B.B. King	95
Best Buy Theater	96
Don't Tell Mama	99
Iridium	100
Swing 46	101

ADDITIONAL VENUES 102-103
Birdland (Theater District)
Gramercy Theater (Gramercy)
Guantanamera (Midtown West)
Hard Rock Cafe (Theater District)
Hiro Ballroom (Chelsea)
Irving Plaza (Gramercy)
Roseland Ballroom (Theater District)

MANHATTAN UPTOWN 105

UPPER WEST SIDE
Beacon Theatre	106
Dizzy's Club Coca Cola	107
P&G Bar	108
Smoke	109

UPPER EAST SIDE
Bar East	110

SPANISH HARLEM
Camaradas	111
FB Lounge	112

HARLEM
Showmans	113
Shrine	114
St. Nick's Jazz Pub	115

ADDITIONAL VENUES 116
Apollo (Harlem)
Cleopatra's Needle (Upper West Side)
Cotton Club (Harlem)
Feinstein's (Upper East Side)
Lenox Lounge (Harlem)

BROOKLYN NORTHSIDE 119

WILLIAMSBURG
Brooklyn Bowl	120
Bruar Falls	122
Glasslands	123
Knitting Factory	124
Music Hall of Williamsburg	125
Lovin' Cup Cafe & Cameo Gallery	126
Pete's Candy Store	128

Continued on next page

Contents

WILLIAMSBURG cont.
Public Assembly	130
Spike Hill	131
The Trash Bar	132
Union Pool	134
Zebulon	136

GREENPOINT
Matchless	137

BUSHWICK
Goodbye Blue Monday	138
Pine Box Rock Shop	139

ADDITIONAL VENUES   140
The Charleston (Williamsburg)
Coco66 (Greenpoint)
Europa (Greenpoint)
The Gutter (Williamsburg)
Tommy's Tavern (Greenpoint)

BROOKLYN CENTRAL   142

PARK SLOPE
Barbes	143
Puppets Jazz Bar	144
The Rock Shop	145
Southpaw	146
Union Hall	148

GOWANUS
The Bell House	150
Littlefield	152

RED HOOK
Bait & Tackle	154
Jalopy	155
Rocky Sullivan's	156
Sunny's Bar	157

DUMBO
Galapagos Art Space	158

ADDITIONAL VENUES   159
BAM (Fort Greene)
Douglass Street Music Collective (Gowanus)
Fifth Estate (Park Slope)
Hank's Saloon (Boerum Hill)
Ibeam (Gowanus)
Sycamore (Ditmas Park)
Tea Lounge (Park Slope)

MAP KEY   160
Downtown	161-163
Midtown	164-165
Uptown	166-168
Brooklyn	169-171

COMMUNITY PAGES   172
Art By The Ferry	173
The Jazz Foundation	174
Music Unites	175
Road Recovery	176
Sickday House Calls	Inside Back Cover

OUR PARTNERS & FRIENDS
BMI	Inside Front Cover
17th Street Photo:	
Audio-Technica	178
Skullcandy	179
Arcadia Media	180
Arlene's Grocery	181
Brooklyn Bowl	182
Pine Box Rock Shop	183
TC Electronic	184
TC Helicon	185
Germ Music	186

REFERENCES   187-189
QUOTES & THANKS   190-192

MANHATTAN DOWNTOWN

	GENRE	PAGE
TRIBECA		
92YTribeca	ALL: ROCK, POP, FOLK, R&B, EXPERIMENTAL	7
Canal Room	ROCK, POP, '80s, TRIBUTE	8
SOHO		
City Winery	ROCK, FOLK, SINGER-SONGWRITER	10
Don Hill's	ROCK 'N' ROLL	12
Jazz Gallery	JAZZ	13
SOB's	WORLD & URBAN: BRAZILIAN, AFRICAN, LATIN, HIP-HOP, R&B	14
NOHO		
Ace of Clubs	VARIOUS: ROCK, POP, INDIE, PUNK, METAL	15
Bowery Poetry Club	ALL: "EXPECT THE UNEXPECTED"	16
CHINATOWN		
Fontana's	VARIOUS: ROCK, POP, INDIE, PUNK, METAL	18
Santos Party House	ALL MODERN MUSIC: ROCK, POP, HIP-HOP, WORLD	20
LOWER EAST SIDE (LES)		
Arlene's Grocery	ROCK, POP, FOLK, INDIE	22
The Bowery Ballroom	ROCK, POP, INDIE	24
Cakeshop	ROCK, POP, INDIE, EXPERIMENTAL	25
The Delancey	ROCK, POP, PUNK, INDIE, METAL, DJ, BURLESQUE	26
Fat Baby	VARIOUS: ROCK, POP, INDIE, DJ	27
The Living Room	ROCK, POP, FOLK, SINGER-SONGWRITER	28
The Local 269	ROCK, PUNK, INDIE, BLUES, JAZZ, SINGER-SONGWRITER	29
Mehanata	WORLD: GYPSY PUNK, CABARET	30
Mercury Lounge	VARIOUS: ROCK, POP, INDIE	31
National Underground	ROCK, POP, FOLK	32
Parkside Lounge	ALL: ROCK, POP, FOLK, WORLD, BLUES, COMEDY	33
Pianos	ROCK, POP, FOLK, INDIE	34
Rockwood Music Hall	INDIE, POP, WORLD, FOLK, JAZZ, R&B, ECLECTIC	36
EAST VILLAGE		
Banjo Jim's	FOLK: BLUEGRASS, ROOTS, ALT. COUNTRY	37
The Bowery Electric	ROCK, POP, PUNK, DJ	38
Dominion	ROCK, POP, JAZZ, R&B, WORLD, DJ	40
Lakeside Lounge	ROCK 'N' ROLL, COUNTRY, GARAGE	41
Lit Lounge	ROCK, PUNK, INDIE, METAL	42
Joe's Pub	ALL GENRES, THEATER, MUSICALS, CABARET	43

Continued on next page

Downtown Manhattan

MANHATTAN DOWNTOWN

EAST VILLAGE cont.	GENRE	PAGE
Jules	JAZZ	44
Nublu	JAZZ, WORLD, DJ	45
Nuyorican Poets Cafe	POETRY, HIP-HOP, WORLD, COMEDY	46
Sidewalk Cafe	ANTIFOLK, INDIE, FOLK, EXPERIMENTAL	47
Webster Hall	VARIOUS: ROCK, POP, FOLK, INDIE, PUNK, ELECTRONIC, DJ	48
The Studio at Webster Hall	VARIOUS: ROCK, POP, FOLK, INDIE, PUNK, ELECTRONIC, HIP-HOP	49

GREENWICH VILLAGE

Bar Next Door	JAZZ	50
The Bitter End	VARIOUS: ROCK, POP, FOLK, R&B, FUNK, BLUES	51
Blue Note	JAZZ (LATE NIGHT: R&B, FUNK, SOUL, HIP-HOP)	52
Cafe Wha?	R&B, WORLD	54
Groove	R&B (SOUL, FUNK), BLUES	55
Kenny's Castaways	ROCK, POP, FOLK, BLUES	56
Le Poisson Rouge	ALL: CLASSICAL, ROCK, METAL, FOLK	58
Sullivan Hall	ROCK, POP, INDIE, JAM, ECLECTIC	60
Red Lion	ROCK, POP, FOLK, COVER, TRIBUTE	62
Terra Blues	BLUES	63
Village Underground	VINTAGE ROCK, FUNK, R&B, REGGAE, COVER	64
Village Vanguard	JAZZ	65
Zinc Bar	JAZZ, WORLD	66

WEST VILLAGE

55 Bar	JAZZ, BLUES	68
Caffe Vivaldi	CLASSICAL, JAZZ, WORLD, COUNTRY, POP, ROCK	69
Cornelia St. Cafe	JAZZ, THEATER, POETRY	70
Fat Cat	JAZZ, WORLD	72
Garage	JAZZ	73
Smalls	JAZZ	74

ADDITIONAL VENUES

	NEIGHBORHOOD	76-77
169 Bar	Chinatown	
ABC No Rio	LES	
Arthur's Tavern	West Village	
B Flat	Tribeca	
Crash Mansion	LES	
The Duplex	Greenwich Village	
Marie's Crisis	West Village	
Otto's Shrunken Head	East Village	
R Bar	SoHo	
Tammany Hall	LES	

92YTRIBECA

200 Hudson St | New York, NY 10013 | 212-601-1000
Hours: Mon-Tue 9a-3p, Wed 9a-10p, Thu-Fri 9a-mid, Sat 5p-mid, Sun 10a-3p
Subway: 1,2 or A,C,E to Canal St
www.92YTribeca.org

Written by: Ben Ramos

DRINKS: $ - $$ Full Bar FOOD: Cafe	ATMOSPHERE Non-Profit Cultural & Community Center	ADMISSION Free - $15 *All Ages	VENUE TYPE Mid-Size Room, Table Seating, VIP Area	MUSIC TYPE ALL: Rock, Pop, Folk, Experimental, Ambient

TRIBECA
Corner of Canal St & Hudson St

92YTribeca is a sophisticated multi-purpose community center with a mainstage, gallery, cafe, lounge, screening room, lecture hall and more. Opened in 2008, the mission of 92YTribeca is to be "a home for artists who are willing to experiment" and "use [their] stage to try something no one has seen before." It is an additional location to the 92Y on 92nd Street, and geared towards singles, couples and families in their 20s and 30s.

The management believes that NYC audiences have broad interests in music, art and film that often transcend a particular genre or scene.

"We present a wide range of artists, cross pollinating between indie rock and dance music, jazz and world, hip-hop, punk and bluegrass, new music and singer-songwriters, at a venue where one can see progressive, contemporary, exciting work," says Michele Thompson, the club's director.

At first glance, the live music space has a sterile feel—but when the performance begins, it becomes apparent that this multi-purpose space at 92YTribeca was designed to establish rapport between the audience and artist. Magenta-tinted up-lighting glows above a comfortable, L-shaped red leather couch. Pendant light fixtures dot the ceiling like stars over little cocktail tables, with candles giving the space a classy lounge-like atmosphere. The unfinished concrete slab floor and slightly raised wooden stage with its simple red curtain and fixed lighting keep the venue grounded in performance functionality. The overall cleanliness and multi-media capabilities suggests an avant-garde rather than frenzied night club experience.

The cafe at 92YTribeca also hosts live performances by emerging musicians, DJs, poets and other artists in a more mellow environment. Music events tend to occur Friday and Saturday evenings with some variation. The Sunday morning all ages/family show is music oriented.

Tech Specs
Mixing Console: Yamaha LS9-32ch
Mains & Monitors: (2) Meyer Sound CQ-1 Active FOH speakers, (2) UPA1-P room fills, (1) EAW LA128Z Subwoofer (6) Mackie SRM-450 active stage monitors, QSC Power Amps
Stage Size: Depth: 14', Width: 26', Elevated 30"
Lighting: ETC Smart Fade Lighting Console, ETC Smart Pack 12 x 10 amp Dimmers, 12 Source Four Jr. Zoom, 8 Apollo Smart Color Scrollers
Recording capabilities: Audio/Video
Video Projection: NEC NP-4000 Projector, Front video Projection Screen 160"W x 90"H, SONY BRC-300 Pan/Tilt Video Camera
Other: Green room, dressing room

Downtown Manhattan

CANAL ROOM

285 West Broadway | New York, NY 10013 | 212-941-8100
Hours: Office 10:30a-6:30p, Doors 7:30 or 8p
Subway: A,C,E to Canal St | 1 to Canal St
N,Q,R or J, or 6 to Canal St
www.canalroom.com

Photo: Rupert Hitchcox

Written by: Jason Siegel

MUSIC TYPE	VENUE TYPE	ADMISSION	ATMOSPHERE	DRINKS: $$
Various: Rock, Pop, '80s, Tribute Bands	Mid-Size Club Capacity 400	$10 - $25	Intimate, Upscale Showcase Venue	Average $6 - $12 FOOD: no

TRIBECA — Corner of West Broadway & Canal St

Canal Room has created a name for itself by hosting big names in music and persevering through challenging years—ultimately, finding its identity.

Situated on the border of Tribeca and SoHo, Canal Room fits well into both neighborhoods being a polished space designed specifically for live performances and DJ shows. The stage is expansive and the focal point of the room; whoever is commanding the stage—independent artist or private event host—is supported by a dynamic sound system and acoustics.

Photo Courtesy of Canal Room

In its exuberant way, Canal Room has brought the vaguely outre tribute band idea back into the mainstream. On Saturday nights the *Back to The '80s* show is a smash hit with the live band, Rubix Kube, playing hits from that glorious decade. The band performs in full costume, while the crowd packs the room, many dressed in '80s-style gear themselves. The venue also hosts band-specific tributes, from U2- imitators to The Police impersonators. During the week NYC-based and touring acts rules the stage.

HISTORY

The Canal Room was opened by Sam Lott and Marcus Linial in 2003. Marcus has been involved in the music business for years, even releasing a rap album on J Records back in 2001. The two men also owned Shine, the club that existed in the same spot before Canal Room. They closed Shine when the lease ended, renovated the space for several months and reopened as Canal Room. While Shine focused on record company events—showcases and release parties for signed artists—Canal Room has become a distinct venue, with a schedule of national and local performers.

In its early days, Canal Room booked national touring acts, such as Jay Z, Elvis Costello and John Legend. Being at the tip of Tribeca also gave Canal Room the opportunity to host the American Society of Composers, Authors and Publishers (ASCAP) Music Lounge Series, which, until 2008, was a part of the Tribeca Film Festival. From '04 to '08, Canal Room hosted five straight days of forty-minute sets all afternoon and evening. Though the film festival has since axed the music portion from its program, it brought more incredible, high-profile artists, like John Mayer, to Canal Room's stage.

Downtown Manhattan

> "It's a very difficult business… it's really tough to run a live music business in New York City, but at the end of the day it's a pleasure, it's an honor, and it's a joy to come to the Room."
>
> Marcus Linial, Co-owner

When several new large-capacity clubs opened in Manhattan, the competition to book the best acts coming through New York became fierce. In response, Canal Room opted to focus on and nurture local acts. Several music venues moved uptown to the fashionable Meatpacking District, but Canal Room decided to stay put. The struggling economy in 2008 added another hurdle, but Canal Room stuck it out, and being one of the few high-profile clubs in the Tribeca/SoHo area, the venue soon found its groove. During Canal Room's revival Colleen Hendricks was hired, who had previously booked the Highline Ballroom and B.B. King.

She quickly affected positive change at the club and strengthened the club's image in the music scene—Canal Room is now a solid participant in the CMJ music festival.

Settled in its identity as an upscale club with high integrity, the room is intent on continuing down the path of hosting parties, finding amazing live bands, and bringing people together in memory of the '80s.

Sound Check

The venue has been redesigned several times over the past decade. With each makeover, it's apparent that the focus is to provide the best possible live music experience for the fan and artist. The stage is large for a mid-size venue, is elevated by several feet and is located near an exit. For fans, sightlines are great and for bands loading-in and -out is convenient. The sound system consists of a modern state-of-the-art EAW line array.

Tech Specs

FOH Mixing Console: Allen & Heath iLive-T112 with the iDR-32 (the i/o dps unit)
Mains: 8 EAW KF730 Compact Line Array Stereo Mains. 4 EAW SB1000z Sub Woofers 4 EAW KF730 Compact Line Array for Dance Floor Fill, 2 EAW DCS-2 Horn loaded Subs for dance floor fill
Monitors: 3 Radian Biradial full range Monitors and 4 EAW SM155HI monitors with 4 independent mixes from FOH
Microphones/DIs: AKG, Shure, Sennheiser, ProCo, Radial
Backline: Pearl Drums (no cymbals), GK Bass Head, Hartke 4x10
DJ System: 2 Technics SL1200 Turntables (3 more as Spare) 2 Pioneer CDJ1000MKII, 1 Denon 2600F Mixer, 1 Rane MP 44 DJ Mixer, 2 EAW JF 60 Monitors (Stereo)
Lighting System: State-of-the-Art
Video System: Optoma DLP Projector, 1 VHS Deck, 1 DVD Player
Stage Size: 9 ft x 26 ft
Soundcheck/Line-check: Per advance
Other: Green room, dressing room

Downtown Manhattan

CITY WINERY

155 Varick St | New York, 10013 | 212-608-0555
Hours: 11:30a-12mid, Music times vary
Subway: 1 to Houston St or Canal St | C,E to Spring St
www.citywinery.com

Written by: Emily Niewendorp

MUSIC TYPE	VENUE TYPE	ADMISSION	ATMOSPHERE	DRINKS: $$-$$$
Rock, Pop, Folk, Singer-songwriter	Mid-Size Club Capacity 327 - 499	Free - $75	Refined, Rustic Charm	$7 - $18, Wine $25+ **FOOD:** Full Menu

SOHO — Between Spring St & Vandam St
Downtown Manhattan

City Winery brings wine country to the heart of New York City. Opened by Michael Dorf in 2008, the city's only fully-functional winery integrates music, fine dining, 500 wines and public wine-making capabilities.

City Winery's red brick structure stands bright and confident on the corner of Varick and Vandam. Cafe curtains add a rustic charm and the large wooden doors open directly into the thick of the 21,000 square-foot venue. Musicians at all levels say it's a fancy room. City Winery is at once a performance space, wine-bar and Mediterranean-inspired restaurant. At the bar, true house wines rush from spigots connected to barrels in the cellar.

Photo by: Alex Baldwin

A winding staircase funnels down to City Winery's winemaking facilities. Glass walls provide glimpses of the processing and storage rooms for the 220 barrels stored in the cellar. Classes, lectures and events are available to the public, some are exclusive to the winemaking members. Anyone interested in making wine can find a winemaking package to suit him or her at City Winery. Packages range from individual barrels, to shared, corporate and others. Barrel ownership offers a slew of perks, such as exclusive offers and first access to music shows. The barrel owner chooses his level of involvement in the process, and is wholly supported by the winemaking staff.

A service feature that contributes to optimizing guests' experience is the venue's ticketing system, which allows for selection of seats or tables on the venue's website. An evening of complete relaxation chiseled out of a hectic schedule will have secured the first important component ahead of time: preferred seating.

Future plans for City Winery include conversion of the second floor to house a members-only locker space for wine storage, an upstairs dedicated restuarant, roof space, a show kitchen, and events space.

Photo by: Alex Baldwin

HISTORY

Opening the Knitting Factory and producing NYC music festivals and concerts introduced Michael as an important player in the city's entertainment industry. His interest

Pictured from Left to Right: Amber Rubarth, JJ Gray, Five for Fighting
Photos above by: Alex Baldwn

in wine began to effervesce when he made his first barrel of wine in California. He was compelled to understand the process better. Supported by friends and associates, Michael began to envision a winery for NYC that offered a luxurious experience.

Michael's extensive search for a building brought him to a non-residential neighborhood, located on top of the Holland Tunnel. The structure had been used for 120 years as a printing facility and offices, but had all the potential Michael needed. On the border of Tribeca and SoHo, the building was large enough to hold winemaking equipment and contained loading docks to accommodate 90 tons of grape deliveries.

After sandblasting away seven layers of painted and plastered history, City Winery's fresh face welcomed its first audience on New Year's Eve 2008, with a concert featuring Joan Osborne. Other music greats have followed, such as, Suzanne Vega, Philip Glass with Patti Smith, Lou Reed and Bobby De Niro.

> "In our overly-hyper, digital world that we're living in, and the ability to replicate almost everything you can't digitize, [it's about] the experience of being in a room with 300 fellow fans, and being with some intimate friends, and being physically with an artist who is performing and hopefully speaking to you in a way that every other music form — if it's not live, really can't."
>
> Michael Dorf, Owner

The music programming is stimulating and high-quality, from folk and rock, to singer-songwriters. An event Michael especially appreciated was a 2010 performance by legendary folksinger/songwriter Pete Seeger, who entertained the audience with beloved classics, and presented contemporary material inspired by the recent Gulf oil spill.

Sound Check
Sound Quality: Great
Stage Lighting: Great
Sightlines: Great
Eardrum Meter: Yellow

Tech Specs
Sound System: Yamaha M7CL
Meyer M'elodie Array, 600-HP, UPQ-1P Fills, MM-4xP Miniature Loadspeakers
Monitors: 7 mixes, Meyer UM-1P Active
Backline: Yamaha Baby Grand Piano
Recording: ProTools HD
Other: Green room

Downtown Manhattan

DON HILL'S

511 Greenwich St | New York, NY 10013 | 212-219-2850
Hours: 11p-4a Daily
Subway: 1 to Houston St or Canal St | C,E to Spring St
www.donhills.com

Written by: Emily Niewendorp

MUSIC TYPE	VENUE TYPE	ADMISSION	ATMOSPHERE	DRINKS: $-$$
Rock 'n' Roll	Dive Bar, Rock-Dance Club	Free - $10	Gritty Rock Club	Average $4 - $12 FOOD: no

SOHO — Corner of Greenwich St & Spring St

A long-running club, Don Hill's is currently experiencing an injection of fresh, impassioned inspiration with the addition of two nightlife impressarios to its team: **Nur Kahn and Paul Sevigny.** The weekend of Don Hill's re-opening featured many A-list bands such as, The Dead Weather, Yeah Yeah Yeahs, Iggy Pop, Hole and Crystal Castles. The idea behind the club's rejuvenation is to bring back a piece of New York City that has gone missing: non-exclusive, gritty rock clubs.

HISTORY

Don Hill, the person, started working on Bleecker Street, among the legendary live music outposts decades ago. He worked at numerous clubs until he became part owner of the Cat Club in the '80s. The Cat Club booked emerging bands such as White Zombie, Sonic Youth and Jane's Addiction. A car accident interrupted Don's life and sidetracked him for several years, until his friend who owned the Ear Inn, offered Don use of a space across the street from the Inn saying, "See what you can do with it." Don named the space Don Hill's, started scheduling shows, and eventually hosted theme nights for which the club became famous.

The buzz surrounding the venue's high-voltage shows and themed-out parties in the '90s was huge and attended by adventurous, nightlife enthusiasts. **Squeezebox!**, a punk drag party, attracted attention for producing the first-ever, drag-queen band. A documentary of Squeezebox! screened at Tribeca Film Festival in 2008. **TISWAS**, an English-themed night, showcased The Strokes and other mod, rocker bands. The **Rock Candy** party, featured rock bands and drew Sylvain Sylvain of New York Dolls fame, The Independents, who were promoted by Joey Ramone, and others.

Sound Check
The sound system has plenty of low-end as well as presence on the top-end to bring the vocals out above the mix no matter how loud it gets on stage. The stage is elevated and it's one of the few small to mid-size venues with a built-in drum riser.

Sound Check
Sound Quality: Great
Stage Lighting: Great
Sightlines: Good
Eardrum Meter: Red

Downtown Manhattan

JAZZ GALLERY

290 Hudson St | New York, NY 10013 | 212-242-1063
Hours: Shows 9p & 10:30p
Subway: C,E to Spring St | 1 to Houston St
www.jazzgallery.org

Written by: Jasmine Lovell-Smith

DRINKS: no FOOD: no "Just Great Music"	ATMOSPHERE Small Intimate Loft Space	ADMISSION $10 - $20 All Ages	VENUE TYPE Small Room Capacity 70	MUSIC TYPE Jazz

Tucked away in an intimate loft space in lower Manhattan, the Jazz Gallery is home to some of New York City's most adventurous jazz programming. This non-profit jazz and cultural center is simply furnished and welcoming to all.

The Gallery's relaxed atmosphere is a change of pace from other Manhattan jazz venues. Director Deborah Steinglass describes the "hominess, and the roll-up-your-sleeves dedication of the staff" as part of the Gallery's charm. White walls display jazz-themed artworks, and folding chairs and benches offer concert-style seating in front of the cozy red, curtain-lined stage. No food or drinks are served, keeping the focus squarely on the music.

A wide range of exciting and innovative music is presented at the Jazz Gallery, which hosts performances three to five nights a week. The venue makes a priority of presenting the work of emerging professional musicians, as well as more established jazz artists. Past performers have included artists such as: Steve Coleman, Ravi Coltrane, Gretchen Parlato and Ambrose Akinmusire. The varied and interesting programming attracts a discerning crowd of music lovers of all ages and nationalities.

Pictured: Singer Sofia Rei Koutsovitis

The Jazz Gallery has had a colourful history, beginning with its musical life in 1995 as a rehearsal space for trumpeter Roy Hargrove and his progressive Big Band. Hargrove's business manager Dale Fitzgerald came up with the idea of using the space as a gallery. Over the next several years the space presented theme-based art exhibits, poetry and live music, arriving at its current focus on live music in 2000.

Beyond presenting performances, the Jazz Gallery is constantly searching for new ways to support the jazz community. The Gallery's initiatives include master classes, jam sessions, an annual new-music commissioning series and an artist residency program. "There's another side to our mission—not just that we present," says Deborah. "We're also serving the jazz musician."

Sound Check
The need for sound reinformcement is minimal–mainly vocals, acoustic and electronic instruments are connected to the sound system. A 7 ft Baldwin Baby Grand piano and a bass amp is provided as backline. The stage is 12'x18', slightly elevated and large enough to accomodate complex ensembles. Thick, plush curtains backdrop the stage adding class to the space, while providing acoustic warmth to the sound of the room.

SOHO
Between Broome St & Spring St

Downtown Manhattan

SOB's

204 Varick St | New York, NY 10014 | 212-243-4940
Hours: Mon-Thu, Sun 7p-2a, Fri-Sat 7p-4a
Subway: 1 to Houston St
www.sobs.com

Full Menu: Latin & Caribbean Cuisine

Written by: Allie Arias

MUSIC TYPE	VENUE TYPE	ADMISSION	ATMOSPHERE	DRINKS: $-$$
World: Brazilian, African, Latin, Reggae, Urban, R&B, Hip Hop	Mid-Size Club Capacity 350	$10 - $25	High-energy, Intimate, Upscale	Average $6 - $13 **FOOD:** Full Menu

SOHO — Corner of West Houston St & Varick St

From its unmusical beginnings as a sandwich shop, SOB's (Sounds of Brasil) has evolved into one of the city's premier world music venues. Early performances from Tito Puente and Marc Anthony put this vibrant venue in the minds of people around the world.

It was thirty years ago that Larry Gold focused on his appreciation for Brazilian music and turned his father's shop into a live music venue, bringing Afro-Latino Diaspora music to New York City at a time when it wasn't readily accessible.

Larry confides that the club is of such a global nature it would thrive in any city with an ethnic population. **Folks from Haiti, Brazil, Senegal, India and more gather at SOB's to celebrate their heritage and mingle with other cultures.** SOB's provides an intimate stage for global talent; from up-and-coming artists looking to familiarize their names with American audiences, to established musicians. **Brazilian legend Gilberto Gil played his first USA gig at SOB's.** Another memorable night at the club included the double billing of jazz singers Abbey Lincoln and Betty Carter. Other notable performers have included John Legend, The Fugees, Celia Cruz and Bebel Gilberto.

SOB's is also known for its excellent contemporary Latin cuisine, which is infused with a Caribbean flair. The cocktails are potent, but who wouldn't want to have a stiff caipirinha or mojito while grooving to some Latin beats? SOB's excels in improvement. One of their latest additions is a Bossa Nova Brunch on Sundays, which includes a three-course meal for under $30, with unlimited sangria. Or, stop by on Fridays for a free salsa class before the show!

Sound Check

This is a spacious room with high ceilings and a sound system capable of filling the space. Acoustically, it's a live room. The sound engineer has a bird's eye view of the stage—located on the balcony level above the bar. Sightlines are excellent from any position as the stage is elevated by several feet and postioned front-and-center.

Tech Specs

Mixer: Allen&Heath ml4000, 32 ch
PA/Mains: (2) EAW mh690T per side (flown), (1) EAW sb250 per side (flown), (2) sb528 subs
Monitors: (6) EAW sm200 iH, 6 mixes, mixed from front-of-house
Backline: Full
DJ Setup: Yes – Technics 1200mk2, CDJ1000 MK2
Recording: Yes
Other: Green room, 2 dressing rooms

Downtown Manhattan

ACE OF CLUBS

9 Great Jones St | New York, NY 10012 | 212-677-6963
Hours: Music times vary
Subway: N,R to 8th St | F to Broadway/Lafayette 6 to Bleecker St
www.aceofclubsnyc.com

Full Menu: Acme Underground, Southern/Cajun Cuisine

Written by: Emily Niewendorp

DRINKS: $-$$ Average $7 - $13 FOOD: Full Menu	ATMOSPHERE Lively Subterranean Rock Club	ADMISSION $8 - $15	VENUE TYPE Basement Capacity 175	MUSIC TYPE Various: Rock, Pop, Punk, Indie, Metal

Ace of Clubs is a basement club with a vibe reminiscent of the grungy, old days of the East Village. The club is stealthily located below ACME Bar & Grill, and sometimes undetectable by those unfamiliar with its location.

Downstairs, a tight foyer between the stairwell and the music room acts as a congregating room for fresh air or a break from the music. The stage is on the far end of the rectangular-shaped space and, though the sound system is decent, it can get loud. The room is well-maintained with dim lighting, brick walls painted black, wood flooring and benches and tables along the walls.

Formerly known as ACME Underground, the club has a laid-back and fun atmosphere with lots of room for dancing. The crowd varies from college kids and hipsters, to 9-to-5ers looking to forget their work day.

Depending on the band and the size of its audience, the room can be raucous, energetic and packed with people. On other nights, it serves as a great spot for a chill night of tunes and drinks.

Indie rock bands play Ace of Clubs primarily, along with alternative, soul, blues and country acts thrown into the mix. Additionally, there are stand-up comedy and theater nights.

The club's staff members are no-nonsense, but pleasant, and the sole bartender is incredibly efficient. The drinks are decently priced, however, all beers are only available by bottle downstairs.

UPSTAIRS

ACME Bar & Grill is a Southern-style, rowdy restaurant, serving up fantastic sandwiches, traditional Southern appetizers and entrees. There is also a wide selection of beers on tap available at the bar. Arriving early for the show and sitting down to nosh on some fried chicken or jambalaya is definitely the right way to start the night.

Sound Check
Sound Quality: Good
Stage Lighting: Good
Sightlines: Good
Eardrum Meter: Red

NOHO Between Lafayette St & Broadway

Downtown Manhattan

Tech Specs
Mixer: 32 Ch Yamaha MG32
Sound System: Mains – 2 JBL Stacks Pro Series 2, Subs – Yorkville SW 1000 2x18s
Monitors: 4 mixes, mixed from FOH 3 Yorkville Elite EM408, 1 EV T15 drum mon
Backline: Partial Backline

15

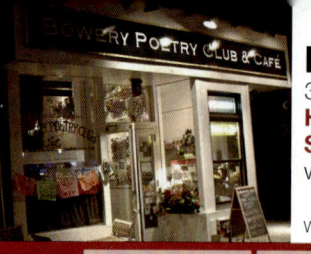

BOWERY POETRY CLUB

308 Bowery | New York, NY 10012 | 212-614-0505
Hours: Weekdays 4p-4a, Weekends 12p-4a
Subway: F to 2nd Ave | 6 to Bleecker St
www.bowerypoetry.com

Written by: Emily Niewendorp & Bill Nevins

MUSIC TYPE	VENUE TYPE	ADMISSION	ATMOSPHERE	DRINKS: $-$$
Everything: "Expect the Unexpected"	Small Club Capacity 125	$5 - $10	Art Bar	Average $3 - $13 FOOD: no

NOHO — Between Bleecker St & Houston St

Downtown Manhattan

Bowery Poetry Club is a one-room venue with brick walls, a bar, a stage, a simple sound system and casual seating.

The programming is overseen by the nonprofit, Bowery Arts & Science, and prides itself on innovative work that is accessible to everyman. When musicians submit their material, the production manager Eliel Lucero and the general manager, David Brouillard, who book the club, encourage the artists to create a show with bands or friends under a like-minded vision. This way the audience can enjoy several hours of music.

Bowery Poetry Club features the Irish punk rockers The Ruffians, and nearly every genre in existence: ska, rockabilly, adult contemporary rock, punk rock, jam bands, hip-hop, bluegrass, blues, even pop singers, who move in sync.

According to the club's owner, Bob, "Monday nights bring Taylor Mead, the octogenarian poet laureate of Andy Warhol's Factory; a cross-dressing Bingo game hosted by downtown superstars Murray Hill and Linda Simpson; and the NYC Talent Show, the best collection of downtown freaks you'll ever see, hosted by Diane O'Debra and Victor Varnado."

"Autumn at the Bowery Poetry Club is just wild and exciting," says Eliel. With CMJ Music Marathon in October, theater festivals, the Urbana series back in swing (they often take summers off) and other popular weekly and monthly shows, vastly different crowds return to the venue. Weekends provide day time programming for high schools or visiting groups.

> Like a proud parent, Bob boasts about his club and the neighborhood, "The lineage of the Bowery Poetry Club is the populist art tradition of The Bowery itself—birthplace of burlesque, vaudeville, Yiddish Theater—and today you'll find all manner of poetry, music, theater, film, and visual art served up warm and friendly by an all-artist staff."

The Art Wall, one of the main walls of the venue, is a place for rotating art. John Simms was the curator of a recent collection: "The Rhythm of Structure: Mathematics, Art and Poetic Reflections." Artwork on the wall above the bar includes portraits of poets by Noah Apple, a few of which are: Ann Sexton, Walt Whitman and owner Bob Holman's late wife, Elizabeth Murray—an amazing artist who has work displayed at the

MOMA and the Whitney. The front cafe changes management often, usually offering snacks, drinks and small meals.

HISTORY

Bob Holman, world famed slam poet, film maker (*United States of Poetry* for PBS) and professor of creative writing for Columbia U and NYU founded Bowery Poetry Club in 2002.

Bob had been running the Nuyorican Poets Cafe and became well-known for his mission of preserving languages and culture.

When talking about Bowery Poetry's steady evolution as a platform for nearly every art form, Eliel says, "I think it's all still poetry. It might not be written poetry, but it's still all an interpretation of what poetry could be. Be it the poetics of music or the poetics of dance, or of burlesque or even comedy, everything has a certain rhythm and poetry to it.

Not everything is good poetry, but everything is always poetry."

> **Be ready to expect the unexpected at Bowery Poetry. Eliel states, "...the shows are always getting...weirder—or just different. So, it's a lot of fun to see."**

Series that have run for many years, such as Diane O'Debra's Talent Show, started because she took initiative and approached the club with the idea.

Not everyone likes every show, but as the long as the audience likes it, then it is serving the purpose for the community. Eliel sums it up well: "Sometimes I'm just weirded out, but it's great. Being challenged like that is healthy."

Sound Check
Sound Quality: Good
Stage Lighting: Good
Sightlines: Great
Eardrum Meter: Green–Yellow

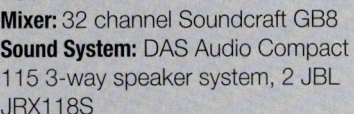

Tech Check
Mixer: 32 channel Soundcraft GB8
Sound System: DAS Audio Compact 115 3-way speaker system, 2 JBL JRX118S
Monitors: 2-3 separate mixes, Yamaha BR15M
Backline: Piano and Drum Kit

Downtown Manhattan

FONTANA'S

105 Eldridge St | New York, NY 10002 | 212-334-6740
Hours: 2p-4a Daily
Subway: B,D to Grand St | F,J,M to Essex St/Delancey St
www.fontanasnyc.com

Written by: Emily Niewendorp

MUSIC TYPE	VENUE TYPE	ADMISSION	ATMOSPHERE	DRINKS: $-$$
Various: Rock, Pop, Indie, Electronic	Basement Capacity 150	Bar, Lounge: Free Music: $5 - $10	Spacious multi-level Neighborhood Bar	Happy Hour until 8p FOOD: no

CHINATOWN
Between Grand St & Broome St

In Chinatown, Fontana's vitality stands out in a neighborhood whose residents honor tradition over trends. This popular bar and music spot was a pioneering music venue in the area below Delancey Street when it opened in 2006—and it is still the only bar on this stretch of Eldridge Street.

Photo by: Rupert Hitchcox

Fontana's entrance sits several steps up from the street. The interior is splashed with color—red-cushioned, u-shaped booths face the bar, and blue walls carry large paintings of movie stars, classic Thunderbird cars and pin-up girls from the '50s and '60s. To top it off, the windows overlooking the street are dressed with Venetian blinds that bring dime novel detective stories to mind. The main bar serves a diverse selection of beers and liquors.

The venue sprawls out over 4,000 square feet beyond the front bar, creating several attractive spaces for enjoying the evening. The Chandelier Room seduces with its faux leopard-upholstered seating and abundant space for mingling. This lounge has its own full bar, a pool table and its sparkling chandelier. Music-themed films flicker on the wall. Upstairs, DJs spin on the balcony and patrons unwind on couches.

The downstairs live music room at Fontana's feels like a special, private room. The room narrows at the back, providing seating for chatting with friends, or with the cool bartenders. Type O Negative, a Brooklyn heavy-metal band, played a memorable, hard-core show at Fontana's several years ago. On other nights, singer-songwriters mellow the crowd, and world music bands make appearances quite frequently.

> I grew up around live music…My dad was a musician and paid the bills by playing out every night. He built a room, filled with equipment, just for his band to have a practice space. As a child, I was always allowed to play in that room anytime I wanted, and without supervision. I used to turn on the PA and play on everything. It was inspiring. That's why it's important to support live music in NYC. Seeing vans full of gear parked in front of bars is always very exciting. It's a part of what makes this city come to life. It takes courage to start a band.
>
> Deannie Fowler, Co-owner

Downtown Manhattan

Photo by: Rupert Hitchcox

HISTORY

The space was for rent when co-owner, Holly, found Fontana's future location on a walk around the neighborhood. She showed the space to the bar's prospective investors, and every one of them fell in love with it. In the 19th century it had been New York City's first police precinct. The large space was "old, creepy, and dirty–but in a good way." The prospective owners had discussed including live music in the venture, but according to Deannie, **"…when we saw the space, we knew right away… the layout is absolutely perfect for having bands."**

Together, the owners worked to give the old building a new life. By choosing a name for the venue that is linked to the building's history, homage is paid to a police officer who walked the neighborhood's streets in the 1800s. Off duty, Sergeant Fontana would surely have enjoyed a cold pint or two over a game of pool with the fellas.

Fontana's marked its place in New York City as one of few music venues owned and operated by women. Unpretentious and slightly off the beaten path, Fontana's provides great music and good times, on- and off-stage.

A staunch promoter of live music, Fontana's is rightfully a popular destination on weekend nights. Co-owner Deannie says, "…sometimes the neighbors yell at us in Chinese, but we don't mind because we love it here and we love them. They are foreigners here, and so are we. That's what makes us fit in."

State of the Bathroom:
Blue, small as f*** with kitty art.

Sound Check
Sound Quality: Good
Stage Lighting: Good
Sightlines: So-So
Eardrum Meter: Yellow–Red

Sound Check
by Rubes Harmon, Sound Engineer
Recent upgrades include a Soudcraft GB4 16ch console and more EQs for 4 monitor mixes. What I like most about the room is the character. I'm able to get a larger room sound with a more intimate feeling (provided stage volume is controlled and the band is tight). I mix at unity and minor adjustments with as little eq as possible. The graphs are always rung out to keep a clean sound so I make light reductions with the parametrics to make things fit better together.

Downtown Manhattan

SANTOS PARTY HOUSE

96 Lafayette St | New York, NY 10013 | 212-584-5492
Hours: 7p-4a Daily
Subway: N,Q,R or J or 6 to Canal St
www.santospartyhouse.com

Written by: Nick D'Amore

MUSIC TYPE	VENUE TYPE	ADMISSION	ATMOSPHERE	DRINKS: $-$$
All Modern Music: Rock, World, Hip-Hop	Mid-Size, 2 rooms Capacity 350 - 600	Free - $15+	Rock-Dance-House Party	Average $5 - $12 FOOD: no

Santos Party House was created to be the place where anyone can let it all hang out, where anyone can "Feel Free to Feel Free" — as a notice posted in the club suggests. Santos rolls with the collective unconscious; think Ken Kesey and the Merry Pranksters. Santos taps into the collective unconscious of what people want and what they're doing, and has turned that openness to discovery into an environment. It's a self-defining, self-rejuvenating art that keeps hundreds of NYC's hippest partiers coming through the doors every night.

Translation: Santos Party House is part rock venue, part dance club and part trippy house party—all at the same time. Blacklight illuminates the venue's dark walls while silvery sparkling disco balls of varying size create their own planetary skyscape overhead. The heart's pulse adjusts to the boom boom boom of the custom-made, full surround-sound speakers housed in massive cabinets suspended from the ceiling on either side of the dance floor. The common vibe is at times trance inducing, yet the flow is good. The custom-built dance floor is supported by spring-loaded shocks; when people jump and dance on the floor, it's like being on a trampoline. **"Santos just feels good when you walk out onto that floor," co-owner Andrew W.K. states. Simply printed signs abound, with lighthearted sentiments like, "Party is our middle name," "Music is a Joy to Behold" and "Let Me Do the Talking."**

HISTORY

Deriving its name from Santa Santos, an imagined spirit of nightlife, Santos' owners have successfully transferred their love of music and passion for fun into the venue since its opening in June 2008. The historic factory building was formerly a retail clothing outlet. Owners Ron Castellano, Larry Golden, Spencer Sweeney, Derek Ferguson, and the inimitable Andrew W.K. built the club from scratch, creating a two-level, 8,000-square-foot entertainment space. Andrew proudly says, "A virgin nightclub seldom opens in Manhattan!"

Located between Chinatown and Tribeca, the club's two levels can operate separately or together, as concert venues or as dance clubs. The owners focused on offering performers and audiences quality sound, lights, stages and dance floors. The ground-floor stage area provides copious amounts of danc-

CHINATOWN — Between Walker St & White St

Downtown Manhattan

Photos by: Rupert Hitchcox

ing space on the floor. The downstairs stage is for smaller acts and is a cozier version of the upstairs area. Both levels include a large bar area. An evening's events can be live bands, DJs, comedy, film screenings and even weddings—Andrew was married there in October 2008. With so many venues catering to certain styles and scenes, Santos strives to be all-inclusive and unpredictable: on any given night, you can see anyone or hear anything. Approaching its third year of existence, Santos Party House remains committed to evolving the venue experience—by staying tapped into the collective unconscious. The venue's atmosphere is as integral to the show experience as the performers themselves.

Some of the more **well-known acts that have played Santos include: the Yeah Yeah Yeahs, Q-Tip, Busta Rhymes, Moby, The Sounds, Meshell Ndegeocello, N.E.R.D., Cro-Mags, The Black Dahlia Murder, KRS-One, Kool Herc, ESG, John Zorn, Thurston Moore, Ash, and Amanda Blank**.

Sound Check
Sound Quality: Great
Stage Lighting: Great
Sightlines: Great
Eardrum Meter: Yellow—Red

The allure of Santos Party House has spread to the famous, as well; Jay-Z has counted the club as one of his favorite spots in the city and Diddy held his Obama election party there. Other notable guests spotted at the club have been Lady Gaga, Beyonce, Mick Jagger, Jack Nicholson, Lindsay Lohan, Mary-Kate and Ashley Olsen, Steve Buscemi, Kirsten Dunst, Björk and Lou Reed.

State of the Bathroom: Modern amenities meet venerable punk rock club grit. decade's worth of tagging and stickers in only two years.

Sound Check: Comments
This venue has the greatest number of speakers per square inch than any other mid-size venue in NYC. The sound in the main space can be loud to extreme, in a good way depending on the style of music and sound engineer. The venue boasts 150,000 watts of sound, 148 light fixtures, video projection and an elevated stage.
One of the best venues in the city to experience live music.

Tech Specs
Sound System: Soundcraft Vi 6
JBL Vertec 4888 and two 4887 line array speakers, JBL Vertec 4880 Ultra Sub Woofers
Monitors: Soundcraft Vi4
JBL STX 812 monitor wedges
Backline: Full Drum Kit, Partial Backline
DJ: Full setup

Downtown Manhattan

ARLENE'S GROCERY

95 Stanton St | New York, NY 10002 | 212-353-1688
Hours: Mon-Sun 6p-2a, Fri-Sat 6p-4a
Subway: J,M,F to Essex St/Delancey St | F to 2nd Ave
www.arlenesgrocery.net

Written by: Emily Niewendorp

Rock 'n' Roll Karaoke Every Monday 10p - 2a

MUSIC TYPE	VENUE TYPE	ADMISSION	ATMOSPHERE	DRINKS: $-$$
Rock, Pop, Folk, Indie	Small Club 129	$5 - $10	Neighborhood Bar Showcase Venue	Average $3 - $13 FOOD: no

LOWER EAST SIDE — Between Orchard St & Ludlow St

Downtown Manhattan

Arlenes is a longstanding showcase venue that embraces young artists as well as touring and established bands. The original three owners of Arlene's Grocery: Dermot Burke, Tony Caffrey, and Shane Doyle, ventured into the 'wild, wild west' of the Lower East Side in the mid-'90s, before any other music venue dared. Crime and drugs burdened the LES, yet they believed, risks aside, that the neighborhood would become New York City's next hip area—and the gamble paid off. Other venues followed Arlene's lead and the LES birthed a flourishing art and music scene.

The three owners converted the prior business, a bodega called Arlene Grocery, into a live music venue, keeping the store's original exterior tropical-themed murals and name. Only recently were the designs modified and an 'apostrophe-s' added to grammatically correct the venue's name, although newcomers still mistake Arlene's for a grocery store.

On Arlene's historic opening night, 30 people gathered to see poet Allen Ginsberg backed by Lenny K on guitar. The new venue functioned with sparse resources for several months; the sound system was problematic and the sound board lived onstage, a less-than-optimal place for sound control. Busboy and eventual booker, Owen Comasky, hustled — simultaneously cleaning beer glasses and running sound. Conditions improved quickly; Shane had discovered Jeff Buckley at his previous club, Sin-e, and Jeff's management agency outfitted Arlene's with a good sound system. The venue began buzzing with activity and it became the place where bands played to self-promote.

It wasn't long before the momentum of Arlene's successes attracted world-famous stars: David Bowie, Ron Sexsmith, David Gray and booking agent Marty Diamond. Then everyone wanted to play there: The Strokes, Vanessa Carlton and Joss Stone. Clive Davis came through— as did Quincy Jones, Paul Simon, Mick Jagger and Michael Stipe with Dashboard Confessional.

Industry people frequented the space and bands were signed, but not everyone was happy. The club gave free admission without

Pictured Left & Center: Zelazowa
Right: Toyeater

paying the bands, which outraged many musicians and led to protests outside the venue. Yet, the formula worked: bands who played Arlene's often found representation, and because it was a cool place with a great sound system, the club became very successful.

Arlene's Grocery expanded next door into a former butcher shop, which serves as the main entrance today. Behind its eye-catching red and yellow awning, the Butcher Bar charges no cover and is a relaxing place to hang-out between sets in the music room. Shane eventually sold his stake in Arlene's Grocery leaving Dermot and Tony's philosophy to fuel the club's continued success. They entrust creative control to the booking agent Julia Darling, and the rest of the crew, which allows for self-initiated endeavors, such as a Germ Recording's studio. Run by Danny Garcia out of a space in the basement, the studio offers live Internet broadcasts and a slew of recording options for bands.

Arlene's charges a door cover these days, though it's one of the lowest in the city, and bands now get paid. Four to five bands play six nights a week and showcases are a constant. Always a great sounding room, Arlene's is now an institution and their legendary jam-packed Monday night rock 'n' roll karaoke kicks ass!

Sound Check
Sound Quality: Great
Stage Lighting: So-So
Sightlines: Good
Eardrum Meter: Yellow—Red

Sound Check
Arlene's Grocery is considered by many, one of the best sounding small venues in NYC. A sand-filled stage helps define low-frequencies. A triple-plyed acoustically treated floating ceiling absorbs sound and sonic reflections. The slightly sloped floor from the rear of the room to the front of the stage and an elevated stage provides for better sightlines. The sound engineers are attentive and helpful in getting the sound right on stage. Arlene's recently upgraded to Turbo Sound as the main speakers.

Tech Specs
Sound System: Midas Venice 320 Turbo Sound tops and bottoms
Monitors: 4 separate mixes, EAW
Backline: Full Backline
Hospitality: Drink Discounts
DJ: 2 Turntables/Mixer
Recording: In-house audio & video recording — nightly
Live Streaming: www.livestream.com/arlenesgrocery

Downtown Manhattan

THE BOWERY BALLROOM

6 Delancey St | New York, NY 10002 | 212-533-2111
Hours: Music times vary
Subway: B,D to Grand St | F,J,M to Essex St/Delancey St
www.boweryballroom.com

Written by: Sarah Oramas

MUSIC TYPE	VENUE TYPE	ADMISSION	ATMOSPHERE	DRINKS: $$
Rock, Pop, Indie	Mid-Size Capacity 550	$10 - $30	Restored Old Time Theater	Average $6+ FOOD: no

LOWER EAST SIDE — Between Chrystie St & Bowery St
Downtown Manhattan

Playing The Bowery Ballroom is a milestone for musicians moving up in their careers; it's a beacon of indie success. With its high quality sound system, professional team of sound engineers and beautiful setting, Bowery Ballroom attracts up-and-coming acts, established bands, and those on the cusp of breaking to the next level.

Frank Bango started at The Bowery Ballroom as a bartender when it first opened in 1998, and has worked his way up to become the general manager. He ascribes the success of the venue to the fact that "it's always had the same caliber of performances."

The entrance of the Bowery Ballroom leads down to a basement level lounge that exudes a sense of the grungy, artistic history of the Lower East Side. It's a hip room with a full bar, plenty of seating and space for socializing before and after the show.

The actual performance space is up a large staircase, lined by performers selling their merchandise. The main floor feels like a restored old time theater with beautifully polished wood floors, long theatrical curtains and great sight lines. Top it off with rock venue sound and you get a sense of what you are seeing matters.

There is a second bar at the back of the sizable dance floor, allowing fans to refresh their beverages without having to miss any of the show. The dance floor is flanked on both sides by staircases leading to the balcony, which houses an inset full bar and private booths on either side. Each side of the balcony accommodates six-eight small tables. For those lucky enough to snag a table, they offer a great vantage point for watching a show with a little distance from the main crowd.

Sound Check
Sound Quality: Great
Stage Lighting: Great
Sightlines: Great
Eardrum Meter: Yellow—Red

Tech Check
Mixer: Yamaha PM3000 40 channels
Sound System: EAW speakers, Crown power, Klark Teknik FOH EQ
Monitors: Soundcraft 40 ch, 8 mixes, 4 stereo, EAW wedges, Crown power
Backline: No Backline
Other: Green room
Comments: Consistently great sounding room, currently looking to upgrade FOH console to a Midas–Heritage series

CAKESHOP

152 Ludlow St | New York, NY 10002 | 212-253-0036
Hours: Cafe 9a-2a | Bar 5p-2a
Subway: F,J,M to Essex St/Delancey St | F to 2nd Ave
www.cake-shop.com

Written by: Emily Niewendorp

DRINKS: $-$$	ATMOSPHERE	ADMISSION	VENUE TYPE	MUSIC TYPE
Average $4+ FOOD: Cafe	Hipster Music Cafe	$5 - $15	Basement Capacity 74	Rock, Pop, Indie, Experimental

Cakeshop specializes in punk, indie and experimental bands, and vegan cupcakes. Established around 2005, this Lower East Side venue seeks to showcase developing bands and encourages debut performances regularly. Cakeshop offers music, a full bar, and cafe services seven days a week.

UPSTAIRS CAFE

Cakeshop charms with a loose indie rock vibe and an odd-ball decor. Art and random objects collect on the walls, shelves and in the storefront window. The cafe offers an assortment of vegan and traditional baked goods, and coffee, teas and espresso all day and night. A selection of vinyl albums, CDs, cassette tapes, small-press zines and more are available for purchase. A cozy, art gallery with seating occupies the rear of the space. During the day, regulars hang out at the cafe for its free Wi-Fi and at night a young crowd enjoys bar drinks at sweet prices.

DOWNSTAIRS MUSIC VENUE

Under a low ceiling the floor slopes steeply downward from the back of the room to meet the slightly elevated stage. For the best view of the band, slip through the crowd to the other side of the bar, or find a perch on one of the many well-used, cushioned benches along the wall. Under the red ceiling, black and red walls sparkle with tinsel and strings of lights.

The types of shows at Cakeshop change quickly from day to day. A California indie-rock band may pack the room full of zealous ladies and tattoo-covered guys for one set, while during the next set an experimental duo will talk to their small crowd of loyal friends as if they are hanging out in the living room.

Sound Check
Sound Quality: So-So/Good
Stage Lighting: Minimal
Sightlines: So-So
Eardrum Meter: Yellow–Red

Tech Check
Sound System: 24ch Mackie, EAW UPJ
Monitors: 3 wedges mixes
Backline: Full Backline
Comments: Small basement venue, low ceiling, generally loud, DJ ready

LOWER EAST SIDE
Between Stanton St & Rivington St

Downtown Manhattan

THE DELANCEY

168 Delancey St | New York, 10002 | 212-254-9920
Hours: 5p-4a Daily
Subway: J,M,F to Essex St/Delancey St
www.thedelancey.com

Year-round Heated Rooftop Garden

Written by: Daniel Morrow

MUSIC TYPE	VENUE TYPE	ADMISSION	ATMOSPHERE	DRINKS: $-$$
Rock, Pop, Punk, Indie, Metal, Burlesque	Basement Capacity 100	Free - $15	Eclectic, Multi-level Art Bar	Average $6-$10 FOOD: no

LOWER EAST SIDE — Between Clinton St & Attorney St

Located next to the Williamsburg Bridge entrance, The Delancey combines the hipness of Williamsburg, Brooklyn with the dynamic party atmosphere of the Lower East Side.

The Delancey boasts three levels for entertainment. Enter the venue through a long, narrow corridor and walk straight down to the basement where the main performance stage features three to eight bands every night. Or, walk in the ground floor where patrons are entertained by singer-songwriters on a small stage with a well-maintained piano. Ample seating is found in the many curtained-off alcoves, or by the window overlooking the bridge. Alternatively, drinks can be ordered at the roof garden's bar, while relaxing at the pond, surrounded by greenery.

The Delancey transforms itself for virtually all occasions. Both the ground and basement levels have a DJ for the later parts of each evening, and on Friday and Saturday nights the venue refashions itself into a veritable nightclub. There are Afro-punk themes, weekly burlesque shows and a fetish night once a month.

The stage lighting in the basement is made more dramatic by the room's otherwise low light levels. Comfortable leather sofas fringe the room and a warm, red glow infuses the space. The crowd stands close to the stage creating an intimate energy. Even on quieter nights the high sound quality gives audience the feel of a much larger space. The in-house sound engineer, Marco, is particular about getting excellent results—as reported by audiences and bands alike. Indie/rock bands take the stage most nights, but the venue maintains a diverse nature with various genres and party nights.

State of the Bathroom: Is too clean for rock 'n' roll possible?!

Sound Check
Sound Quality: Good
Stage Lighting: Good
Sightlines: Good
Eardrum Meter: Yellow—Red

Tech Check
Sound System: Midas Venice 320, Yorkville Unity Series Speakers
Monitors: 4 wedges mixes, Yorkville/JBL
Backline: Full Backline
Comments: Basement venue, low ceiling, generally loud, DJ ready

Downtown Manhattan

FAT BABY

112 Rivington St | New York, NY 10002 | 212-533-1888
Hours: 7p-4a Daily
Subway: J,M,F to Essex St/Delancey St | F to 2nd Ave
www.fatbabynyc.com

Written by: Emily Niewendorp

DRINKS: $-$$$	ATMOSPHERE	ADMISSION	VENUE TYPE	MUSIC TYPE
Bottle Service FOOD: no	Hip, Fashion-conscious Dive Bar	Free - $15	Basement	Various: Rock, Pop, Indie, DJ

LOWER EAST SIDE — Between Ludlow St & Essex St — **Downtown Manhattan**

Fat Baby emerged onto the scene in 2005 as a chic, dance spot and (some would argue) dive lounge. The venue's popularity has grown, via word-of-mouth and blogs, perpetually buzzing with activity, through holidays and rainy weekends alike.

The ground level of Fat Baby boasts a multilevel bar and lounge, decked out with specialty hard-woods and vintage wallpaper. A mezzanine with booths often serves as a VIP area and overlooks the dance floor. The music room downstairs carries a different, more creative atmosphere. The darkly lit room houses a small stage, a few couches, and a small bar with room for dancing. A side entrance for performers gives them a direct means of access and egress from the venue.

The hip, fashion-conscious staff at Fat Baby manage the day-to-day operations, while the booking agents keep the club on the cutting edge of New York's music scene. Indie rock bands are featured the most, but jazz, funk, soul, and world music artists also crop up from time to time. Each week night, four bands play to neighborhood crowds, while the weekend bridge-and-tunnel patrons get only three bands—to allow for late-night DJ parties.

HISTORY

Co-owner, Rob Shaliman, previously owned a bar on Ludlow St. called Dark Room. He sold his stake in the company, in the hopes of using the capital to fulfill a dream: to own and operate a multi-floored, live music club.

The gentrification upheaval spawned by a real estate boom provided him with an ideal opportunity: a catering company had just vacated some highly coveted, Lower East Side real estate. Although the architectural framework of the building was sound, the rest of it was completely unsalvageable; the entire space had to be gutted and its layout completely altered to satisfy Rob's vision of the new place.

An actual baby was the source of inspiration for the venue's name. Fat Baby's owner, Rob, and his wife were visiting with a relative and parent of a chubby little child, when his wife made an innocuous request: "Let me hold that fat baby!" From this incident the venue's name was born.

Sound Check
Sound Quality: Good
Stage Lighting: Good
Sightlines: Good
Eardrum Meter: Yellow–Red

Tech Check
Sound System: 16ch Allen&Heath, EAW
Monitors: 3 wedges mixes, JBL Eon/Mackie
Backline: Minimal – Drums only
Comments: Small basement venue, low ceiling, generally loud, DJ ready

> *The energy of live music transfers to little kids…toddlers… you play music for them and they will dance. Music is innate in people. It moves everyone.*
> Rob, Co-owner

THE LIVING ROOM

154 LUDLOW ST | New York, NY 10002 | 212-533-7235
Hours: Mon-Sun 6p-2a, Fri-Sat 6p-4a
Subway: J,M,F to Essex St/Delancey St | F to 2nd Ave
www.livingroomny.com

Written by: Emily Niewendorp

MUSIC TYPE	VENUE TYPE	ADMISSION	ATMOSPHERE	DRINKS: $-$$$
Rock, Pop, Folk, Singer-songwriter	Small Club Capacity 130	Free - $15 1 Drink Min. per set	Casual and Inviting	Average $3 - $14 FOOD: no

LOWER EAST SIDE
Between Stanton St & Rivington St

In a neighborhood full of similar sounding live music venues, The Living Room sings to its own tune, creating a different vibe in the process. Housed originally a few blocks away, the club, now on Ludlow St., has held on to its familial, down-home vibe for over 10 years. In contrast to its neighbors (Pianos and Cakeshop), The Living Room is more low-key and subtle—drawing folk musicians, singer-songwriters, blues singers and smaller-sounding rock bands.

The Living Room consists of an active neighborhood bar, a large back room with its main stage, and the lesser-known Googie's Lounge upstairs. In both music rooms, seating is available and drinks are ordered from a cocktail waitress.

The main stage is only slightly elevated, but a generous seating increases sightlines for those standing in the back of the room. By encouraging folks to take a seat and relax, The Living Room compels the audience to direct their attention to the artists.

Upstairs, Googie's Lounge offers a more intimate environment for all sorts of small and up-and-coming artists that use the space to fine-tune their craft. The space is enclosed in heavy blue drapes, with round tables, couches and living room-style end tables. The small stage has a white, baby grand piano and matching white, mod light fixtures hang throughout the little space.

Many shows at The Living Room are free. A suggested $5 tip bucket is passed, unless the band requests a door cover. Jim Campilongo's Monday night residency, going strong since 2004, is a treat that should not be missed. Every other Saturday night there is a musical-comedy act, The Renaldo The Ensemble, fronted by the spectacular Aldo Perez. During the rest of the week, four to five bands play both rooms each night, offering a variety of pickings.

In connection with **Sirius XM Radio**, an hour of live recordings from The Living Room play on The Loft program, which features celebrated artists such as Brendan O'Shea, The Frames, Spottiswood and His Enemies, and Cat Martino.

And to include everyone, The Living Room schedules **all-age shows for kids** on Saturday or Sunday afternoons. Working with Kidrockers, who have brought bands like The Hold Steady and Nada Surf, as well as, Beatles cover band, Bubble, the club markets the shows as a place to, "get your kids out of the house, out of your hair, and come hear and see some great music!!!"

Sound Check
Sound Quality: Great
Stage Lighting: Good
Sightlines: Great
Eardrum Meter: Green–Yellow

Downtown Manhattan

THE LOCAL 269

269 Houston St | New York, NY 10002 | 212-228-9874
Hours: 4p-Late, Daily
Subway: J,M,F to Essex St/Delancey St | F to 2nd Ave
www.thelocal269.com

Written by: Ruth-Anne Damm

DRINKS: $-$$	ATMOSPHERE	ADMISSION	VENUE TYPE	MUSIC TYPE
2 for 1 until 8pm FOOD: no	Neighborhood Dive Bar	Free - $10	Small Room Capacity 70-100	Rock, Punk, Indie, Jazz, Blues

LOWER EAST SIDE
Corner of Suffolk St & Houston St

Downtown Manhattan

Do you crave variety in your live music experience? The Local 269, located in the pulsating neighborhood of the Lower East Side, features a carousel of talent and genres, seven nights a week.

Home to many musicians, The Local 269 is a place where, in a single night, you could see the next rising band or singer-songwriter, plus an all-star jam, featuring members from The Levon Helm Band, UFO, The Manhattan Blues Connection, Gary Lucas, Stiff Little Fingers, and Kraut.

Out of its windows, jazz and blues tones ring, as well as the sounds of rock, reggae, and soul. "All types of quality music plays here," says Jules, bartender of The Local. Experienced musicians create fabulous sounds on the slightly-elevated stage and new musicians find their way to the venue every Saturday night. Les Chalimon, drummer of the Blues Connection, is both a performer and patron at the venue. "This place is more magical than others," he asserts, "because of the variety of music." His appreciation is genuine: hours after his own performance, you can later find him in the audience, listening to a newcomer act onstage.

The Local 269 features a mix of free and general admission shows, priced around $10. The bar is in a single large room, equipped with an excellent sound system. Seating is limited, but the standing room is welcoming to hip shakers, toe tappers, and other kinds of dancers. The atmosphere has a warm and well-used feel to it; old chandeliers feature some broken light bulbs, while the brick walls and wooden furniture underscore the venue's rustic charm.

Sound Check
Sound Quality: Good
Stage Lighting: So-So
Sightlines: Good
Eardrum Meter: Yellow—Red

Sound Check
Primarily a vocal PA but capable of mic'ing everything and running it through FOH. The venue provides a full backline consisting of Orange, Fender, Marshall guitar amps, Fender Basic 40 bass amp and Ludwig drums. The sound in the room depends on the band. Overall, a great place to discover a new band and a perfect sized venue for a touring band working on their fan base.

Photo by Ruth-Anne Damm

MEHANATA

113 Ludlow St | New York, NY 10002 | 212-625-0981
Hours: Thu-Sat 8:30p-4a
Subway: J,M,F to Essex St/Delancey St | F to 2nd Ave
www.mehanata.com

Written by: Emily Niewendorp

MUSIC TYPE	VENUE TYPE	ADMISSION	ATMOSPHERE	DRINKS: $-$$
World: Gypsy-Punk, Cabaret	Restaurant, Club Capacity 300	$10 after 10pm	Fun!	Average $4 - $12 **FOOD:** Full Menu

LOWER EAST SIDE — Between Rivington St & Delancey St

Mehanata is a notorious, glorious, disco dive-bar where you can experience "Balkans Gone Wild." The venue's ramshackle storefront leads into a dining area evocative of a European wine garden; sapling branches and greenery decorate the balcony and the walls. Early in the evening, folks dine on Eastern European and Middle Eastern cuisine. Disco and laser lights dance on the floor and the stage, as harbingers of the excitement to come.

While the ground floor exudes celebratory warmth, the basement channels an ice world—a cavern in the wintry mountains of Bulgaria, complete with frosted branches along the ceiling. The bar features a spectacular mosaic of frozen, mismatched tiles.

The highlight of this Carpathian scene is the Ice Cage, a subzero, glass-enclosed freezer room that holds top-shelf vodka and several adventurous patrons. Entrance to the Ice Cage is $20, and its rules read like a script for a James Bond movie: "...you are clothed in a Russian military uniform and handed an ice shot glass. You have two minutes to drink six shots." Photographers are on staff to document your escapades (or ice-capades, in this instance).

Most of the venue's patrons are Eastern European; many bands play Euro-pop. Gypsy-punk band Gogol Bordello got its start here. Eugene Hütz, the band's frontman, occasionally DJs, and always generates a raging, partying atmosphere.

Mehanata moved from its original home in Chinatown to Ludlow St. around 2006. It has been said that the parties are tamer at the new location, although that may seem unbelievable after experiencing a night of the festivities. The energetic dancing that builds to ecstasy by night's end excludes no one. Don't miss the man who dances with a chair on his chin.

Sound Check
Sound Quality: So-So
Stage Lighting: Minimal
Sightlines: So-So
Eardrum Meter: Yellow

Sound Check
Basic PA setup on stage is used mainly for vocals and acoustic instruments. The vocals tend to be inaudible and distorted, but oddly enough, the fans are having too much fun to notice!

Downtown Manhattan

MERCURY LOUNGE

217 Houston St | New York, 10002 | 212-260-4700
Hours: 6p-3a Daily
Subway: J,M,F to Essex St/Delancey St | F to 2nd Ave
www.mercuryloungenyc.com

Written by: Brian Thunders

DRINKS: $-$$	ATMOSPHERE	ADMISSION	VENUE TYPE	MUSIC TYPE
Average $6+ FOOD: no	Showcase Venue	$8 - $10	Showcase Room Capacity 250	Various: Rock, Pop, Indie

At the crossroads of the Lower East Side, Houston and Essex, stands a former tombstone shop turned rock club, The Mercury Lounge, home to a unique history. Once upon a time it housed the servants to the Astor Mansion and a labyrinth of tunnels below ground connected the two buildings.

Opened in 1993 by The Bowery Presents, The Mercury Lounge is long established as the premier small-size LES live music venue, catering to New York's rock and indie scene.

The space is akin to the great NYC rock clubs—a long, wooden bar with lighting that allows you to see and be seen. On any given night you can rub shoulders with the band before they perform. The bar has typical rock-club fare: reasonably priced bottles and tap beers, as well as a full liquor selection.

Past the bar through swinging double doors is the live room, a large space that's acoustically treated for some of the best sound in NYC. The stage is lit tastefully, without any overly attention grabbing strobes or spots. It is the perfect sized room: you're never too far from the band, but the place holds a decent amount of people—and gets packed often—so, everyone in the room is there for the same purpose, enjoying the same thing. It adds to the experience. The outer edge of the live room is lined with couches and a server near the entrance will give your drink orders to the bartenders through a cut-out in the wall.

The Mercury Lounge has been host to some of the biggest names in music, including Radiohead, 30 Seconds to Mars, Lou Reed, Joan Jett, Jeff Buckley, The Strokes, Jim Jones, Interpol, Tony Bennett, the Dandy Warhols, Broken Social Scene, The Killers, Lady Gaga, and more.

LOWER EAST SIDE
Between Essex St & Ludlow St

Downtown Manhattan

Sound Check
Sound Quality: Great
Stage Lighting: Good
Sightlines: Great
Eardrum Meter: Yellow–Red

Tech Check
Sound System: Exceptional—Midas Verona, EAW JF200i/SB250 Mains, Crown power
Monitors: 4 wedges mixes, EAW SM500i
Backline: Drums
Comments: Sets the standard for purpose-built, acoustically treated showcase venues.

NATIONAL UNDERGROUND

159 Houston St | New York, NY 10002 | 212-475-0611
Hours: 12p-4a Daily
Subway: F to 2nd Ave
www.thenationalunderground.com

Written by: Mark Osborne

MUSIC TYPE	VENUE TYPE	ADMISSION	ATMOSPHERE	DRINKS: $-$$
Rock, Pop, Folk	Small Club Capacity 70	$5 - $11	Southern-spirited Neighborhood Bar	$3+ Happy Hour **FOOD:** yes

LOWER EAST SIDE — Corner of Houston St & Allen St

The Mississippi River does not flow near New York but its musical spirit pervades this Houston Street establishment. The name 'National Underground' is homage to the famed National guitar, which was used widely in country, bluegrass, and blues music. True to its name the National Underground features a variety of country, alt rock, and roots bands, seven days a week. The National Underground was established by brothers Gavin and Joey Degraw both accomplished and celebrated musicians in their own right.

The venue itself is split into two spaces, a main floor at street level, and a basement which can be accessed by a door next to the main entrance. The security people are friendly, and there is often no cover charge to either space.

The main ground floor is the larger of the two rooms and is an unpretentious mix of exposed stone wall sprinkled with decor that could have been picked from a trailer park yard sale in Alabama. But, its not about the surroundings; the National Underground focuses on the music and creating a vibe that is seldom found north of the Mason Dixon line: eats, inexpensive beer, and some good-ole Southern rock.

The basement is what realtors euphemistically call charming, but in reality is very small. There is a tiny bar and a tiny stage, and a small area to congregate. It is open, however to all styles—the venue encourages "anything goes." Neither space seems to attract the typical LES crowd on the weekends, but tends towards a variety of ages, who all appear to be there to focus on the music. The main space has a jam night every Tuesday which also brings in a great crowd of roots music aficionados.

Sound Check (2 Rooms)
Sound Quality: Good
Stage Lighting: Minimal
Sightlines: So-So
Eardrum Meter:
Downstairs, Yellow-Red
Upstairs, Yellow

Tech Check
Mixer: Upstairs-Mackie, Downstairs-Yamaha
Sound System: QSC K-Series
Monitors: Minimal
Backline: Full Backline
Comments: 1 sound engineer for both rooms

Downtown Manhattan

PARKSIDE LOUNGE

317 East Houston St | New York, 10002 | 212-673-6270
Hours: 1p-4a Daily
Subway: F to 2nd Ave
www.parksidelounge.net

Written by: Sari Henry

DRINKS: $-$$	ATMOSPHERE	ADMISSION	VENUE TYPE	MUSIC TYPE
1p-8p Happy Hour FOOD: no	Neighborhood Dive Bar	Free - $7	Small Club	Rock, Pop, Folk, World, Blues, Comedy

Inviting, welcoming, inclusive. Parkside Lounge prides itself on being a place where all different types of people can have a good time. The venue offers performances for every type of taste: music ranging from bluegrass to local indie rock and an open-mic night, and comedy and cabaret shows. The club's come-as-you-are atmosphere is the result of a seemingly unlikely partnership between Karen Waltermire, known locally for years as the "Blonde Bombshell of Bleecker Street," and former Parkside bartender, Christopher Lee.

The spirit of Parkside is embodied in its eclectic mix of patrons: locals, tourists, music-lovers, drag queens, stockbrokers and frat boys, who all enjoy Parkside's distinctive offerings of performances and drink specials—Sunday's all-day Liquid Brunch, Manhattan Mondays and Tuesday Brewsdays. Some fun side distractions include the foosball game, Pac-Man, board games and a photo booth.

Performances go up in the tiny back room of the bar, which are as distinctive as the crowd itself. The space is attractive to musicians and fans because it places the monetary responsibility of the show in the hands of the performers: the performers set admission prices and keep the profits from the show. According to guitarist James MacCarthy from Band of Outsiders, he and other musicians enjoy playing Parkside because the amps are good, the back room is cozy and the management is accommodating. What the club may lack in sound quality, it more than makes up for in ambience. Indeed, the bar is often quite crowded, the shoulder-to-shoulder crowd attesting to the popularity of the venue.

HISTORY

Parkside started life in 1908 as an ice house on Allen Street several blocks west. Soon after it became a bar taking its name from the small park near the median on Houston. In 1996, the venue moved to its current location on Houston Street when Karen purchased it from the Gellerman Family. Christopher became a partner in 2009 and his influence is apparent in the venue's southwest accents. In particular, Christopher believes that the city is in need of better Bloody Marys and that they are far superior in New Orleans and his native Texas. To give the drinks more bite and flavor, Lee concocts Cajun Bloody Marys that feature pickled green beans instead of celery.

Sound Check
Sound Quality: Good
Stage Lighting: Good
Sightlines: Good
Eardrum Meter:
Green–Yellow

Tech Check
Sound System: Yamaha EMX 860
Monitors: Ceiling Mounted
Backline: Full Backline
Comments: Sound mixed from stage
Other: Greenroom available

LOWER EAST SIDE
Corner of Houston St & Attorney St

Downtown Manhattan

PIANOS

158 Ludlow St | New York, NY 10002 | 212-505-3733
Hours: 3p-4a Daily
Subway: J,M,F to Essex St/Delancey St | F to 2nd Ave
www.pianosnyc.com

Written by: Emily Niewendorp

MUSIC TYPE	VENUE TYPE	ADMISSION	ATMOSPHERE	DRINKS: $-$$
Rock, Pop, Folk, Indie	Small Club Capacity 150	Free - $10	Indie Rock Club, Showcase Venue	Happy Hour 3p-7p **FOOD:** Full Menu

LOWER EAST SIDE — Between Ludlow St & Rivington St

Downtown Manhattan

Pianos is one of the liveliest music venues in the Lower East Side and it has been since it opened in 2002. The venue's unique bright-colored schemes, light-hearted decor, full schedule of DJs and live music acts attract crowds night after night.

Pianos appeal is astonishing, yet rightly so: there are always people spilling out its doors, milling around outside and waiting in line for entry. Through the large, front windows, people can be seen laughing, socializing and moving to the DJ's beats. Inside, the bar has an inviting demeanor of white painted brick and wood beams, with shades of blue highlighting the window frames and the floor. This space is barely large enough to allow for the large amounts of traffic flow, but the surfer photos on the wall, the curvy packed bar and high tables, perfect for sampling from the menu with friends, all induce a congenial tone.

The live room is the driving force at Pianos. It has its own pint-size bar for the ardent music aficionados, who don't want to miss a beat. Multiple bands play nightly, ranging from indie rock to singer-songwriter. The capabilities for sound are excellent; the speakers are all top notch and the stage is sand-filled to absorb sound and reduce echoing. The colors are bolder and darker in this room pointing attention to the musicians, who can command the small room and be seen by everyone on the surprisingly high stage.

> Franz Ferdinand played Pianos in their first U.S. show, right before they popped. P.J. Harvey has played there. Another memorable show was a New Year's event: Tinkle Show with comedian David Cross from Arrested Development, and Wilco.

The upstairs area has a slight jungle theme. Some stuffed animals silently watch the room's activities from an alcove near the stairwell. This 2nd floor space operates as a disco, dance party, karaoke room and second stage for acoustic set-ups, sometimes as many as seven in an afternoon and evening. Low-key in the early evening, it is ideal for a quiet dinner at the bar. Later at night, particularly during special events, it can become a raging dance party.

Pianos' intentional beach house designs are a much welcomed contrast from the common 'dark and dirty bar.' The venue has also fine-tuned its operations, retaining what is a hit among its patrons and benefits the business most. Four-dollar frozen margaritas are a smash at happy hour. Most of the staff are like-minded artists and surfers themselves. And the gastro-pub menu has been narrowed down to the popular items such as burgers, seared tuna salad and sandwiches.

Something interesting is always going on at Pianos. People walking by, look in and think, "I want to go in there."

HISTORY
Pianos fashioned its name from the previous business's trade—piano-refurbishing. Before the change-over the shop looked like a piano graveyard with strings, pieces of wood and piano frames lying around. For a short while, Pianos was used as a do-it-yourself performance space, until the live room was built for the bands. Intended to be a multi-room venue, the upstairs floor and its bar/lounge and smaller playing area was developed a short time later.

Pianos has never attached itself to certain music genres. The venue has had different bookers, but the focus throughout the years has always been on booking bands that draw people, as well as, bands that have potential to attract attention. **Developing bands is important to Pianos, as is trying to predict what the next good sound is going to be.** The bookers at Pianos are constantly scouting, listening to 100s of submissions each week and reaching out to agents.

Sound Check (2 Rooms)
Sound Quality: Main Room–Great, Upstairs–Good
Stage Lighting: Main Room–Good, Upstairs–So-So
Sightlines: Main Room–Great, Upstairs–So-So
Eardrum Meter:
Main Room, Yellow–Red
Upstairs, Yellow

Tech Check
Mixer: Midas Venice 320
Sound System: Downstairs, EAW EP3/EP1
Monitors: 4 mixes, EAW
Backline: Full Backline
Comments: 16 track recording available

Downtown Manhattan

ROCKWOOD MUSIC HALL

196 Allen St | New York, NY 10002 | 212-477-4155
Hours: 6p-4a Daily
Subway: F to 2nd Ave | F,J,M to Delancey St | B,D to Grand St
www.rockwoodmusichall.com

Written by: Erika Omundson

MUSIC TYPE	VENUE TYPE	ADMISSION	ATMOSPHERE	DRINKS: $-$$
Indie, Pop, World, Jazz, R&B, Eclectic	Small Club Capacity 50 - 200	Free - $20	Intimate Listening Room	Average $6+ FOOD: no

LOWER EAST SIDE — Between Houston St & Stanton St

Rockwood Music Hall initially opened as a small, intimate room with deep red hues, exposed brick, candlelight, three small rows of tables and a grand piano that occupies most of the stage. Named after its owner, Rockwood Music Hall has quickly developed a reputation for impeccable booking of the most talented musicians. With a new act every hour, audience members may come for one specific act, but end up staying for another. It is a place to discover emerging artists and a place where established artists feel comfortable playing an intimate acoustic set or joining with other musicians to experiment with new sounds.

Maintaining incredibly high musical standards and quality facilities has resulted in devoted audience-goers and repeat performances by some of most talented musicians from New York and beyond. The consensus among those who frequent Rockwood Music Hall is that it is the perfect cozy space to sit down, relax, listen to great music and discover new artists such as Julia Darling, Megan Palmer and many others while choosing from an impresive list of wines and imported beers. At the end of the set, they pass a silver bucket to collect tips (a $5 suggested donation) for the bands.

In April 2010, Rockwood Music Hall expanded to a space directly next door and added a second space called Rockwood Music Hall Stage 2. This new space is more than twice the size of the original Rockwood Music Hall, but manages to maintain much of the charm and intimacy of the original space. Stage 2 includes a catwalk-like baclony whichs adds a slightly grander feel to the new space.

Some of the more well-known artists that have played at Rockwood include: Grace Potter & the Nocturnals, Eli "Paperboy" Reed, Wakey! Wakey!, Chris Thile, Teddy Thompson, Amos Lee, Richard Julian, Jim Campilongo, Brendan James, Elizabeth & the Catapult, James Maddock, Sonya Kitchell, Jamie McLean, and Peter Salett. Bluegrass guitar virtuoso Michael Daves and the experimental jazz great Dred Scott Trio continue to play long-standing Tuesday night residencies at Rockwood. Several famous artists and actors have made special appearances at Rockwood in guest appearances or under various pseudonyms including Chrissie Hynde, Norah Jones, Sharon Jones, Ari Hest, Rufus Wainwright, Jeremy Sisto and others.

Tech Check
Sound system: New York's best kept secret!

Sound Check (2 Rooms)
Sound Quality: Stage 1–Great, Stage 2–Great
Stage Lighting: Stage 1–Great, Stage 2–Great
Sightlines: Stage 1–Great, Stage 2–Great
Eardrum Meter:
Stage 1–Yellow
Stage 2–Yellow

Downtown Manhattan

BANJO JIM'S

700 E 9th St | New York, 10009 | 212-777-0869
Hours: Sun-Thu 6p-4a, Fri 5p-4a, Sat 2:30p-4a
Subway: F to 2nd Ave | L to 1st Ave
www.banjojims.com

Written by: Heather McCown

DRINKS: $-$$ Cash Only FOOD: no	ATMOSPHERE Lovingly Preserved Neighborhood Bar	ADMISSION Free, Tip Jar, One Drink Minimum	VENUE TYPE Small Club	MUSIC TYPE Folk: Bluegrass, Roots, Alt Country

Stepping up on the small front porch into Banjo Jim's is synonymous with entering a lovingly preserved museum of the musician, Banjo Jim Croce.

Created by owner Lisa Zwier-Croce in late 2005, this humble venue ensures the longevity of Jim's positive attitude toward life and the wonderful memories he left behind. The club's motto, "Feel the Love," defines the feeling Jim invoked in people that he met. When discussing the motivations behind opening the cozy joint, Lisa emphasized: "Our focus is to make a welcoming space for the musicians to play."

Inside the club, the tiny bar top winds through the back of the small room beneath the banjos and signed posters scattered against the red walls. Tables and a couch-like bench on the wall provide seating. Perfectly positioned on the corner, the venue's front windows allow both patrons and musicians a view of the beautiful community gardens during the day,

and allow pedestrians to check out what's happening inside at night.

One of the bartenders, Bill Bell, comments that Banjo Jim's is a staple for neighbors and those, "who don't mind wandering east of the nearest subway station." The audience on any given night is mostly comprised of locals, but certain acts also bring in their own crowd.

On a Monday, one can sit down to an empty place at 7 p.m., order a can of Dale's Pale Ale for $4, to accompany the live music, and look up to find the place mysteriously packed within short order. It is apparent in the mesmerized faces that folks are enraptured by the excellent musicianship presented each night, and Jim's lingering good vibes.

With reasonable prices, the one-drink minimum per set is easy on the wallet and yet another nod to a place which wants to embrace folks rather than turn them away.

Sound Check
Sound Quality: Good
Stage Lighting: Minimal
Sightlines: Good
Eardrum Meter:
Green–Yellow

Tech Check
Mixer: Mackie 1604
Monitors: Minimal
Backline: Upright Yamaha Piano, Full Backline
Comments: The bartender doubles as the sound engineer. The mixer is behind the bar.

EAST VILLAGE
Corner of Avenue C & 9th St

Downtown Manhattan

THE BOWERY ELECTRIC

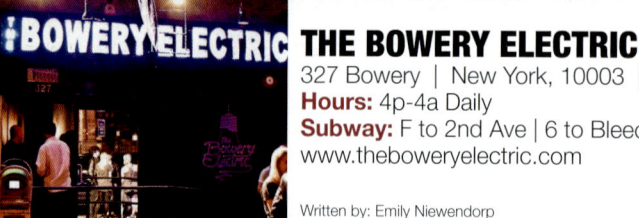

327 Bowery | New York, 10003 | 212-228-0228
Hours: 4p-4a Daily
Subway: F to 2nd Ave | 6 to Bleecker St or Astor Place
www.theboweryelectric.com

Written by: Emily Niewendorp

MUSIC TYPE	VENUE TYPE	ADMISSION	ATMOSPHERE	DRINKS: $-$$
Rock, Pop, Punk, DJ	Basement Club Capacity 150	Free - $20	Rock 'n' Roll Spirited	Happy Hour 5p-9p FOOD: no

EAST VILLAGE
Corner of Bowery & 2nd St

Downtown Manhattan

"New York's in my blood," says Jesse Malin. The owner of The Bowery Electric, Jesse supplies the rock 'n' roll spirit that courses through the club. A big-hearted rocker in his own right, Jesse has toured as a musician since the age of thirteen, as a solo artist and in bands such as Generation D and Heart Attack.

An advocate of any downtown scene, Jesse emphasizes, "Wherever I go in the world I always look for the underground. Where are the artists?" In New York City, Jesse funnels his energy into building a supportive downtown community for rock, punk and indie artists. He owned hard-core, punk venue Coney Island High on St. Mark's Place (a few blocks NE of The Bowery Electric) in the mid-'90s. Former Coney Island High patrons recall waiting in line outside the club conscious of nearby drug addicts. The much-loved club closed during its fight for a dancing license under Mayor Rudy Guiliani's 'clean up New York' campaign. Jesse went back to touring, still desiring a rock club.

When Jesse talks, his excitement about being back downtown is evident. NYC's current popular and polished downtown appearance is a vast contrast from its unrefined condition in the '90s. The grit and rawness that Jesse remembers remains close, he says—in the reformed CBGBs space down the block and the ever-present homeless population. Regardless of these environmental changes, **The Bowery Electric attracts rock 'n' roll artists and enthusiasts of all ages, their 'attitudes' and big hearts included. Jesse hopes to provide a place where young kids can grow musically, and learn from their elders how to blow off steam in a positive way: "Meeting a guy, meeting a girl—being social impacts people's lives."**

The building The Bowery Electric occupies supplied electrical parts for many years, followed by the short-lived Remote Lounge. Partnering with one of the lounge's owners, Jesse and

38

some investors turned the space into a rock 'n' roll club and kept some of the building's history in its name. The coolest aspect of The Bowery Electric is the sunken stage and floor. Stone walls and a 19th century vaulted ceiling add to the venue's old-NY vibe, while the finished wood floors and clean space identify with the neighborhood's reformation. The smaller room-size limits capacity, but there is no lack of rocking-out under the sidewalk of New York City. Behind the stage, a proper green room and dressing rooms accommodate the bands. In addition, a private space called the Vault Room that features cavernous walls, can be reserved for private parties. The venue's two floors allow people to wander and not get bored. The chic upstairs bar is lined with mirrors, musicians' artwork and photographs.

Music at The Bowery Electric focuses loosely around rock 'n' roll. Jesse encourages bands to play set lengths determined upon the amount of material in their repertoire, rather than squeeze another band into the evening's line-up. Celebrities, as performers and spectators, pass through The Bowery Electric often. Patti Smith has read poetry and played. Secret shows of well-known artists are common and draw lines of waiting fans, amping up the energy on the block. One hot surprise was a two-hour show by Foxboro Hot Tub, Green Day's side project. Bill Murray and Joan Jett both attended that event. Frequently, Jesse will perform on his own stage, where his energetic spirit projects throughout the room.

On the weekends, DJs host dance parties that are strictly rock 'n' roll—no rap or house music. People surprisingly find themselves loosening up on the dance floor, having a great time. The venue attracts patrons of all financial levels and cultures—men in suits, goth chicks, etc.—and features special nights for ages 18 – 21 on occasion.

Sound Check
Sound Quality: Good
Stage Lighting: Good
Sightlines: Good
Eardrum Meter:
Yellow

Tech Check
Sound System: 32ch Yamaha Mackie SR1530 speakers
Monitors: 4 mixes, JBL MRX
Backline: Full Backline
DJ: Full DJ setup
Other: Green room, dressing room

DOMINION

428 Lafayette Street | New York, NY 10003 | 212-473-1698
Hours: Music times vary
Subway: 6 to Astor Pl | N,R to 8th St
www.dominionny.com

Written by: Daniel Morrow

MUSIC TYPE	VENUE TYPE	ADMISSION	ATMOSPHERE	DRINKS: $$-$$$
Rock, Pop, Jazz, R&B, World, DJ	Club, Theater & Lounge	$10+	Elegant	FOOD: no

EAST VILLAGE — Between 4th St & Astor Place

Dominion NY is a fresh face to New York City, having opened its doors in January 2011. Despite describing itself as a multi-purpose venue, it clearly places a weighty emphasis on live music. For its size, the venue boasts one of the finest sound systems in New York, including one of the most advanced recording systems: 64 Track Digidesign Pro Tools HD, purpose-built to record the shows.

Upon entry to the venue, there is a spacious bar outfitted with seats and tables. This has a cocktail lounge feel, with comfortable seating and a menu of enticing cocktails. A mini corridor lined with loveseats leads to the live music space in the back.

The performance space is larger than expected for a self-designated "intimate venue" and, although the stage is too low to guarantee excellent sightlines for a fully packed audience, there is ample room for the musicians. The artist/VIP suite above the stage offers a full bathroom and is a luxurious highlight of Dominion. A beautifully designed spiral staircase leading down from the green room onto the stage should certainly make for grand stage entrances!

What is even more impressive about Dominion is that it uses a concert arena-type sound system for a music room of its size. The investment on sound treatment also leaves little to be desired; the curtains surrounding the entire room, for example, are of the thickest material available on the market. The lighting is also well above NYC's usual standards. It is perfectly well equipped to provide for full-scale theater shows.

As well as music and theater, the venue's flexibility and seemingly limitless resources enable it to cater to dinners, buffets, private parties, DVD screenings, comedy shows, web broadcasts and DJ shows.

Sound Check
Sound Quality: Great
Stage Lighting: Great
Sightlines: Good
Eardrum Meter: Yellow

Photo courtesy of Dominion

Tech Check
Mixer: Midas Venice 320, Mackie Onyx 4880
Sound System: Turbo Sound Floodlight 5 way, EAW SB 1000 Subwoofers, Crown power
MONITOR SPEAKERS: JBL SRX 700 SERIES, 12 discreet mixes
BACKLINE: Full Backline, Kawai 7' Grand Piano
WIRELESS SYSTEMS: Shure UHF, 6 U1UA transmitters/receivers, 6 Beta87 heads, 2 SM58, DPA Wireless, 4 4065 headsets & body packs, Countryman, 2 Isomax headsets & body packs
DJ EQUIPMENT: Rane SL3, (2) CDJ1000mk3, (2) Technics 1200
AUDIO RECORDING: 64 track ProTools HD4
VIDEO RECORDING: 3 Panasonic AG-HVX200 HD Cameras, 13' HD projector

Downtown Manhattan

LAKESIDE LOUNGE

162 Avenue B | New York, NY 10009 | 212-529-8463
Hours: 4p-4a Daily
Subway: F to 2nd Ave | L to 1st Ave
www.lakesidelounge.com

Written by: Sari Henry

DRINKS: $-$$	ATMOSPHERE	ADMISSION	VENUE TYPE	MUSIC TYPE
Cheap / FOOD: no	Neighborhood Dive Bar	Free, Tip Jar	Small Club Capacity 160	Rock 'n' Roll, Country, Garage Rock

The Lakeside Lounge has a unique philosophy: one band per night. Avoiding the typical band-after-band deluge was a key ideal for owners Eric Amble (former Joan Jett and the Blackhearts guitarist) and friend Jim Marshall who opened the venue 15 years ago in their own neighborhood of the East Village.

Lakeside Lounge is an intimate space—dark and homey. Yet the club is large enough to pack in a crowd and resourceful enough to have Tabletop Ms. Pac Man, a nifty black & white photo booth and one of the best jukeboxes around. The stage sits directly in front of the street window, encouraging the occasional passerby to stop for a while and peer at the musicians on stage.

Artists such as Steve Earle, Joey Ramone, Ryan Adams, Jewel, Waco Brothers, The Fleshtones, and Wayne Kramer have gigged at Lakeside. It has also seen surprise performances by artists such as the North Mississippi All-Stars and Robert Randolph.

As a guitarist, Grammy Award winning producer and studio owner (Cowboy Technical Services), Eric's raison-d'etre is music. This passion is reflected in his efforts to have a simple and non-pretentious venue with no cover charge. Eric feels that many clubs reach too far and overbook bands; he says, **"Great bands should be great when it's empty and great when it's full."**

Lakeside Lounge pays homage to Eric's favorite bar in Wisconsin called Chuck's. In fact, the venue's logo is a representation of Lake Geneva, where Chuck's is situated in the town of Fontana. At Lakeside, Eric has created his dream of a Chuck's-like tavern atmosphere in New York. Lakeside Lounge is a relaxed environment and a great place to see a band.

State of the Bathroom:
Nouveau vieux, dive-bar. (What does that even mean?!)

Sound Check
Sound Quality: Good
Stage Lighting: Minimal
Sightlines: Good
Eardrum Meter:
Green–Yellow

Tech Check
Sound System: Minimal
Monitors: JBL 15" EON
Backline: Full Backline
Comments: Audio recording available

EAST VILLAGE
Between 10th St & 11th St

Downtown Manhattan

LIT LOUNGE

93 Second Ave | New York, NY 10003 | 212-777-7987
Hours: 5p-4a Daily
Subway: F to 2nd Ave | 6 to Astor Place
L to 3rd Ave or 1st Ave
www.litloungenyc.com

Written by: Laura Sherman

MUSIC TYPE	VENUE TYPE	ADMISSION	ATMOSPHERE	DRINKS: $-$$
Rock, Punk, Indie, Metal on Mondays	Small Basement	$5 - $13	Artistic, Dark, Friendly if you get in	$4+ FOOD: no

EAST VILLAGE — Between 5th St & 6th St

Created and designed specifically for the East Village underground elite, Lit Lounge is strictly for those who unabashedly revel in their counterculture status. Its mostly young patrons are a mix of college students, skaters, hipsters and gutter punks. Many village bars get co-opted by the casual bohemian; Lit Lounge staunchly maintains its fringe identity.

Back in 2002, the Lit Lounge opened its doors with the aspiration to be a real dive bar. Now affirmed by its outward appearance—a sign-less entryway accompanied by a lone, velvet-roped corral for smokers—Lit Lounge represents itself as a post-punk, indie music venue and art gallery: **"a place for painters, musicians, writers and performers whose visions are not accepted by the mainstream to hang out and build a community."**

The club is housed in a cave-like basement, with an accompanying vibe that makes guests want to party as if their parents went away on vacation. It boasts a 35 foot-long bar, with a lounge/dance area on the upstairs level, and another bar, stage and dance area below. The Fuse Gallery, attached to the rear of the club, features modern art works that reflects the club's atmosphere. Prior to the venue's opening, co-owners Max Brennan and Eric Foss gave the space a 'thoughtful' renovation, thus rendering it an authentic, Village Underground look.

"We don't want any Top-40 wannabes. In fact, we don't want any band who has formed for the sole purpose of financial gain, and we definitely don't book cover bands," says the owners, who instead favor music genres like new wave, no wave, noise rock, math rock, electro dance rock, brit-pop, psychedelic, experimental, abstract folk, etc.

State of the Bathroom: Use if and only if it is an emergency.

Downtown Manhattan

Tech Check
Sound System: Mackie SR
Monitors: JBL (small and mean!), 3 mixes
Backline: Full Backline
Comments: Tiny stage

Sound Check
Sound Quality: So-So
Stage Lighting: Minimal
Sightlines: Minimal
Eardrum Meter: Yellow—Red

Sound Check
Sound Quality: Great
Stage Lighting: Great
Sightlines: Great
Eardrum Meter:
Yellow

JOE'S PUB
425 Lafayette St | New York, NY 10003
212-539-8778
Hours: Mon-Sun 6p-2a
Subway: 6 to Astor Pl | N,R to 8th St
www.joespub.com

Written by: Emily Niewendorp

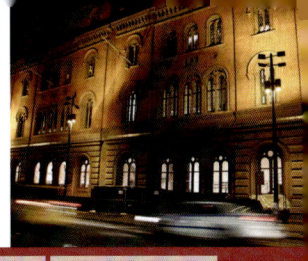

DRINKS: $$-$$$ $12 Table Minimum FOOD: Full Menu	ATMOSPHERE Upscale, Casual	ADMISSION $12 - $25	VENUE TYPE Supper Club Capacity 150-180	MUSIC TYPE All genres, Theater, Musicals, Cabaret

EAST VILLAGE — Between 4th St & Astor Place

Downtown Manhattan

Joe's Pub is a gift to New York City. An off-shoot of The Public Theater, which is rented from the City of New York for $1 a year, this upscale music venue has become an important outlet for live music shows, and a jumping-off point for new theatrical performances that might then run at The Public.

The music program at Joe's Pub represents NYC's diverse citizenry. The mix of genres in the club's repertoire includes: classical, singer-songwriter, jazz, avant-garde, world music, hip hop and one-person shows. An impressive array of musicians have played Joe's Pub, including David Byrne, Bono, Elvis Costello, Mos Def, Alicia Keys, Emmylou Harris, David Gray, Amy Winehouse and Fiest—just to name a few.

HISTORY

The Public Theater used to be one of the City's first libraries: Astor Library, built in 1854. In the mid-1960s, New York Shakespeare Festival founder Joseph Papp discovered the building. It had fallen into disrepair and was close to demolition, when it was preserved under the NYC's new landmark law. It was the first building saved under the ruling and the City entrusted the renovated building to Papp for the low-priced rental. Papp dedicated the beautiful structure to the people of New York City and all aspects of the theater community. The theater is known for specializing in unconventional performances, which reflect the social and political concerns of the times.

In 1998, Joe's Pub was converted from office space attached to the side of the main theater building. Initially, the new space was used for musical and play workshops, but it was after these evening events—when the space was turned over to the bar—that it quickly became a hot NYC night club. In 1998, Joe's Pub offered 200 shows; today, it produces more than 800 shows per year, attended by over 100,000 people annually.

Joe's Pub is nonprofit organization supported by donor/partner programs rooted from The Public's first days. The club's current director Shanta Thake states, **"Anyone who has an artistic sensibility can immediately connect to the space. As an artist you walk in and realize this is part of something much bigger."**

Tech Check
Sound System: Midas Verona EAW speakers, Crown power
Monitors: 4 mixes, EAW
Backline: Grand Piano, Full Backline
Other: Green Room
Comments: Professionally designed stage for a wide array of performance events. DJ ready.

JULES

65 St. Marks Place | New York, NY | 212-477-5560
Hours: Mon-Thu, Sun 11a-12mid, Fri-Sat 11a-1a
Subway: 6 to Astor Pl | N,R to 8th St
www.julesbistro.com

Written by: Heather McCown

MUSIC TYPE	VENUE TYPE	ADMISSION	ATMOSPHERE	DRINKS: $$
Jazz	Restaurant Capacity 50 - 75	Free	Cozy Bistro	Average $7-$12 FOOD: Full Menu

EAST VILLAGE
Between 2nd Ave & 3rd Ave

Downtown Manhattan

Jules Bistro is nestled in the heart of the East Village. For 15 years it has been home to nightly jazz and delicious French cuisine, in a restaurant-style setting.

Jules is part of the Forgeois family of restaurants (others including, Bar Tabac and Cafe Noir), offers frog legs, duck and veal, with the requisite salade Niçoise and steak frites. Don't be fooled by the excellent dishes; this is a neighborhood spot with a laid-back atmosphere. The white stucco walls contrast with the dark wood of the bar and exposed beam floors, all of which are enhanced by the festive candlelight. Established in 1993, this spot is a haven for those looking for good food, camaraderie and excellent jazz music.

This is also a musician's joint where acts are scheduled months in advance. Jules paints the palate with a comfortable ambiance of warmth and appreciative patrons, while the musicians provide a complement of rich tones and lilting melodies. "The musician's get to control the sound of the room," states bass player Pat Ryan, as the instruments are acoustic or enhanced by small amplifiers. Jerome, one of Jules' bartenders states, **"We try to keep the music at a comfortable level where everyone can talk at the bar or tables,"** which are placed within feet of the musicians.

On any particular evening, patrons delight in the excellent music; including, the gypsy swing sounds of the band, Lower East Side Hot Club. Each note seems to playfully mingle with the aromas of food and warm conversation. During interludes, Jerome shaves a delicate morsel of Tête de Moins cheese for those seated at the bar. Jules feels comfortable alone, or with a group. The venue provides a delicious combination of food and drink that is only enhanced by the artistry of the musicians.

Sound Check
Sound Quality: Good
Stage Lighting: Minimal
Sightlines: Minimal
Eardrum Meter:
Green

Sound Check
Marvin Sewell, guitarist Cassandra Wilson
"Atmosphere is good and the music is good. You feel like you are somewhere else–another place in time when in that spot. The confines are small but nice."

NUBLU

62 Avenue C | New York, NY 10009 | 212-375-1500
Hours: 8p-4a Daily
Subway: L to 1st Ave | F to 2nd Ave
www.nublu.net

Written by: Allie Arias

DRINKS: $$	ATMOSPHERE	ADMISSION	VENUE TYPE	MUSIC TYPE
Average $6-$12 FOOD: no	Intimate, Worldly, DIY	$10	Small Club Capacity 80	Jazz, World, DJ

"This is what the East Village used to be," is a phrase Nublu's owner Ilhan Ersahin hears frequently about his quietly removed bar on Avenue C.

The phosphorescent, blue light above the tattered, plastic entryway between 3rd and 4th streets downplays the raw talent inside the unmarked door. The stage is past the bar, near the back of the room, and only slightly elevated. The audience can either sit near the music, or enjoy it from a distance. Seating at the bar is limited, but couches or cool chairs that look like oversized tennis balls are available. At one point or another, dancing is a must, so don't get too comfortable.

Depending on the night, Nublu offers live psychedelic funk or jazz jams, and DJs spin electronic or samba that encourages even arrhythmic folks to get up and groove. The environment is relaxed and friendly. Ilhan's motto is "aim locally, think internationally," which is evident in the East Village regulars and the international clientele that slightly alters the vibe from night to night.

Nublu evolved from simple gatherings of Ilhan and his musician friends, to a home away from home for artists and people from around the world. Nublu represents in Ilhan's eyes, "the sound of today."

DJs play a huge role at Nublu. A DJ spins between bands so the music never stops and Ilhan handpicks DJs that are unique in their musical expression. At Nublu, you won't hear top-40s songs, instead the blends of funk, hiphop, jazz, soul, Latin and more.

Nublu also has its own record label, so be sure to check out the array of albums and merchandise on the wall behind the bar for sale. Forro In The Dark, Wax Poetic, Hess Is More and 3 Na Massa are a few of the Nublu bands.

Sound Check
Sound Quality: Good
Stage Lighting: Minimal
Sightlines: Good
Eardrum Meter:
Green–Yellow

Tech Check
Sound System: Mackie CFX
Monitors: Minimal
Backline: Basic but full backline
Comments: Consistently showcasing the best musicians in the world.

EAST VILLAGE
Between 4th St & 5th St

Downtown Manhattan

45

NUYORICAN POETS CAFE

236 3rd St | New York, NY 10009
212-505-8183
Hours: Wed-Sat 7p-1a, Sun-Tue 7p-11p
Subway: F to 2nd Ave | L to 1st Ave
www.nuyorican.org

Written by: Sari Henry

Sound Check
Sound Quality: Good
Stage Lighting: Good
Sightlines: Good
Eardrum Meter:
Green

MUSIC TYPE	VENUE TYPE	ADMISSION	ATMOSPHERE	DRINKS: $
Poetry, Hip Hop, World, Comedy	Small Club Capacity 120	$5 - $20 Student Discount	Timeless, Diverse, Inviting	Average $4 - $6 FOOD: no

EAST VILLAGE — Between Avenue B & Avenue C

Downtown Manhattan

The Nuyorican is quite large for a New York City venue. The space has a raised stage, table seating, and a second floor balcony with seats. Food is not available, but they do serve wine, beer, coffee and soft drinks during events. The Cafe is only open when an event is scheduled on the calendar.

Executive director Daniel Gallant describes the Cafe's vibe as "high energy, yet supportive." Intended as an outlet for under represented Puerto Rican artists, the Cafe provides a nurturing place for new and established artists—of all ethnic backgrounds. Veteran Beat writers including Allen Ginsberg and William S. Burroughs, as well as poetry impresario Bob Holman have been associated with the Cafe, linking it to enduring bohemian traditions.

The Friday night poetry slam always fills the house. Slams are a sort of tournament in which judges are chosen from the audience and poets compete against each other in three minute slots. There are also open mic nights, at which anyone can perform, and from which slam performers are chosen for future features and slams.

The Cafe also hosts live music performances, ranging from hip hop through singer-songwriter acoustic sets to Latin jazz and Yerbabuena, the Puerto Rican roots style of music.

HISTORY

Nuyorican, a mysterious name to many, is hip short-hand for "New York Puerto Rican," a designation coined by New York's post-Beat Puerto Rican writer/poets Miguel Algarin, Pedro Pietri and Miguel Piñero. A gathering of writers started circa 1973 in the apartment of Miguel Algarin as a salon outlet for the East Village literary and spoken word artists. It soon outgrew Miguel's living room. By 1975 it relocated to an Irish bar called the Sunshine Cafe on East 6th Street, which was christened the Nuyorican Poets Cafe. In 1980 overflow audiences inspired the purchase of Nuyorican's present building at 236 E. 3rd St.

The neighborhood has transformed since Miguel et al conceived of their showcase. Due to gentrification many venues and stores have opened shop in the East Village; regardless, up-and-coming spoken word artists from all over the city, and the country, still travel to the Nuyorican Cafe to present their work.

Tech Check
Sound System: Toft A6B mixer, JBL monitors 2 Mixes, Video projector, DJ ready

Sound Check
Sound Quality: Good
Stage Lighting: Good
Sightlines: So-So
Eardrum Meter:
Green

SIDEWALK CAFE
94 Avenue A | New York, NY 10009
212-253-0036
Hours: 9a-4a Daily
Subway: F to 2nd Ave | L to 1st Ave
www.sidewalkmusic.net

Food Served Late

Written by: Kyle Benson

DRINKS: $-$$	ATMOSPHERE	ADMISSION	VENUE TYPE	MUSIC TYPE
$3+ FOOD: no	Antifolk	Free 2 Drink Minimum	Small Club Capacity 100	Antifolk, Indie, Experimental, Roots

Sidewalk is a cafe, bar and music venue, ideal for exploration and new music experiences. Ben Krieger, the current music handler, likens the spot as, "traditionally, a place where good people get their first gigs."

EAST VILLAGE
Between 6th St & 7th St

Downtown Manhattan

Six nights a week, bands of various music styles take to the stage, while on Monday nights a spattering of genres is on display for the infamous open mic, arguable the longest-running in New York. Anybody that sticks around longer than an hour on any given night will see a variety of performances, from unknown duos to Jason Trachtenburg of the Trachtenburg Family Slideshow Players. It is this diverse talent that gives Sidewalk Cafe its magnetism.

HISTORY
Much has changed in the East Village's Alphabet City over the last three decades, but despite restaurant booms and gentrification, this venue has outlasted many of its neighborhood counterparts. When it opened in the '80s, Sidewalk operated solely as a restaurant, but for the past 15 years the back room has become a reputable venue, helping to ignite many notable musicians including Regina Spektor, The Moldy Peaches, Beck and Nellie McKay.

This small, 100-person music space with a humble stage is also responsible for ushering in a new niche genre called antifolk. The story goes that Lach, a local musician, working to break into the West Village folk circuit, had been rejected because his sound was too 'edgy.' So, with a classic dose of American 'screw-off,' Lach searched for a place where a greater freedom of expression could live. After a short stint in the Lower East Side, he found his home at Sidewalk Cafe. It was here that he cultivated an artist sanctuary for anyone with a song to sing. As the antifolk genre grew, the venue built a semi-annual festival. In February and August of each year, a roster of active regulars and returning participants gather for a week of stomping-ground gigs. Lach resided as the curator for 15 years before stepping down in 2008.

Tech Check
Mixer: Mackie 1640
Monitors: JBL JRX112M
Backline: Piano, Drumkit, Marshall Amp
Comments: Audio Recordings, DVD player and screen/projector available

47

WEBSTER HALL

125 East 11th St | New York, NY 10003 | 212-353-1600
Hours: Music times vary
Subway: N,Q,R,4,5,6 to Union Square
R to 8th St | 6 to Astor Pl
www.websterhall.com

Written by: Laura Sherman

MUSIC TYPE	VENUE TYPE	ADMISSION	ATMOSPHERE	DRINKS: $$
Various: Rock, Pop, Folk, Indie, DJ	Mid-Size Club Capacity 1400	Free - $30	Iconic	FOOD: no

EAST VILLAGE — Between 3rd Ave & 4th Ave

Webster Hall events are all the rage with music enthusiasts age 18 and up. Going to Webster Hall on the weekend is a sweaty and magical experience; the light shows alone are worth the price of admission.

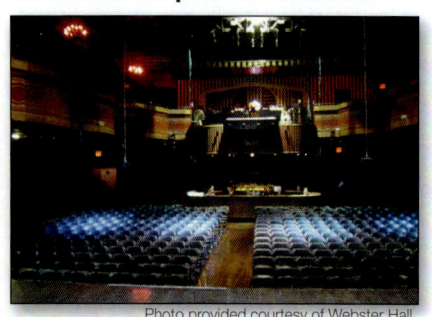

Photo provided courtesy of Webster Hall

Webster Hall creates magic on a daily basis. People show up to dance, dressed to impress, and performing there live as a musician is extraordinary.

The club fuses state-of-the-art audio, video and lighting technology, creating a playground for the ultimate party. Webster Hall can cater to groups of 100 to 2,000, with crazed dancing capacity for 1,400 on the Grand Ballroom's suspended floor system. With 40,000 square feet, split among four floors, and seven event rooms there's always a lot going on at Webster Hall.

HISTORY

Webster Hall has helped to create history in more ways than simply music. Built in 1886 by Charles Rentz, it was originally used to host society balls and political rallies. It is said that the women's right to vote was unofficially decided in the Grand Ballroom, and during the prohibition period it was Al Capone's speakeasy. During the 1950s, RCA Records became the "acoustical integrity" of the Grand Ballroom at Webster Hall, and the venue became the home of the east coast recording studio. The club was graced by the presence of artists such as Ray Charles, Elvis Presley and Frank Sinatra. In 1980, The Ritz opened at Webster Hall as the famous showcase for emerging rock acts and featured such amazing artists as Tina Turner, Eric Clapton, B.B. King, Sting and Guns 'n' Roses. After Prince performed on the stage

Tech Check: Webster Hall

Mixer: Midas Heritage 3000 - 44 ch
Sound System: Stereo 3-way line array – each array has 12 L-Acoustics dV-DOSC and 4 L-Acoustics dV-SUB enclosures, Subwoofers 6 L-Acoustics SB218, Amplification (15) L-Acoustics LA48A, Processing Dolby Lake Contour
Monitors: Midas XL250 - 48 ch
Drum Fill L-Acoustics dV-SUB enclosure, L-Acoustics ARCS, Clair Bros. 12AM floor monitors, **Side Fill** Clair Bros. R4 III
Lighting Control: High End Systems Wholehog III console (V3.1.6) with DP2000, 2 external touch screens, 2 playback wings, High End systems Hog iPC Console, DFD 4-Universe DMX Switch, DFD Bi-Directional hubs, DFD Isolation Amplifier
Other: Stage 36' W x 12'6" D x 4'3" H, dressing rooms, 9 65" Sharp Aquos LCD TVs, 2 NEC LT260 projectors
Comments: State-of-the-art concert hall

Downtown Manhattan

THE STUDIO AT WEBSTER HALL

125 East 11th St | New York, NY 10003 | 212-353-1600
Hours: Doors 8p, Music times vary
Subway: N,Q,R,4,5,6 to Union Square
R to 8th St | 6 to Astor Pl
www.websterhall.com

Written by: Laura Sherman

DRINKS: $$ FOOD: no	ATMOSPHERE Premier Showcase Venue	ADMISSION Free to $15	VENUE TYPE Mid-Size Club Capacity 300	MUSIC TYPE Various: Rock, Pop, Folk, Indie, DJ

EAST VILLAGE
Between 3rd Ave & 4th Ave

Downtown Manhattan

he claimed it was, "The best stage in New York City." The Ritz relocated in 1986, which allowed Webster Hall to be reborn.

The Ballinger family of Toronto, Canada, rewrote the rulebook on New York City nightlife when it purchased the club in 1990, and restored the name to the original Webster Hall. The venue has gone through several significant changes, but somehow managed to keep most of its original design. The ceiling dates back to 1886, and is Art Deco at its finest. The preserved decor allows your imagination to run free through history.

Photo provided courtesy of Webster Hall

Tech Check: The Studio at WH
Mixer: Yamaha M7CL-48 ch
Sound System: L-Acoustics ARCS Active 2-way, SB28 subwoofer enclosures, L-Acoustic power
Monitors: Mixed from FOH, L-Acoustics 12XT, 115 HiQ, L-Acoustic power, 5 mixes
Backline: Full Backline - Tama Superstar, Marshall JVM210H, (2) 4x12 speaker cabinets, VOX AC30 H2 combo, Markbass 104 HR with 4x10 cabinet, Korg M50
Lighting: Martin LightJockey 2.8.1 with touchscreen, 8-Faders DMX-IN console, (6) Martin Mania SCX600 Scanners, (24) Par 56
Comments: Best-in-class venue

In 2008, the New York City Landmarks Preservation Commission designated Webster Hall as a historical landmark. The Ballinger family stays involved with the club on a daily basis, and several of the nighttime managers are family members.

The Studio at Webster Hall is a smaller space with a capacity for 300, which opened its doors to up-and-coming artists in 2008. The space is sponsored by retailer Best Buy and has one of the best PA systems for its size. It is equipped with high-end recording equipment, and capabilities for multi-track live recordings of performances in the Grand Ballroom as well as The Studio itself.

The Studio carries on the legacy of the 1950s when Webster Hall was the home of RCA Records. Recently, The Studio teamed up with another icon in music, MTV, to present a digital web cast "Live From The Studio." The webcast showcases indie rock acts, including both unsigned and established acts. Trevor Silmser, a co-founder of The Studio, says the partnership "will help establish opportunities for young bands to monetize their music." The first band to be featured on the web cast was The Drums. Some of the other acts that have performed at The Studio include Keane, Against Me!, Vampire Weekend, Shwayze and many others.

49

BAR NEXT DOOR

129 MacDougal St | New York, 10012 | 212-529-5945
Hours: Sun-Thu 10a-3a, Fri-Sat 10a-4a
Subway: B,D,F,M,A,C,E to West 4th St
www.lalanternacaffe.com

Written by: Emily Niewendorp

MUSIC TYPE	VENUE TYPE	ADMISSION	ATMOSPHERE	DRINKS: $$-$$$
Jazz	Small Restaurant 28 Seats	$10/$25 per set One Drink Minimum	Elegant, Earthy, Welcoming	$7+ FOOD: Full Menu

GREENWICH VILLAGE
Between West 3rd St & West 4th St

Offering an elegant yet earthy and welcoming atmosphere, The Bar Next Door consistently draws the finest known and unknown talent in NYC. The signature group is the trio and according to the booker, Peter, is "the leanest full group in jazz."

HISTORY

The Bar Next Door is tucked away in the English basement of a charming restored Federal Period townhouse built in 1829 that also houses its parent, the restaurant La Lanterna di Vittorio. The music began in this cozy basement restaurant when Jonathan Kreisberg, Joel Frahm and Peter Mazza took initiative and approached the owner, Vittorio, requesting each their own night to perform live—Joel on Tuesdays, Jonathan on Wednesdays and Peter on Sundays. When the musicians were still sustaining themselves a few years later and attracting crowds and choice reviews, Vittorio became open to filling the remainder of the week with music. Peter began booking jazz groups and musicians and today, ten years later, Jonathan, Joel and Peter continue to play their ongoing respective nights.

> "I'm a native New Yorker... this room is my love as my heart goes into EVERY personal gig or booking. I've aspired to have the room uphold the creative integrity and welcoming energy that is truly NY."
>
> Peter Mazza, Booker/Musician

Tech Check
Sound System: No sound system, acoustic

Downtown Manhattan

THE BITTER END

147 Bleecker St | New York, 10012 | 212-673-7030
Hours: Mon-Thu, Sun 7:30p-2a, Fri-Sat 7:30p-4a
Subway: A,C,D,E,F to West 4th St | 6 to Bleecker St
www.bitterend.com

Written by: Rachel Antonio

DRINKS: $-$$	ATMOSPHERE	ADMISSION	VENUE TYPE	MUSIC TYPE
Average $6 - $11	Legendary	$8 - $10	Small Club	Various: Rock, Pop,
FOOD: no	Showcase Venue	1 to 2 Drink Minimum	Capacity 230	Funk, Blues, R&B

New York City's oldest rock venue, The Bitter End, still draws crowds no matter how trendy other music venues get. This Bleecker St. landmark is almost as much a legend as some of the stars whose careers were launched here—a seemingly endless roster of music giants, such as: Arlo Guthrie, Carly Simon, Bo Diddley, Peter, Paul and Mary, Billy Joel, Linda Ronstadt and Stefani Germanotta (Lady Gaga).

The Bitter End hasn't changed its look since 1961. Its practical clapboard frame exterior and blue awning have marked the club's location for 50 years. Inside, the worn wood paneling, exposed brick and Tiffany-style lampshades give the space a rustic, dated feel. Faded and peeling posters decoupaged onto the walls further emphasize the venue's age. *Billboard* magazine articles, autographed photos, records and ticket stubs adorn the walls as badges of honor, heralding the dues paid here.

Free of obstructed views, the stage is set up for musicians to command the focal point in this venue. Colored stage lights brighten up the space, which is home to a baby grand piano. Tables are available close to the stage, or many people prefer to stand and dance in the back near the bar. The Bitter End was founded on rock music, although it is common to hear other genres such as pop, country, folk and soul.

Table seating requires a two-drink minimum per show and bar seating one drink. The bartenders, manager and bouncer all help make The Bitter End a relaxed and casual environment. Co-owner and manager Paul Rizzo says: "I just want everyone to have a good time on all levels."

On Sunday evenings, The Bitter End hosts a singer-songwriter night, giving amateurs a chance to strut their stuff. Musician Emma Lov says: "It feels really good to be in front of an audience. The Bitter End treats you like a professional."

GREENWICH VILLAGE
Between LaGuardia Pl & Thompson St

Downtown Manhattan

Sound Check
Sound Quality: Good
Stage Lighting: Good
Sightlines: Good
Eardrum Meter: Yellow

Tech Check
Mixer: 24ch Allen&Heath GL2400
Sound System: EAW LA325 Mains
Monitors: Mixed from FOH, JBL wedges
Backline: Yamaha Baby Grand Piano, Full Backline
Comments: Large stage, Audio recordings available

BLUE NOTE

131 West 3rd St | New York, NY 10012 | 212-475-8592
Hours: Mon-Sun 8 & 10:30p, Fri-Sat 12:30a, Sun 12:30p & 2p
Subway: A,C,E,F,B,D to West 4th St
www.bluenote.net

Sunday Jazz Brunch 12:30p & 2:30p

Written by: Emily Niewendorp & Monica U. Garcia

MUSIC TYPE	VENUE TYPE	ADMISSION	ATMOSPHERE	DRINKS: $-$$$
Jazz (Late Night: Funk, Soul, R&B, Hip-Hop)	Supper Club Capacity 186	$8 - $65 $5 - $25 Minimum	World-renowned	$5 - $30 FOOD: Full Menu

GREENWICH VILLAGE — Between MacDougal St & 6th Ave

Downtown Manhattan

The Blue Note Jazz Club's jazz persona sizzles like a long, high hat brush roll. The club seems to have always existed. Blue Note's notoriety stems from the void it filled in New York City's music scene when it opened in 1981. Most supper club-type venues, like Blue Note, had all but disappeared from NYC, leaving jazz venues that existed on two levels: smoky, basement clubs or large concert halls. **Legendary musicians, such as Dizzy Gillespie, Sarah Vaughan, Oscar Peterson, Carmen McRae and Betty Carter were retreating from public view. Blue Note was born fully formed, with no question about its identity.** The club emanated a sense of home to jazz artists, immediately attracting luminaries back to the small stage.

In the club's beginning years, cherished relationships created fond memories between the musicians and the Blue Note staff. Owner Steve Bensusan, says, **"I remember hanging out with Dizzy as a young kid. It was amazing. All the musicians—this was kind of like a home for them, outside of just performing here. They would come here during the day and hang out—poker games in the dressing rooms, things like that."** A small jazz club with dressing rooms was a great perk, but a no-smoking policy such that Blue Note had was unheard of at the time, and very favorable to singers.

The popular restaurant and bar brought in sufficient revenue with its 185-seat space, which enabled Blue Note to be generous toward its musicians. Every seat in the house had an excellent sightline, making for an intimate atmosphere. Blue Note became a destination for folks, even those who were not already jazz sophisticates, yet wanted exposure to the genre. The Blue Note educated many people in this way, contributing to the rekindling of the jazz scene.

Although jazz music has naturally changed since its Golden Era, Blue Note artists continue to experiment musically and impassion the crowds. **Over the years the big evolution at Blue Note has revolved around the range of**

Photo provided courtesy of Blue Note

jazz-influenced music it books. In the '80s, the club showcased traditional jazz; in the '90s, it experimented with smooth jazz, R&B and blues. Presently, Blue Note's music programming is diversified—from Mos Def to Chick Corea—running the gamut of jazz and jazz-related music. **Hip-hop, soul and funk artists take the stage in the wee hours of the night, drawing a younger demographic into the room.** The end result is an infusion of younger audiences who come back to see the more established jazz artists on other nights.

The Blue Note staff creates a welcoming experience in Greenwich Village, a historically relevant birthing ground for jazz. Ticket prices and minimums are competitive with other jazz clubs. Detailed artist biographies appear in Blue Note programs, creating healthy anticipation over future visits. First-time patrons may come initially because they are curious about Blue Note, but on succeeding visits they will be curious about the musician and his or her music.

The Blue Note shares its name with Blue Note Records. When the club opened in 1981, Blue Note Records was defunct, which legally enabled Blue Note Jazz Club to use the name. Later the record label resumed business and the club and the label have since shared the same name. Blue Note records its albums under the Half Note Records label.

Blue Note Jazz Clubs are also in Nagoya and Tokyo, Japan, and Milan, Italy. The owners also own B.B. King and the Highline in NYC.

Sound Check
Sound Quality: Great
Stage Lighting: So-So
Sightlines: Great
Eardrum Meter:
Green

Tech Check
Mixer: Yamaha M7CL
Sound System: SLS ribbon based main speakers, d&b Audiotechnik B4 subs
Monitors: 3 mixes, JBL ceiling mounted speakers, mixed from FOH
Stage: 21.5' (W) x 9' (D) x 21" (H)
Backline: Yamaha C7, Yamaha Maple Custom drums, Aguilar 500SC bass amp
Other: Dressing room, green room

Downtown Manhattan

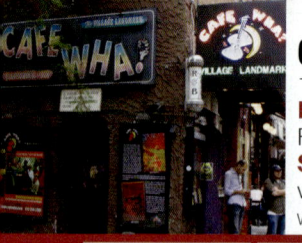

CAFE WHA?

115 MacDougal St | New York, NY 10012 | 212-254-3706
Hours: Mon 9p-2:30a, Tue-Thu, Sun 8:30p-2:30a, Fri-Sat 8:30p-4a
Subway: A,C,E,F,M,B,D to West 4th St
www.cafewha.com

Written by: Nick D'Amore

MUSIC TYPE	VENUE TYPE	ADMISSION	ATMOSPHERE	DRINKS: $-$$
R&B, World	Basement Club Capacity 299	$5 - $15 1 Drink Minimum	Energetic Club	Average $5 - $12 FOOD: Full Menu

GREENWICH VILLAGE
Between Bleecker St & West 3rd St

Downtown Manhattan

A rare intimacy exists between the band and the audience at Cafe Wha?. Large bands occupy a small stage, playing almost literally in the lap of the audience. The club packs in as many people as possible, but it is never uncomfortable. The space's layout guarantees a seat near the action on stage, or a place to dance.

Cafe Wha? offers three resident bands each week: Brazooka, a Brazilian jazz band; Disfunkshun, a Brazilian dance band; and the 10-member Cafe Wha? Band. Guest bands fill the remainder of the schedule. To simply label the house band a cover band would be akin to calling Guinness just a beer, or calling New York just another city. Cafe Wha?'s players are masters of their craft, performing as a tight, creative group and offering infectious interpretations of many rock and pop standards.

Cafe Wha? continues to reinvent itself—now a venue offering a raucous good time, attracting visitors and college students alike.

HISTORY

Cafe Wha? carries on as a vibrant New York City institution with a rich past. In its heyday, the venue helped launch some of the most legendary artists in popular music, such as Bob Dylan, Jimi Hendrix, The Velvet Underground and Bruce Springsteen. Writers and artists of the Beat Generation met at Cafe Wha? in the 1950s. During the social upheaval of the 1960s, Greenwich Village, and Cafe Wha? in particular, remained a safe haven for the revolutionary thinkers of the era.

As the times and tastes of the public changed, so, too, did the entertainment provided at the venue. While you might not discover the next revolution in popular culture at the club these days, what you will experience are three excellent bands offering crowd-pleasing music that gets the floor rumbling under dancing feet.

Sound Check
Sound Quality: Good
Stage Lighting: Good
Sightlines: Good
Eardrum Meter: Yellow

Tech Check
Mixer: Mackie TT24
Sound System: QSC K-Series
Monitors: 6 mixes QSC K-Series, JBL EON, Mackie SRM
Backline: Full Backline
Comments: Efficient stage for size and amount of backline

GROOVE

125 MacDougal St | New York, NY 10012 | 212-254-9393
Hours: 3p-4a Daily
Subway: A,B,C,D,E,F,M to West 4th St
www.clubgroovenyc.com

Written by: Nick D'Amore

DRINKS: $-$$	ATMOSPHERE	ADMISSION	VENUE TYPE	MUSIC TYPE
Average $5 - $12 FOOD: Full Menu	Spontaneous, Jamming	Free - $7	Restaurant Club Capacity 84	Classic R&B, Soul, Funk, Motown

GREENWICH VILLAGE
Corner of West 3rd St & MacDougal St

Downtown Manhattan

Groove opened its doors in 1997, a natural progression by a collective of musicians from the 101 Bar, a venue further uptown on 7th Avenue. The club's name explains its philosophy: performances are loose and organic.

Bands jam and swing spontaneously, interacting with the audience in the intimate room. On any given night, guitarists bring their solos off stage—in between the rows of tables—or an audience member jumps on stage to wail along with the band. The musicians never stop laying down thick grooves, showcasing tight playing to a crowd of hand-clappers and head-bobbers. Joy for the music overrides any air of pretension at Groove; the bands are excited to play and the audience happy to be a part of the performance.

Groove focuses primarily on R&B, blues, soul and funk music. The rhythms wafting out into the streets of Greenwich Village beckon people inside, if they aren't already intrigued by the colorful mural of legendary musicians painted on the club's exterior wall. Inside, artwork and pictures tastefully decorate a good portion of the walls. They serve to commemorate the superstars who have been drawn to the tunes at Groove, including Chaka Khan and Shaquille O'Neal. Groove's affordable menu, the room's ambience, and sultry soundtrack provide a great date spot.

Groove schedules jazz artists, spoken word performers, DJs and even some rock bands in addition to the club's house bands throughout the week. Local and developing musicians perform in the early time slots, and inspire moving and grooving in the crowd.

Outdoor seating is available before the music starts. Groove opens early for happy hour specials, followed by big-time talent in a warm and harmonious setting.

Sound Check
Sound Quality: Good
Stage Lighting: Good
Sightlines: Good
Eardrum Meter: Yellow

Tech Check
Mixer: Presonus Studio Live
Sound System: JBL VRX Mains
Monitors: 3 mixes, JBL 712N
Backline: Full Backline
Comments: Mainly cover bands playing classics R&B, Soul, Funk

KENNY'S CASTAWAYS

157 Bleecker St | New York, NY 10012 | 212-979-9762
Hours: 12p-4a Daily
Subway: A,C,E,B,D,F,M to West 4th St
www.kennyscastaways.net

Written by: Sari Henry

MUSIC TYPE	VENUE TYPE	ADMISSION	ATMOSPHERE	DRINKS: $-$$
Rock, Pop, Folk, Blues	Multi-Level Capacity 200	Free - $15	Classic Greenwich Village	Average $3 - $10 FOOD: Full Menu

GREENWICH VILLAGE — Between Sullivan St & Thompson St

Kenny's Castaways stakes its claim as a major tent peg in New York City's rock 'n' roll history. In business for 43 years, Kenny's exudes an 'old-time' New York feel and is an attraction for tourists, due to its glorious days of yonder past.

The owner, Maria Kenny, describes Kenny's decor as "classic and timeless with a downtown contemporary feel." Kenny's dimly illuminates its two-level, New Orleans-style architecture, which houses collectible antiques and memorabilia from the club's illustrious past. The combination of tantalizing history and the venue's musician-friendly policies embrace visitors and New Yorkers alike.

Kenny's Castaways is quite large for a medium-sized venue with occupancy at 200. Generally there is no cover charge although that policy seems to shift depending on the performers. Their kitchen serves affordable Cajun and bar-type food and the bar-drinks are just as reasonable.

All in all Kenny's is a fine place to go to experience a venue with a truly "old time" New York feel. If you are in the mood to take a chance on the level of experience and the genre of music you want to hear this is the place for you. You will be supporting an authentic New York music club which encourages new talent in the old ways. And who knows? You might see the next Bruce Springsteen.

HISTORY

The club was established by Irish immigrant Patrick Kenny on the Upper East Side in 1967 and moved to its present location on Bleecker St. in 1974.

The venue's historically-preserved second location had been a 19th century gay bar called The Slide. In 1890 the *New York Press* reported that the dive bar was: "The wickedest place in New York," due to its patrons' flaunting homosexuality. Artifacts on display from that era still entertain visitors.

Downtown Manhattan

Patrick loved and appreciated music and musicians deeply. He opened his nightclub for musicians to showcase their music, and a variety of genres from jazz to hard rock fills Kenny's Castaways.

Patrick's words live on to this day: **"[the club] is about creating memories for people and creating a sense of possibility."**

Many of the most talented and most famous rock 'n' roll musicians in history played or started their careers at Kenny's. A sampling of these musicians include, **Aerosmith, The Marshall Tucker Band, Patti Smith, Blues Traveler, Bruce Springsteen, the New York Dolls, Jerry Jeff Walker, Willie Nile, Steve Forbert, Bonnie Raitt, The Smithereens, Rod Stewart, Professor Longhair and more, ranging in attitude from Phoebe Snow to Rage Against the Machine.**

Patrick passed away in 2002, but his legacy carries on through his daughter, Maria, who runs the club. Maria seeks to further perpetuate her father's dream by encouraging local and promising bands to share their talents, rather than demand that they fill the seats. To counter the venue's reputation among locals as a tourist attraction, she invites musically-inclined neighbors to the club. A great opportunity fell into her lap when Ben Harper, who lives nearby, visited the club one night and, in liking what he saw, asked to try out some of his material. That led to impromptu gigs by established musicians such as Ben Harper or Tom Morello from Rage Against the Machine. Kenny's also hosts weekly residencies.

State of the Bathroom:
Pleasant, clean and historic in a good way, not in a CBGBs historic kind of way.

Tech Check
Mixer: Soundcraft GB4-32ch
Sound System: QSC Main speakers
Monitors: N/A # of Mixes, QSC
Backline: Partial Backline
Comments: The performance area–stage and layout is great. A 2nd level balcony with seating surrounds the performance area. The potential for an exceptional venue exists.

Sound Check
Sound Quality: Good
Stage Lighting: So-So
Sightlines: Good
Eardrum Meter:
Yellow

Downtown Manhattan

LE POISSON ROUGE

158 Bleecker St | New York, NY 10012 | 212-505-3474
Hours: Music times vary
Subway: A,C,E,B,D,F,M to West 4th St
www.lepoissonrouge.net

Written by: Jason Siegel

MUSIC TYPE	VENUE TYPE	ADMISSION	ATMOSPHERE	DRINKS: $-$$$
ALL: Classical, Rock, Metal, Folk	Mid-Size Venue Capacity Up to 700	$5 - $30	Quintessential Live Performance Venue	Average $6 - $12+ FOOD: no

GREENWICH VILLAGE
Between Sullivan St & Thompson St

Le Poisson Rouge, French for 'The Red Fish,' was so named as a bit of a joke. When co-owners David Handler and Justin Kantor were brainstorming venue names, they were aiming for pretension. It was a conscious effort to belie the true nature of their endeavor: to deliver, eclectic, varied music to the masses. Being classical musicians themselves, David and Justin are passionately committed to their genre, but in a decidedly unpretentious way.

A tilted, fish tank greets patrons as they descend the broad staircase to LPR. The large room is sleek and black, without engendering too much darkness. Red highlights—Le Poisson is 'rouge,' after all—spice up the visual aesthetic. The main stage faces the room diagonally from the corner and a roll-out stage tucks underneath when not in use. This smaller, moving stage allows for varied seating configurations, much like a black-box theater. Black couches and bar tables line the back wall, and modern-styled chairs and tables fill up the space directly in front of, or around, the stage. The bar serves as a multi-use space—for drinks at night, as a cafe by day, and continually as an open, art gallery. Past the gallery, two vast, medieval thrones with fish-shaped arms guard the bathrooms.

Acoustics are paramount to LPR's design; the performance space was engineered by legendary architect John Storyk, who designed the world famous Electric Lady Studios for Jimi Hendrix, Jazz at Lincoln Center, and private studios for numerous artists: Bob Marley and Bruce Springsteen, among others.

David and Justin, consider Le Poisson Rouge a 'gateway club.' LPR has entertained audiences with a plethora of musical styles: opera and other classical forms, indie rock, hardcore metal and rap, along with additional fringe genres. David grins, recalling, "five to seven hundred people, twenty- and thirty-somethings, standing through a forty-minute-long symphony, beers in hand…pierced

Downtown Manhattan

and tattooed to the nines," for the New York premiere of sacred music composer Arvo Pärt's newest piece. **David and Justin are adamant about their 'no-limits' policy on the types of genres featured at LPR; their only condition is that the music be *magnificant*.**

HISTORY
Le Poisson Rouge occupies the same building that once housed the Village Gate, a Greenwich Village mainstay from 1958 to 1993. The Village Gate hosted such remarkable acts as Jimi Hendrix, Allen Ginsberg, Dizzie Gillespie, John Coltrane, Thelonius Monk, Billie Holiday, Duke Ellington, Nina Simone, Ella Fitzgerald and Aretha Franklin. So, as David puts it, LPR has "a lot of ghosts in here… really good ghosts." In the interim, the space served as an off-Broadway theater and a night club.

Upon graduation from the Manhattan School of Music in 2004, David and Justin began looking for the perfect space in which to open a modern, funky venue. The Greenwich Village, once an über-bohemian and gritty neighborhood, further transitioned during the '90s and '00s into an upscale version of its former self. This evolution in the neighborhood suited David and Justin's pseudo-pretentious idea for a venue and also inspired them to ensure the continued production of rich music in the Village. Fast forward a few years: David and Justin received the keys to the space in the fall of 2007, remodeled the entire interior in a few short months and opened LPR in the summer of 2008.

Sound Check
Sound Quality: Great
Stage Lighting: Great
Sightlines: Great
Eardrum Meter:
Yellow—Red

Sound Check Comments
by Justin Hosek, Sound Engineer
Mixing FOH on a D-Show at Le Poisson Rouge is a great experience. The sound system is very responsive and with the large variety of musical genres performing it is an unbelievably versatile system that can make the most quiet, classical show sound acoustic, and the most heavy rock or electronic music sound huge. There is a Yamaha M7CL controlling LA Acoustic monitors on stage, leaving the FOH mixer nothing to worry about except engineering the perfect mix.

Tech Check
Mixer: Digidesign D-Show Profile, 48 ch
Sound System: , Meyer Line Array, M'elodies/M1D's
Monitors: Yamaha M7CL, 7 discrete wedge mixes, L-Acoustics Active wedges
Lighting: ETC Ion console with fader wing
Recording: ProTools HD3, Mac Xeon quad-core desktop
DJ: Serato setup
Backline: Yamaha S6B 7' Concert Grand Piano, Full backline
Other: Green room

Downtown Manhattan

SULLIVAN HALL

214 Sullivan St | New York, 10012 | 212-477-2782
Hours: Sun-Thu 7p-1a, Fri-Sat 7p-3a
Subway: A,B,C,D,E,F,M to West 4th St
www.sullivanhallnyc.com

Written by: Emily Niewendorp

MUSIC TYPE	VENUE TYPE	ADMISSION	ATMOSPHERE	DRINKS: $-$$
Rock, Pop, Indie, Jam, Eclectic	Mid-Size Club Capacity 345	$10 - $25	Jam-friendly Rock Club	$5+ FOOD: no

GREENWICH VILLAGE — Between Bleecker St & West 3rd St

Sullivan Hall has as rich a history as the performers who have played it. The remodeled, state-of-the-art Sullivan Hall was once a rugged club known as Lion's Den, which attracted a variety of people and musicians for 20 years. Compared to the old days of Lion's Den, Sullivan Hall may be cleaner and more polished, but the jam-friendly, grooving and worn-in vibe of the club remains.

Lion's Den opened in the early '90s and became a hang-out for locals, college students and hippies, who heard great, under-the-radar music and forged new friendships. Students from nearby New York University could afford the $10 cover and would wander in just to check out the intriguing sounds coming from the club. **Among the now-famous talent that graced the stage of Lion's Den were Alice in Chains and Ben Folds in his first New York City performance.**

The men that would eventually convert the space to Sullivan Hall had invested years of passion and energy into Lion's Den. The club's current owner, Howie Schnee, began booking Lion's Den in 1996. At the same time, he and Mike Maietta developed a managing company, Creative Entertainment Group, and fostered strong working relationships with bands and people in the music industry. As the years went by the club developed a lot of 'character' as it fell into disrepair. Howie noticed that musicians began responding unfavorably to playing there, so he approached the club's then-owner regarding its conditions and possible upgrades, but *years* went by, until in 2007, the owner agreed to the transformation. With the owner's consent, Howie and Mike invested the money to completely overhaul the venue, and became part owners in the process.

Many folks resisted changing Lion's Den, but there was no denying that business was on the decline. As Howie explained: "It had never been upgraded over the years, so it started to develop the feel and smell of a frat house." A proper upgrade would turn the club into a state-of-the-art spot, where bands would again be excited to play. In the summer of 2007, Lion's Den closed for one month and was completely gutted and remodeled.

When Lion's Den reopened, the club's upgrades were impressive. A first-class Meyer sound system replaced outdated equipment and a larger, front-and-center stage gave the audience an excellent live music experience. A new hardwood floor was installed, the stage lights were upgraded, and the band greenroom was improved. An audio and video recording system was also installed to provide recording options for bands.

The club continued as Lion's Den until the owners finally decided to disassociate themselves with the name altogether. At midnight Jan. 1, 2008, the old Lion's Den awning was taken down and Sullivan Hall's awning was put up. The New Orleans band, Big Sam's Funky Nation, who frequently perform at the venue, helped christen the club as Sullivan Hall. On New Year's Day, the grand opening festivities continued with veteran jam band Tea Leaf Green performing, and keyboard virtuoso Marco Benevento of Benevento Russo Duo beginning a month-long residency. Marco performed many memorable sold-out shows that January, partnering with singer-songwriter Kaki King, singer-songwriter Sonya Kitchell, and drummer Billy Martin from the jazzy trio Medeski, Martin & Wood.

Since the venue's overhaul, its audience has expanded, though still attracting a base of bands and students from NYU.

The variety of music at Sullivan Hall reflects the taste of both the owners and of the audience. Howie and his partners are producing a higher standard of live music culture. Their plan to continually upgrade Sullivan Hall and provide the best possible live music experiences will be a treat for musicians and music enthusiasts alike for many years to come.

Sound Check
Sound Quality: Good
Stage Lighting: Great
Sightlines: Good
Eardrum Meter:
Yellow—Red

Tech Check
Mixer: Midas Venice 320
Sound System: Meyer MSL-4/700-HP/UPJ-IP, DBX processing
Monitors: 4 mixes, mixed from FOH Meyer UM-IP, EV, Yorkville
Lighting: Elation Operator Pro DMX Lighting, Ness SC-1230 console
Backline: Full Backline
Other: Green room, dressing room
Comments: Recording capable, 20'x20' stage

Downtown Manhattan

RED LION

151 Bleecker St | New York, 10012 | 212-260-9797
Hours: 11a-4a Daily
Subway: A,B,C,D,E,F,M to West 4th St
www.cvmwebhosting.com/redlion/

Written by: Emily Niewendorp

MUSIC TYPE	VENUE TYPE	ADMISSION	ATMOSPHERE	DRINKS: $-$$
Rock, Pop, Folk Cover, Tribute	Restaurant Bar Capacity 176	Free - $15	Pub Culture	Average $5 - $10 **FOOD:** Full Menu

GREENWICH VILLAGE
Corner of Thompson St & Bleecker St

Sports bar by day, music venue by night: the Red Lion brings traditional English pub culture to Bleecker Street. The venue attracts students from NYU, and a lively mix of American and European professionals. At night's end, everyone from avid sports fans to dancing couples mix together in rowdy fun.

The Red Lion opened in 1983. Ten years later, current owner Andrew Breslin took over, inspired to support local musicians. Red Lion has a neighborly and low-key feel during the week when it features original music and singer-songwriters. Its weekend line-up attracts large crowds from the NYC area—some are 'dressed to the nines'—who come out to hear familiar cover songs played by a live band. The Dugger Bros Band with its dynamite, rhythm and blues show is a Sunday night staple.

Throughout its history, Red Lion has lent its stage to several, notable names in music: Bob Dylan hung out here in the '80s; John Mayer has also stopped by. Musicians that often play here include: Gavin DeGraw, Milo Z, Dana Fuchs, The Nerds and Michael Brunnock, among others.

Upon entering the venue, the small stage sits to the left backdropped in bold colors. The bar stretches across the length of the room, staffed with friendly bartenders who converse with regulars on a first-name basis. Seating is provided throughout the wood-paneled room, under tiled murals of legendary musicians. Red Lion also has outdoor seating, a perk that few other Bleecker Street venues can provide.

The kitchen is open until midnight. It serves American-European cuisine, an all-day English breakfast and brunch on Saturday and Sunday. (Note: the Bloody Marys are great.)

An ATM is housed in an old-fashioned, red telephone booth in the back.

Sound Check
Sound Quality: Good
Stage Lighting: Great
Sightlines: Good
Eardrum Meter:
Yellow

Tech Check
Sound System: Allen&Heath GL2200, Celestion Mains
Monitors: N/A # of Mixes, JBL
Backline: Drums and bass amp
Comments: Stage size is 17'x9'

Downtown Manhattan

TERRA BLUES

149 Bleecker St | New York, 10012 | 212-777-7776
Hours: Showtimes 7p & 10p, Open late
Subway: A,C,E,B,D,F,M to West 4th St
www.terrablues.com

Written by: Rachel Antonio

DRINKS: $$ Average $7 - $12 FOOD: no	ATMOSPHERE Old-fashioned Blues Saloon	ADMISSION Average $10	VENUE TYPE 2nd Floor Club Capacity 74	MUSIC TYPE Blues

If blues is your preference, then Terra Blues is your place. Often touted as *the* place to go for an authentic, blues experience, Terra Blues is an old-fashioned saloon for modern-day times.

The great blues players who have played here: Little Milton, Edgar Winter, Johnny "Clyde" Copeland, Kenny Neal, James Armstrong and The Holmes Brothers, are a few of the many national acts that appear year-round at Terra Blues. Local blues musicians like Clarence Spady and Junior Mack are honored with weekly residencies and render equally satisfying shows.

Perched on a second floor above Bleecker St. in the heart of Greenwich Village, Terra Blues seems to call out to pedestrians below. On warm nights, music spills out onto the street through large, open windows draped with lush, reddish curtains. Its dim lighting and laid-back rhythms generate an open and inviting atmosphere. Votive candles dot the internal landscape, quietly illuminating the wood-work and framed photos discreetly recount the venue's impressive history.

It is the mission statement however that defines the venue more than its ambiance and decor: Terra Blues runs on "booze and blues." The music club's bartender, Gabriel Aldort, will attest that this motto has endured for over two decades. The saloon features a full bar and consistently delivers quality shows daily. For over fifteen years, its gothic arch ceiling—complete with gargoyles, it's an interesting visual tangent—has carried the best blues sounds in NYC to date.

Pictured: Michael Powers

The summer of 2010 marked Terra Blues' 20th anniversary. Michael Powers has been playing there since its opening. On Monday evenings, Powers and his band take the stage. When asked what one of his performances is like, he comments: "...[It] runs on spontaneity...It runs on '60s influence. It runs on what we like." The same could be said of Terra Blues.

Tech Check
Sound System: Mackie, EAW JF-560 Mains speakers
Monitors: N/A # of Mixes, Yamaha SM12V
Backline: No
Other: Green room available
Comments: The stage is 5'x17' and is elevated by approximately 3'

Sound Check
Sound Quality: Good
Stage Lighting: Good
Sightlines: Good
Eardrum Meter:
Yellow

GREENWICH VILLAGE
Between LaGuardia Pl & Thompson St

Downtown Manhattan

VILLAGE UNDERGROUND

130 West 3rd St | New York, NY 10012 | 212-777-7745
Hours: Tues-Sat 9p-4a, open Sun
Subway: A,B,C,D,E,F,M to West 4th St
http://www.thevillageunderground.com

Written by: Emily Niewendorp

MUSIC TYPE	VENUE TYPE	ADMISSION	ATMOSPHERE	DRINKS: $-$$
Vintage Rock, Funk, R&B, Reggae, Cover	Basement Club Capacity 230	Free - $10	High-energy, Diverse	Average $5 - $10 FOOD: Full Menu

GREENWICH VILLAGE — Between MacDougal St & 6th Ave

Downtown Manhattan

The Village Underground brings to life music and memories from the past four decades. The entryway is demure and understated compared to its neighbor and sister-bar, The Fat Black Pussycat. Downstairs, the dark brick walls and columns exude a hip, basement environment. This medium-sized room provides a variety of seating: large booths in the back and small tables that skirt the stage. On the walls, posters of prominent '60s rock and folk musicians recall the venue's former activities.

The Village Underground played an important role in the modern, folk-rock era. Originally known as Gerde's Folk City, from 1970 to 1987, the venue yielded up such legends as Bob Dylan and Elvis Costello. In 2000, Noam Dworman, who formerly owned Cafe Wha? around the corner, opened The Village Underground to revive the live music scene in Greenwich Village. The space was given an overhaul, and bands—now playing a variety of music genres—began to groove on the large, well-lit stage.

The Village Underground is not known for folk music these days, but instead hosts rock, R&B, funk, reggae, world and country music. The venue has a namesake in its own band: The Village Underground, which performs popular covers every Wednesday through Friday. The large band invigorates the room and people jump to their feet, dancing and getting 'down 'n' dirty' in the aisles. DJs spin on Saturday night and individual musicians take to the open mic on Sundays. The Cheryl Pepsii Singers, followed by guest bands, jam on Mondays, and world music takes over on Tuesdays.

All the musicians create remixes in their own styles and bring their own recipes from time to time, diffusing creative energy around the room—and the crowd loves it.

Sound Check
Sound Quality: Good
Stage Lighting: Great
Sightlines: Good
Eardrum Meter: Yellow—Red

Tech Check
Sound System: Mackie TT24, Bose
Monitors: EAW SM200ih
Lighting: Light Jockey track spots
Backline: Full Backline
Comments: DVD & 24 track Nuendo recording available, the stage is 20'x10', SUBs & speaker fills positioned throughout venue provides a full and balanced sound

Sound Check
Sound Quality: Great
Stage Lighting: Minimal
Sightlines: Good
Eardrum Meter:
Green–Yellow

VILLAGE VANGUARD
178 7th Ave | New York, NY 10014
212-255-4037
Hours: 8p-1a Daily
Subway: 1,2,3 to 14th St
www.villagevanguard.com

Written by: Daniel Morrow

DRINKS: $-$$	ATMOSPHERE	ADMISSION	VENUE TYPE	MUSIC TYPE
Average $5 - $12 FOOD: no	Iconic	$30 - $35	Basement Club Capacity 123	Jazz

GREENWICH VILLAGE
Between 11th St & Perry St

Downtown Manhattan

The Village Vanguard is the oldest continuously operated jazz club in the world[1] and has stood at its current location on 7th Avenue in the West Village, since 1935. When walking into the basement level venue, its history is immediately apparent. Photographs and posters of famous Vanguard sessions and musicians cover the walls; they are, in the words of owner Lorraine Gordon, "photos of great artists that are no longer with us, who are here in spirit."

Although Village Vanguard has come a long way from its beginnings in 1935 as a variety performance and dinner venue, its enduring success can be largely attributed to its owners and their unadulterated passion for jazz. It was the original owner Max Gordon's love for jazz that led to the Village Vanguard becoming a jazz-only venue in the early 1950s. Lorraine Gordon married Max during this period and took over running the venue after his death in 1989.

Though Lorraine makes all the decisions at the venue, she gets a lot of help from her daughter Deborah and from Jed Eisenman, a life-long Vanguard fan who began working there before Max died.

Today the Vanguard is as lively and popular as it has ever been. There's a healthy mix of music students, locals and international jazz fans visiting the venue every night. The venue still attracts celebrity musicians; *and* the booking is adventurous and often risky by inviting occasional unknown artists to perform. **As Jed explains, "Lorraine is the sole arbiter of what we end up booking, she does it all herself; that's how you can tell how passionate she is about the music."** It is thanks to her life-long passion for jazz and her ability to keep up with the latest in the jazz scene, that she has consistently been able to pick out some of the world's best jazz talent to play at the venue.

The greatest of memories and moments belong to the stage. The room's oddly triangular-shape means that there are no parallel walls and few reflective surfaces. Most venues are inevitably square in nature and it is often the case that hundreds of thousands of dollars are spent on acoustic treatment. This room has never been touched; it is quite by accident, one of the most transparent and natural sounding jazz rooms that can be found in the city.

(1) NPR Music, "The Village Vanguard: A Hallowed Basement," NPR Music, http://www.npr.org (accessed February 2011).

65

ZINC BAR

82 West 3rd St | New York, NY 10012 | 212-477-9462
Hours: Sun-Thu 6p-2:30a, Fri-Sat 6p-3a
Subway: A,B,C,D,E,F,M to West 4th St
www.zincbar.com

Written by: Nick D'Amore

MUSIC TYPE	VENUE TYPE	ADMISSION	ATMOSPHERE	DRINKS: $$
Jazz, World	Small Club Capacity 150	$10	Intimate Jazz Club	Average $8 - $12 FOOD: no

Down a few steps and through the red velvet curtain and you're transported to a time when jazz ruled the cultural landscape. Zinc Bar contains all the elements of a great jazz club: cozy atmosphere, stunning acoustics, subtle accoutrements and stiff cocktails. The only things missing are rings of cigarette smoke.

A night at Zinc is not a sentimental trip down memory lane. Instead, you will hear brilliant musicians taking the vast vocabulary of jazz to exciting and different places. Though the music genre's roots are distinctly American, jazz is truly global music. Performers at Zinc come from varying backgrounds and nationalities, flavoring the language of jazz with their native tongues, resulting in fresh and eye-opening performances. Throughout the week, there are Brazilian, African, Caribbean and Latin performers exploring the music of jazz. Besides its inclusion of world musicians, the club also welcomes free jazz artists, stand-up comedians, poets, cabaret acts and vocal performers.

For the full music experience, walk past the bar to the audience area; though only a few steps away, the music suddenly swells all around you. It is obvious the principals behind Zinc paid particular attention to the club's sound, which creates a rich, full and crisp sonic atmosphere. You can hear the nuances and dynamics of each instrument from any table near the stage: the melodious fingering of a twelve-string guitar; the hushed brushstrokes on a snare; the subtle plucking of a bass; the brassy punches of a trumpet; the expert tickling of piano keys. "The Zinc family of staff, musicians and music fans all truly share a love for the music," says the club's owner, Alex K.

Located a few short blocks away from the hubbub of the university bars and tourist attractions of the West Village, Zinc is an underground

GREENWICH VILLAGE
Between Thompson St & Sullivan St

Downtown Manhattan

oasis of cool. But, there are no pretentions, no airs, no put-ons.

> *"Live music conveys a feeling that does not come through in recorded music. It's like a sixth sense that cannot be captured on tape. It happens every night at Zinc but only in the moment."*
>
> Alex K, Co-owner

HISTORY

Like jazz music itself, Zinc Bar is influenced by the music's history, but is still creating an experience that is attractive and seductive. Zinc's origins are on Houston Street, where the club was located for nearly 20 years.

Zinc began in 1993, when Alex saw that the jazz talent in New York needed a home, but also one that a younger audience could afford. Constructing the venue has continually been a family affair. The club's name is a reference to the "jazz caves" of Paris, where Hemmingway would meet friends. He wrote, "Let's meet at the zinc" because the bars were zinc-topped. Alex's sister and co-owner, Kristina K, was reading Hemmingway in Paris and brought the idea home with her.

The owners recently moved the venue to the heart of Greenwich Village. During the Golden Age of jazz, Zinc's current site was known as The Cinderella Club, a cabaret and jazz club that was active from the 1930s to the 1950s. The venue was home to such jazz luminaries as Thelonious Monk and Billie Holiday. "Every major jazz cat played there," says Alex. One fixture at The Cinderella Club, legendary jazz guitarist George Benson still visits Zinc when he is in town. One night, he took the stage for an impromptu, hour-long performance. The late, great jazz drummer and composer, Max Roach, also used to drop by the club, encouraging the owners to "keep on keepin' on." The impressive list of visitors to Zinc includes: Gil Goldstein; Flora Purim and Airto Moreira; Astrud and Bebel Gilberto; Jeff "Tain" Watts; Ravi Coltrane; and Branford Marsalis.

Sound Check
Sound Quality: Good
Stage Lighting: Minimal
Sightlines: Good
Eardrum Meter: Yellow

Tech Check
Sound System: Behringer, EAW mains
Monitors: N/A # of Mixes, Various
Lighting: Light Jockey track spots
Backline: Sauter piano, Canopus Drums
Comments: 7'x18' slightly elevated stage, surrounded by red velvet curtains located in tiered sub-basement venue.

55 BAR

55 Christopher St | New York, NY 10014
212-929-9883
Hours: 3p-2a Daily
Subway: 1 to Christopher St
www.55bar.com

Written by: Rachel Antonio

Sound Check
Sound Quality: Good
Stage Lighting: Good
Sightlines: So-So
Eardrum Meter:
Green–Yellow

MUSIC TYPE	VENUE TYPE	ADMISSION	ATMOSPHERE	DRINKS: $$
Jazz, Blues	Basement Club Capacity: 75	Free - $10	Heart of Jazz, Soul of Blues	Average $7 - $10 FOOD: no

WEST VILLAGE — Between 7th Ave & Waverly Place

Downtown Manhattan

55 Bar embraces new musicians as well as world-wide veterans of the jazz sphere. The venue schedules two acts daily, often offering the early 7 p.m. show free of charge. Drinks are cheap, making 55 Bar affordable to everyone.

It is a half-basement, true bar (no actual stage for the bands exists), lit with Christmas lights. The manager, Mark Kirby, attributes the high sound quality to the low ceilings and wood floors and paneling.

55 Bar's cutting-edge jazz reputation is so renowned that the club is referenced in music textbooks in the Netherlands. Famous for its nurturing environment of experimental jazz, performers often try out new material written earlier the same day. In this way audiences experience new jazz in the making. "There's all types of jazz trying to get out there," Mark says, "not just sweet and mellow." Up-and-coming jazz musicians who mix elements of jazz with trip hop, electronica, etc. are also welcomed. It's not much of a 'talking bar,' but rather a bar for soaking up the sounds.

HISTORY

55 Bar has come a long way since its 'neighborhood bar' days. The scene back then was wild; alive until the wee hours of the morning, and the type of place where undercover cops roamed.

Its reputation today can be attributed to the late Queva Lutz, who took over the venue more than a decade ago. Back then, the bar featured a popcorn machine and an aged jukebox, filled with 45s of Duke Ellington and old-school jazz. Queva cleaned up the place, mandating that all laws would have to be obeyed. In the words of 55 Bar's 'go-to' man, Mark Kirby: "More importantly, she made it into a serious jazz venue with shows every day—early shows and late shows. She really built it up to be what it is now. I call it 'an internationally-famous, jazz dive'." Queva's son, Scott Ellard owns and books the club now, continuing her vision.

Tech Check
Sound System: Yorkville mixer, Yamaha speakers

Sound Check
Sound Quality: Good
Stage Lighting: Good
Sightlines: Good
Eardrum Meter:
Green–Yellow

CAFFE VIVALDI

32 Jones St | New York, NY 10014
212-691-7538
Hours: 6pm Daily
Subway: A,B,C,D,E,F,M to West 4th St
www.caffevivaldi.com

Written by: Daniel Morrow

DRINKS: $-$$	ATMOSPHERE	ADMISSION	VENUE TYPE	MUSIC TYPE
$5	Bohemian, Cozy	Free	Listening Room,	Classical, Jazz, World,
FOOD: Full Menu		7 nights a week	Restaurant	Country, Pop, Rock

At Caffe Vivaldi, owner Ishrat Ansari has created an inspiring community for musicians to gather and perform. Ishrat describes it as an all-genre music venue, delivering "everything from bluegrass to opera," and that it is more of a listening room than a 'cafe'. Many musicians are handpicked by Ishrat to play, some through the open mic session he holds every Monday.

The venue epitomizes warmth and a home-like atmosphere with a fireplace, plants, and candlelit tables, plus a grand piano. In the stage-less room musicians perform only feet away from regulars, who gather at the tables and snack on Italian and Mediterranean dishes.

HISTORY

Ishrat is an old-time West Village resident, since 1973, when he opened a small bookstore that quickly became a hangout for writers, poets and artists. It was after a visit to Europe with its many cafe style restaurants that he decided to open a cafe with music.

During construction of Cafe Vivaldi in 1983, a local lady approached Ishrat with a sketch given to her many years before. It was of her grandfather, an enthusiast of the composer, Antonio Vivaldi, and the owner of the Laundromat that once stood where the cafe is now. In the sketch, "he irons with his right and leads the philharmonic with his left, augmented by a radio above him" *(quote from the inscription of the sketch)*. Ishrat was so moved by the sketch and the story he named the place Cafe Vivaldi.

The venue aims to carry on the vibrant glory days of the neighborhood. A music lover, Ishrat has sacrificed financial gain in his passion for musicians. Open now for 28 years, Ishrat recalls many famous moments that have taken place in this small room. From Bette Midler's birthday party and visits from Andy Warhol to Joseph Brodsky's interviews after he won the Nobel Peace Prize. Woody Allen has also shot two movies here, *Bullets Over Broadway* and *Whatever Works*. In fact, Ishrat liked the decor from the set design of the latter film so much that he has left much of it intact to this day.

Tech Check
Sound System: 8 Channel Mackie
Backline: Yamaha Recital Grand Piano
Stage Size: 10'x8'

WEST VILLAGE Between Bleecker St & West 4th St

Downtown Manhattan

CORNELIA STREET CAFE

29 Cornelia St | New York, 10014 | 212-989-9319
Hours: Open all day, Shows at 6p & 8:30p
Subway: A,B,C,D,E,F,M to West 4th St
www.corneliastreetcafe.com

Written by: Sarah Oramas

MUSIC TYPE	VENUE TYPE	ADMISSION	ATMOSPHERE	DRINKS: $$
Jazz, Theater, Poetry	Basement Club Capacity 65	$10 - $15 1 Drink Minimum	Upscale, Casual, Intimate	Average $6 - $12 FOOD: Full Menu

WEST VILLAGE
Between Bleecker St & West 4th St

Cornelia St. Cafe is steeped in Greenwich Village history. Located just off Bleecker Street in the heart of the Village, it is the quintessential successful artists' cafe-turned-restaurant. It manages to keep its 1970s performance-space charm in the downstairs venue, while providing an upscale dining experience in the main restaurant.

The music room is intimate; it seats just 55 patrons with space for an additional 10, or so, to stand. The narrow room affords a certain distance from the stage, while providing a closeness that does not feel crowded, but cozy. What can only be described as 'Superman blue and red' decorates the room, but the soft lighting and small tables create a warm, inviting space. With over 35 wines by the glass, a cabaret menu, and a full bar, this venue is an ideal place to settle in for a complete evening.

Cornelia St. Cafe offers material for a wide-ranging audience; line-ups that include every style of jazz from traditional to avant-garde, theatrical performances, and poetry readings in more than six languages. In addition, Tom Chang, who is currently charged with booking the jazz acts, plans to expand the musical offerings to include a broader range of styles.

> "One of the first events that I booked that reflected this shift in focus, was a Southern Indian, Carnatic percussion ensemble that featured the mridangam and tabla, as well as two violinists and a cellist. I will try to book Brazilian artists as well as African, ragtime and more Indian forms, and generally bring to light the vast talent that exists all over the city."
>
> Tom Chang, Booker

With its rich history and constantly-updating performance offerings, Cornelia St. Cafe is a Greenwich Village staple that shouldn't be missed.

Downtown Manhattan

HISTORY

Greenwich Village has always been the center of the New York art scene, and at one time, in the mid '70s, it was undeveloped enough that three artists were able to purchase a small cafe and turn it into a performance space. Cornelia St. Cafe started out this way; where little-known artists came to meet other artists and perform. It was opened in 1977 by a writer and director, Robin Hirsch; an actor, Charles McKenna; and a visual artist, Raphaela Pivetta.

With over thirty-three years' experience in the business, Cornelia St. Cafe has an amazing performance repertoire of many well-known groups, both musical and theatrical. Some notables include The Royal Shakespeare Company, Monty Python and Suzanne Vega. One such noteworthy performance—a poetry reading by Senator Eugene McCarthy—helps explain how this one-room cafe became the flourishing venue it is today:

A poet from the neighborhood introduced herself to co-owner Robin Hirsch and said she wanted to perform. When he asked her, who she would like to perform with, she replied, "Eugene McCarthy." Once it was clarified that she meant Senator Eugene McCarthy from Virginia, they were scheduled and the news began to spread. Robin says, "Word got out and we knew we wouldn't be able to fit everyone in the cafe. So we began to excavate the basement. He flew in from Virginia specifically to perform at this little cafe."

In the years since that poetry reading, Cornelia St. Cafe has further developed its reputation among artists and performance art enthusiasts as a great venue. With an intimate, basement cabaret that boasts over 700 live performances per year and an open-minded philosophy towards new and differing performances, it is no surprise that this venue has remained vital to the artistic community.

Sound Check
Sound Quality: Good
Stage Lighting: Good
Sightlines: Good
Eardrum Meter:
Green–Yellow

Tech Check
Sound System: Mackie 1604VLZ3, JBL Dual 8"
Monitors: 2 mixes, JBL EON G10
Backline: Yamaha G2 Piano, Full Backline
Other: Green room available
Comments: Elevated stage, 12'x15'

FAT CAT

75 Christopher St | New York, NY 10014 | 212-675-6056
Hours: Mon-Thu 2p-5a, Fri-Sun 12p-5a
Subway: 1 to Christopher St
www.fatcatmusic.org

Written by: Heather McCown

MUSIC TYPE	VENUE TYPE	ADMISSION	ATMOSPHERE	DRINKS: $-$$
Jazz, World	Basement Club Capacity 150 - 200	$3	Romper Room for Adults	$5+ FOOD: Snacks

WEST VILLAGE — Corner of 7th Ave & Christopher St

Downtown Manhattan

Upon descending the stairs of Fat Cat on Christopher Street, one may expect the darkened atmosphere of a pool hall; instead sounds similar to Coltrane and Lonnie's Lament are first noticeable. Inside, jazz musicians share the space with pool tables, chess boards, and ping pong tables. Jazz musicians deftly play, oblivious to the action happening around them. Their lyrical notes and deep melodies float past the exposed pipes and spot lights. Part of the crowd sits on corduroy sofas and chairs, while others engage in shooting pool, drinking beer and hanging with friends.

The din from the crowd can be heard only when the band pauses between songs. It is then that one realizes this is a pool hall. Instead of competing for attention, the two complement each other. "The venue is totally unique, because you never see any place that includes table games with live music," says Sheldon Yellowhair, Fat Cat's sound engineer. And, the musicians love it too. Stand-up bassist, Joseph Lepore, remarks: "It's a great place for steady gigs—to work out the music before recording."

Fat Cat is not 'hip'—it doesn't have to try that hard. Rather, it is a place to hear amazing live jazz in a dynamic atmosphere. The mix of live jazz and pool-hall action gives Fat Cat its edge and authenticity, separating it from other West Village, college hang-outs.

According to the manager, Ben, the long-term goal of Fat Cat is to become a non-profit, and give back to the community through equipment donations and musical education programs. For now, Fat Cat continues to, as doorman Charlie Brown puts it, "keep the right kind of people here and the wrong kind out" by embracing diversity and an overall pleasant atmosphere.

Sound Check
Sound Quality: Good
Stage Lighting: Good
Sightlines: So-So
Eardrum Meter: Green-Yellow

Tech Check
Sound System: Mackie ONYX
Monitors: N/A
Backline: Leslie Cabinet, A100 Hammond Organ, Yamaha C3 piano, full backline
Stage Size: 12'x14'

GARAGE

99 Seventh Ave | New York, NY 10011 | 212-645-0600
Hours: Sun-Thu 5p-1a, Fri-Sat 5p-3a, Open for Lunch
Subway: A,B,C,D,E,F,M to West 4th St
1 to Christopher St
www.garagerest.com

Weekend Jazz Brunch

Written by: Sarah Oramas

DRINKS: $$-$$$ Average $7 - $14 FOOD: Full Menu	ATMOSPHERE Sleek, Upscale, Casual	ADMISSION Free	VENUE TYPE Large Restaurant Total Capacity 744	MUSIC TYPE Jazz

Many venues offer live jazz, but few offer high-quality live jazz, seven nights per week, with no cover charge. A sleek jazz venue and restaurant that has been open since 1984, Garage attracts a younger crowd than one might imagine.

Garage's secret to keeping it fresh is booking talented groups for regular weekly or bi-weekly performances. The manager, Juan Carlos Briones, explains, "they all have their own following, so we bring them back."

On any given night, the crowd is a mix of tourists, jazz fans, and jazz musicians who gravitate to Garage to hear high-quality performances in a comfortable atmosphere. "This is a place [where] people come to hear the music," said Juan Carlos. After their set, many of the musicians who've just performed stick around to hear the next set and enjoy a drink.

While the restaurant and lounge maintain a sleek and upscale look the venue is by no means intimidating or stuffy. The staff goes out of its way to be friendly and make visitors feel welcome. The bar is an inviting place to grab a drink while strategically offering a great view of the stage. It boasts an impressive list of artfully crafted martinis, eight draught beers and a wide selection of wines.

For those looking for a more romantic evening or a quiet meal with friends, the restaurant specializes in steaks and seafood. Every seat in the restaurant provides a view of the stage and no table is so far removed that it feels far from the action. A balcony at the back of the restaurant allows patrons access to comfortable booth seating without compromising the view of the stage.

Garage has a very popular jazz brunch on Saturdays and Sundays that features live music and all-you-can-drink mimosas, screwdrivers and Bloody Marys. The patio in front of the venue provides seating as well, and is a great spot to enjoy a meal while watch the bustle of Village night life.

WEST VILLAGE
Between 9th Ave & 10th Ave

Sound Check
Sound Quality: Minimal
Stage Lighting: Minimal
Sightlines: Good
Eardrum Meter:
Green—Yellow

Tech Check
Sound System: Minimal
Monitors: N/A
Backline: No
Stage Size: 10'x8'

Downtown Manhattan

73

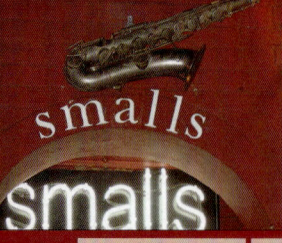

SMALLS

183 West 10th St | New York, NY 10014 | 212-252-5091
Hours: 7:30p-4a Daily
Subway: A,B,C,D,E,F,M to West 4th St | 1 to Christopher St
www.smallsjazzclub.com

Written by: Rachel Antonio

MUSIC TYPE	VENUE TYPE	ADMISSION	ATMOSPHERE	DRINKS: $-$$$
Jazz	Basement Club Capacity 60	$10 - $20	Friendly, Unpretentious	$4 - $16 FOOD: no

WEST VILLAGE — Between 7th Ave & West 4th St

Downtown Manhattan

Smalls contributes in a huge way to the artistic, downtown music scene. What lies beneath the foot traffic in its 10th St. locale leaves a lasting impression.

The guys that have shaped the business are as friendly and cool as college buddies; co-owners Spike Wilner, Lee Kostrinsky, and Mitch Borden have been running Smalls together since 2007. They are jacks-of-all-trades and can be found at Smalls nightly, either greeting folks at the door, managing the bar or playing a set. Mitch's eclectic style, Lee's Fedora, and Spike's curly locks are hard to miss.

Smalls basement space is meant to feel like a rumpus room in a house.

The uniqueness of Smalls can be felt immediately upon entering the venue. Its space welcomes all, evoking an intuitive understanding of decorum. All levels of musicianship are respected, while the hodge-podge of decor defines the room and adds a level of intrigue. The musicians face the entrance, playing from the other side of the room. The bar lines one wall and people fill in the rest of the space, sitting in chairs or leaning into their sweetheart. Pretty much anyone who is a name in jazz has been through the door of Smalls.

From Wynton Marsalis to Roy Hargrove, and Eric Reed, it is not uncommon for one of them to pop in at any given night and perform a set.

Spike credits it all to Mitch, who has a 'flea market' mentality. Mitch picks up anything of value, builds sculptures and puts artwork up all over the place. The club has mismatched curtains, various styles of rugs and one-of-a-kind chairs. Strategically placed mirrors reflect key strokes on the baby grand piano and the beating on the drums. Spike explains:

"We want to get away from the air of formality because right now all of the jazz clubs are so formal. You're not allowed to talk. At Smalls

the music earns the respect of the people naturally, but they're not forced to be quiet"

[FirstLive Note: In fact, Spike was kindly 'shushed' by the audience when we visited Small's to discuss FirstLive Guide.]

Smalls is building a community that encourages global participation and artistic growth. Small's website streams live video and audio of performances nightly, and a database stores musicians' bios and live recordings. One of Small's new ventures is SmallsLIVE, a record label that showcases emerging musicians and features their performance at Smalls. The club also participates in many fundraising efforts for the jazz community. The club has come a long way from its early days, due to the collaboration of three down-to-Earth guys named Mitch, Spike and Lee.

HISTORY
Before Spike and Lee came into the picture, Smalls thrived in the '90s as a bring-your-own-beer jazz club. Mitch was the original and sole owner at the time. The club stayed open 24 hours a day, seven days a week. Spike, who is also a professional pianist, started playing gigs at Smalls in the first month it opened in 1994. He describes the venue's scene as a group of anti-society musicians, saying "[there was] always this extremely dynamic lifestyle going on there."

Smalls met its fate when the club went bankrupt in 2000 and then reopened in 2006 as a Brazilian bar. One year later, Spike and Lee teamed up with Mitch to revamp the place and revitalize Smalls.

Smalls now operates with a formula: a cover fee is charged, which allows patrons to come and go as they please. There are three acts each night. Seasoned musicians play early evening, and the budding artists play after-hours and jam sessions. After midnight admission is half price. Smalls is no longer BYOB, having since acquired a liquor license.

Sound Check
Sound Quality: Good
Stage Lighting: Good
Sightlines: Good
Eardrum Meter:
Green–Yellow

Tech Check
Sound System: Mackie
Monitors: N/A
Lighting: Minimal
Backline: Steinway Piano, Fender Guitar amp, canopus jazz drum kit, Fat Cat bass amp, Fender Rhodes amp
Recording: Audio/Video

ADDITIONAL VENUES

169 Bar
169 East Broadway | New York, NY 10002 | 646-833-7199
www.169barnyc.com

A New Orleans-style dive bar with personality, 169 Bar attracts the curious and the regulars. It promotes: cheap drinks; go-go dancing; DJs who spin '60s soul-jazz, funk, boo-ga-loo and '30's Harlem swing/funk/soul/disco; acoustic Latin, R&B, soul and jazz-funk bands; a pet fish named Jeff; and darts, pool and more. Events typically occur Wed – Sat.

ABC No Rio
156 Rivington St | New York, NY 10002 | 212-254-3697
www.abcnorio.org

Since 1980, ABC No Rio has been a welcoming and inclusive venue for emerging artists, performers and musicians. In its new building, it will continue its Hardcore/Punk Matinees and COMA concerts. COMA is a Sunday evening concert series of experimental and improvisational music. ABC No Rio's weekly Saturday matinees were founded in 1990 in response to the racist, homophobic and misogynistic violence occurring during the late-eighties.

Arthur's Tavern
57 Grove St | New York, NY 10001 | 212-675-6879
www.arthurstavern.com

Open since 1937, Arthur's Tavern is an original experience. In a historically designated building, Arthur's looks like a saloon, and acts like a jazz club. Year-round festive decorations and tight quarters attract all types to its line-up of: jazz, including Dixieland and New Orleans style; Chicago blues; R & B and more.

B Flat
277 Church St | New York, NY 10013 | 212-219-2970
www.bflat.info

In this posh basement space, take your pick between the Monday night four-piece be-bop band and Wednesday night's funky trio. An excellent cocktail list and dinner menu blends American, Italian and Asian ingredients, and the low lighting and superb staff create an easy atmosphere for friendly excursions or a first date.

Crash Mansion
199 Bowery | New York, NY 10002 | 212-982-7767
www.crashmansion.com

Crash Mansion is a true rock club with stone walls, low ceilings, a large open space and leather couches.

Duplex
61 Christopher St | New York, NY 10014 | 212-255-5438
www.theduplex.com

Duplex is a piano bar and cabaret venue that attracts the kings, queens and loyal fans of New York. On the ground floor piano bar, the staff—some between jobs on Broadway—sing as they work. Upstairs, the cabaret dates back to the '50s, boasting performances by Barbra Streisand, Woody Allen, Joanne Worley and more. Duplex also hosts new work on Mondays and encourages submissions.

Marie's Crisis
59 7th Ave South | New York, NY 10014 | 212-243-9323

Contrary to its name, Marie's Crisis is a happy place, where musical theater enthusiasts gather around adept pianists, taking turns singing solos and gathering for sing-a-longs. Once the home of Thomas Paine, the 18th century revolutionary, and named after his pamphlet, "The Crisis," the venue honors those of radical nature in gracious fun.

Otto's Shrunken Head
538 East 14th St | New York, NY 10009 | 212-228-2240
www.ottosshrunkenhead.com

Otto's Shrunken Head rolled onto NYC's night life scene in response to the closure of two Tiki bars uptown. Otto's mixes Hawaiian decor, stiff rum-based cocktails and alternative hedonists. It is not considered a conventional live music venue, but the bar host many bands and events, a few being: exotica, rockabilly, punk, metal, surf and acoustic music; and DJs, open mics, literary readings and film screenings.

R Bar
218 Bowery | New York, NY 10012 | 212-334-0484
www.rbarnyc.com

R Bar mixes the glam of SoHo, the indie-ness of the LES and a hint of rawness from The Bowery. The venue is spacious with ornate chandeliers, stripper poles and chain mail 'curtains' that section off private areas. Open mic is every Tuesday through Thursday followed by live bands. All genres are encouraged.

Tammany Hall
152 Orchard St | New York, NY 10002 | 212-982-7767
www.tammanyhallny.com

Formerly known as The Annex, Tammany Hall converted the space consisting of a basement, ground floor and balcony level into distinct rooms. The upstairs ground-floor space is where live bands perform. The lounge in the basement has it's own street level entrance.

Photo by Jasha Boudard

MANHATTAN MIDTOWN

	GENRE	PAGE
GRAMERCY		
Jazz Standard	JAZZ	80
Rodeo Bar	AMERICAN ROOTS, ROCK 'N' ROLL	82
MURRAY HILL		
The Kitano	JAZZ	84
CHELSEA		
Highline Ballroom	VARIOUS: ROCK, POP, FOLK, INDIE, PUNK, ELECTRONIC, HIP-HOP	85
Hill Country	AMERICAN ROOTS, ROCK 'N' ROLL	86
GARMENT DISTRICT		
Madison Square Garden	VARIOUS	88
Manhattan Center	VARIOUS	89
MIDTOWN		
Carnegie Hall	CLASSICAL, WORLD, JAZZ, POP	90
Miles' Cafe	JAZZ	91
Radio City Music Hall	VARIOUS	92
Terminal 5	ALL MODERN MUSIC	93
Tutuma Social Club	WORLD, AFRO-PERUVIAN JAZZ	94
THEATER DISTRICT		
B.B. King	VARIOUS: ROCK, POP, FOLK, WORLD, BLUES, METAL, HIP-HOP	95
Best Buy Theater	VARIOUS: ROCK, POP, FOLK, WORLD, BLUES, METAL, HIP-HOP	96
Don't Tell Mama	CABARET, COMEDY, MUSICALS	99
Iridium	JAZZ	100
Swing 46	BIG BAND, SWING	101

ADDITIONAL VENUES	NEIGHBORHOOD	102-103
Birdland	Theater District	
Gramercy Theater	Gramercy	
Guantanamera	Midtown West	
Hard Rock Cafe	Theater District	
Hiro Ballroom	Chelsea	
Irving Plaza	Gramercy	
Roseland Ballroom	Theater District	

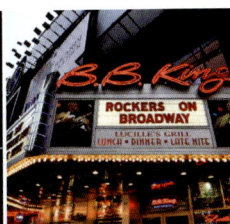

JAZZ STANDARD

116 East 27th Street | New York, 10016 | 212-576-2232
Hours: 6p-3a Daily
Subway: 6 to 28th St
www.jazzstandard.net

Written by: Emily Niewendorp

MUSIC TYPE	VENUE TYPE	ADMISSION	ATMOSPHERE	DRINKS: $-$$$
Jazz	Supper Club Capacity 125	$15 - $30 Student Discount	Casual Supper Club Kid-friendly	Average $5 - $25 **FOOD:** Full Menu

GRAMERCY — Between Lexington Ave & Park Ave

Visiting Jazz Standard is a reward at the end of a long day. The venue's remarkable highlights include owner Danny Meyer's winning hospitality, amazing jazz music, and real pit BBQ from the upstairs restaurant, Blue Smoke.

Photo provided courtesy of Jazz Standard

The stairwell winds down to the club past black and white photos of great jazz musicians from the last century. As the designs and wall coloring turn red—the standard color at Jazz Standard—the air begins to carry an element of anticipation.

When walking into the Jazz Standard, low voices and the soft tinkling of utensils on tableware are audible.

There is a subdued, yet expectant excitement waiting for the music to begin. The staff does its best to accommodate the many seating choices: the bar area; a front section positioned perpendicular to the stage for close views; and tiered platforms.

The black and red stage is simple and intimate, and the roster of talented musicians that play the room means that the shows are nearly always a joy; soft and sweet, and dissident and aggressive. A show at Jazz Standard will carry away any daily strife and charm in the meantime.

Some highlights have included: Bill Charlap with Jim Hall and Frank West; and a Fred Hersch duo series with Kenny Barron, Jason Moran and Ethan Iverson as guests.

The club hosts birthday celebrations and benefits: Preservation Hall Band from New Orleans did a weeklong benefit that hosted numerous Louisiana musicians. Regular events include the Maria Schneider Orchestra's annual Thanksgiving week residency, and the Mingus Mondays weekly residency. The latter residency showcases Charles Mingus' music in three rotating ensembles—Mingus Big Band (winner of Grammy Award for Best Large Jazz Ensemble Album), Mingus Orchestra, and Mingus Dynasty.

Midtown Manhattan

The club has formed its identity by providing opportunities to emerging artists. Luciana Souza is one of many musicians who had her initial, multiple night, jazz-club engagement at Jazz Standard. The club encourages musicians to experiment and present new projects, resulting in shows that are exciting for both the public and the musicians.

Jazz Standard also nurtures the next generation of musicians through the Jazz for Kids program. Conductor David O'Rourke auditions student-musicians from surrounding high schools and junior highs and forms a group. From October to June the kids play a Sunday brunch performance. A $5 donation to see the show has created scholarship opportunities for young musicians to attend college.

There are no table minimums at Jazz Standard, and discounted student tickets are also available. Live recordings of many shows, such as the Grammy nominated duo of Fred Hersch and vocalist Nancy King, are available both at the venue and online.

HISTORY

Known as The Jazz Standard in late '90s, Danny Meyer took over operations in 2001, changed the name to Jazz Standard and closed the space for renovations. It turned out to be fortunate timing, as shortly afterward 9/11 occurred. The venue escaped the loss of business that most NYC companies experienced after the attacks.

A long time enthusiast of jazz since his days as a jazz DJ in college, Danny was also excited about bringing one of the first real pit BBQs to NYC. Long-recognized as a creator of hospitality-driven establishments with excellent cuisine, Danny opened Blue Smoke and Jazz Standard in March 2002. Though live jazz and BBQ may seem like an unlikely pair, both are undoubtedly Danny's passions.

The most proficient musicians and dynamic shows were naturally scheduled for the venue's launch, and since then that high standard has continued.

Tech Check
Technical specs not available

Sound Check
Sound Quality: Great
Stage Lighting: Good
Sightlines: Good
Eardrum Meter:
Green–Yellow

RODEO BAR

375 3rd Ave | New York, NY 10016 | 212-683-6500
Hours: Sun-Tues 9p-12a, Wed 10p-12a, Thu 10p-1a, Fri-Sat 10:30p-1:30a
Subway: 6,R,W to 28th St
www.rodeobar.com

Written by: Emily Niewendorp

MUSIC TYPE	VENUE TYPE	ADMISSION	ATMOSPHERE	DRINKS: $$
American Roots, Rock 'n' Roll	Restaurant, Bar Capacity 150	Free	Honky-tonk	Happy Hour 4p-9p FOOD: Full Menu

GRAMERCY — Between 27th St & 28th St
Midtown Manhattan

Like the music it promotes, Rodeo Bar itself is a no-nonsense, good-times place to eat and drink well, and experience a rock 'n' roll spot with American roots flavor. Folks from out of town that love roots music plan visits to Rodeo Bar when they come to the city.

Peanuts by the basket are available for the taking, and by the end of the night the floors are littered with shells. In the music room, the horse trailer covered in bumper stickers has a bar built inside. When the music and the energy in the room gets cranking, there is no other place like it: the bartenders pound on the roof of the trailer like a big booming battle cry and dancing patrons get in touch with their wild sides. Patrons love the combination of roots music, New York energy and distinctive atmosphere.

HISTORY

Since its inception, Rodeo Bar has been kicking out great American roots music, seven nights a week. In the '80s and '90s, Rodeo Bar was the only cool place in the neighborhood. The area's cheap rents drew artists and other like-minded creative folk, creating a true community.

Established in 1986 as a restaurant called Albuquerque Eats, the owners, Ark Restaurants, quickly converted the space into the Rodeo Bar. The company decorated the bar with stuffed animals and buffalo that are still there and made the back space a live music room.

In 1996, Mitch Pollak was in the process of buying a restaurant named Museum Cafe from Ark and Rodeo Bar was offered as an afterthought. When he saw the menu of Texas-style BBQ and heard the music coming from the back, Mitch was blown away.

Mitch spent years booking bands and promoted concerts in college, so owning a music venue was a natural progression in his career.

Rodeo Bar Photos by: Rupert Hitchcox

Three years later, he sold Museum Cafe, but has held onto Rodeo Bar ever since.

Like many areas of New York, the neighborhood has changed (it is not as dynamic as it once was), but the bar has not. The club's stuffed animals and no-cover policy have remained the same. The establishment also adheres to the ideals practiced by the venue's original booker, Mark Campbell. Mark took great care in respecting musicians, giving bands the entire night to play their music and being the place in NYC that treated touring bands decently.

Rough patches have attempted to throw the Rodeo Bar off its stride, but Mitch has toughed it out. Known for paying bands fairly, the club has had to lower its pay guarantee for bands in order to address higher rent costs. Though that standard is still important, everyone involved has pitched in to keep the venue vibrant. Fortunately for Rodeo Bar, its restaurant sales help keep the doors open. Mitch and the current booker, Jack Grace have talked about making other changes, such as charging a cover for the music, but they always return to the same philosophy: "The venue works as it is, so don't mess with it."

> Musicians around the United States cite Rodeo Bar as their favorite place to play. Bands that now have a following too big for the venue, enjoy returning and playing under disguised names—a surprise treat for those lucky enough to be in the audience on those nights. Rodeo Bar can boast that stars, such as Joan Osborne who got her start playing there every Monday, and Lucinda Williams, launched their careers from the venerable club.

Sound Check
Sound Quality: Good
Stage Lighting: Good
Sightlines: Good
Eardrum Meter:
Green—Yellow

Tech Check
Sound System: Midas Venice, Bose
Monitors: N/A
Backline: No backline

Midtown Manhattan

83

THE KITANO

66 Park Ave | New York, 10016 | 212-885-7000
Hours: Wed-Sat 5p-12mid
Subway: 4,5,6,7,S to Grand Central
www.kitano.com

Written by: Mark Osborne

MUSIC TYPE	VENUE TYPE	ADMISSION	ATMOSPHERE	DRINKS: $$-$$$
Jazz	Small Bar, Lounge Capacity 70	Free Wed - Thu, $15 Fri - Sat	Intimate, Sophisticated	Average $8 - $15 FOOD: no

MURRAY HILL — Corner of 38th St & Park Ave

Midtown Manhattan

"Location, location, location" is the mantra of the real estate business; however at this Park Avenue jazz location, the mantra becomes "intimate, intimate, intimate."

Located in a mezzanine above the lobby of The Kitano Hotel, this unheralded jazz venue dedicates itself to providing quality jazz performances to a small, but loyal, group of jazz followers.

A list of those who have, or are slated to perform at The Kitano, reads like a who's who of contemporary jazz players; most of whom have played with legends such as Freddie Hubbard, Wynton Marsalis, Benny Carter and Randy Brecker. Better yet, the performances are free Wednesday and Thursday, with a small cover charge on the weekends.

The stage is nestled into a corner of the room and surrounded by a random order of small tables and chairs. Seating at the small bar also gives customers a view of the proceedings. A small crew of waitpersons keeps the customers satisfied; but it's not the food and drink that attracts, it's the quality of the performances.

The booking manager, Gino Moratti, approaches his mission of providing loyal aficionados with great jazz by way of an almost evangelical zeal. A jazz pianist himself he prides himself on providing his players with the "best sounding piano in New York," having it tuned three times a week to ensure the integrity of the sound.

The Kitano continues in the rich tapestry of jazz history; the tradition of salon style performances where every breath and every note has meaning and resonance. This Park Avenue jewel is a splendor that needs to be experienced, not just for jazz savants, but for all fans of great music.

Tech Check
Steinway Baby Grand Piano, Vocal PA only

HIGHLINE BALLROOM

431 West 16th St | New York, NY 10011 | 212-414-5994
Hours: Music times vary
Subway: A,C,E to 14th St | L to 8th Ave
www.highlineballroom.com

Written By: Emily Niewendorp

DRINKS: $$-$$$	ATMOSPHERE	ADMISSION	VENUE TYPE	MUSIC TYPE
Average $7-$13	Quintessential Live	$10 - $60	Mid-Size Club	Various: Rock, Pop,
FOOD: Full Menu	Music Venue	Plus Minimum	Capacity 800	Folk, Indie, R&B

CHELSEA
Between 9th Ave & 10th Ave

Highline Ballroom occupies a 2nd and 3rd floor space on the border of the fashionable Meatpacking District and west Chelsea. This premier, large-capacity venue is surrounded by refurbished, hip, living spaces, Chelsea Market and High Line Park.

Opened in 2008, Highline puts on a wide variety of shows. Some of the acts that have performed here include: Lou Reed, Paul McCartney, Donna Summer, Amy Winehouse, The Roots, Santana, 50 Cent, Nas, Al Di Meola, McCoy Tyner, Lady Gaga, Justin Bieber, Indigo Girls, Stevie Wonder, Reverend Horton Heat, Cracker, Prong, Sick of It All, Hot Chip and Super Furry Animals.

Highline's versatile vibe adapts to suit these varied musical genres and their fans. The one-room venue is clean and industrial, yet also has a familiar lodge-look with its high, peaked roof, exposed rafters and finished wood floor. Highline can be set up with tables as a fully-serviced supperclub, or on other occasions the tables can be removed for standing-room concert space. The large, high stage features a killer lighting and sound system. Three bars including one on the balcony provide seamless service and almost all seats and standing positions at Highline offer fine views of the shows.

The menu offers salads, small plates, steak, burgers, fish and vegetarian meals. Bottle service is available. Private parties are encouraged and group rates are available.

Highline Ballroom is named after the newly renovated High Line walkway that runs north and south near the venue. The preserved elevated train line now serves the local community as a park that links several West side neighborhoods: Clinton, Chelsea and the Meatpacking District.

Sound Check
Sound Quality: Great
Stage Lighting: Good
Sightlines: Good
Eardrum Meter:
Green—Yellow

Tech Check
Sound System: Yamaha PM5D-RH
JBL VT4888DP, ASB6128V, ASB6128, VP7212/95DPAN (hole fills), Balcony delayed spkrs VT4888DP, VT4882DP
Monitors: Yamaha M7CL-48
JBL VRX [8 mixes], VRX 915M [reference], SRX725F [side fills], VP7215/64DPAN [drum mon],VPSB7118DPAN [drm]
Lighting: Leprecon Lighting Console LTX48
Backline: Full backline
Other: Green room
Comments: Stage dimensions 30'W x 20'D x 40"H, DJ ready, best-in-class venue

Midtown Manhattan

HILL COUNTRY

30 W 26th St | New York, NY 10010 | 212-691-0507
Hours: Shows: Tues-Thu 9p-12mid, Fri-Sat 10p-1a
Subway: 1,R to 23rd or 28th St
www.hillcountryny.com

Written by: Emily Niewendorp

MUSIC TYPE	VENUE TYPE	ADMISSION	ATMOSPHERE	DRINKS: $-$$
American Roots, Rock 'n' Roll	Mid-Size Club Capacity 299	Free	Good Clean Fun	$2+ FOOD: Full Menu

CHELSEA — Between 6th Ave & 5th Ave

Hill Country brings true central-Texas culture—savory dishes and hot, gritty music—to New York City: dry-rub BBQ with all the fixin's and American roots music—indie rock, southern rock, folk, blues and country.

Hill Country is a large, bi-level restaurant connected by a broad staircase. There are two huge screens upstairs featuring sports, especially Texas-related events and teams. The music venue downstairs is laid out with family-style, wooden tables in front of the stage. The space feels like a finished basement with brick and wood-paneled walls and a large patch-worked Texas flag hangs at the back of the stage.

The music offerings at Hill Country are intentionally as tasty as the food, and most often free of charge. Well-known Austin acts like the honky-tonk, The Derailers, and Heybale, who play on the venue's anniversary each year, alternate with regional and local acts six nights per week. Rock and swing karaoke are a hit on Tuesdays. Hill Country's music booker, Jack Grace, is a cowboy at heart and a professional musician himself, who says his philosophy is, "Never book a bad band and let the good ones play all night long."

Hill Country feeds and cares for its bands, according to Jack, who says, "The younger musicians are blown away because they didn't know they could be treated like that, and the older bands say, 'Wow, I haven't been treated this well since 1986.'"

Hill Country patrons love to choose their brisket, sausage, ribs and other dry-rub BBQ meats and classic southern sides, and then pick them up at the counter, wrapped in brown paper— true Texas road house fashion. Waiters bring drink orders to the table. The feeling is relaxed, greasy, bluesy and just deliciously Texan. Long-necked Lone Star

Rodeo Bar Photos by: Rupert Hitchcox

Beers, Texas craft brews and wines or fine tequilas and bourbons help wash it all down and keep customers coming back for more. Hill Country is a fun, down home place where the live music continues into the night, long past dinner time.

HISTORY

Hill Country is inspired by founder Marc Glosserman's childhood visits to his father's family south of Austin in Lockhart—the BBQ capital of Texas. Texas BBQ's natural partner is Texan music—folk and southern rock, country and Austin City Limits—and young Marc developed an affinity for both. In 2004, after returning from several years' work as an entrepreneur in London, Marc found himself at a family reunion savoring seasoned ribs with the owner of Austin's famous Kreuz Market BBQ, while listening to some down-home Texas music. Thinking out loud, Mark commented that opening a Texas BBQ-style restaurant somewhere else—like NYC—would be a great idea. Today he says, "I had no idea at the time that I would be the one to end up doing it."

Marc found an old manufacturing building in the Flatiron/Chelsea district that was well-suited for Hill Country's concept, but needed proper restaurant utilities, like three 12-story smoke stacks for barbecuing. The building's brick walls and old skylights fit well with the comfortably worn look Marc wanted—like a favorite pair of cowboy boots!

Plans for Hill Country's future are bright. A venue in D.C. has opened and there are ideas for other markets too. A music CD compilation that inspired Hill Country is coming out and there is talk of its own record label.

State of the Bathroom: High ceilings and wooden doors—looks like a luxurious horse stable.

Sound Check
Sound Quality: Good
Stage Lighting: Good
Sightlines: Good
Eardrum Meter:
Green=Yellow

Tech Check
Sound System: Mackie SR 24-4 VLZ Pro, Tannoy V12 mains
Monitors: 3 mixes, Tannoy V12
Lighting: LED lighting, Midi-controlled
Backline: Full backline—Drums, keyboard, bass, guitar amps, *no cymbals/snare
Other: Green Room, meal tickets provided
Recording: Audio stereo board mix, Video projection, DJ ready

Midtown Manhattan

87

MADISON SQUARE GARDEN

4 Penn Plaza | New York, NY 10121 | 212-465-6000
Hours: Music times vary
Subway: A,C,E,1,2,3 to 34th St (Penn Station)
www.thegarden.com

Written by: Emily Niewendorp

MUSIC TYPE	VENUE TYPE	ADMISSION	ATMOSPHERE	DRINKS: $$
Various	Arena	Varies	Multi-purpose Complex	FOOD: no

GARMENT DISTRICT — Between 7th Ave & 8th Ave

Midtown Manhattan

Madison Square Garden, or MSG, is a world-famous sports arena and concert hall, home to the New York Knicks and Liberty basketball teams, and the Rangers hockey team. Housed in four locations over a span of 131 years, it is the longest active major sporting facility in the greater metropolitan area, with a flexible seating capacity in the tens of thousands.

The current facility, situated above Pennsylvania Station, opened on February 11, 1968, with certain technological advances leading its design. Suspension cables, just like those on the Brooklyn Bridge, literally hang the ceiling like a canopy from above, thereby removing the need for columns or similar supports that would normally obstruct a spectator's view.

The Garden, as the venue is also called, is the third busiest arena in the world in terms of ticket sales, hosting 400 events annually. A fight shortly after opening between Mohammed Ali and Joe Frazier set a ticket sales precedent for future shows. In the years that followed, music icons like Michael Jackson and Elvis Priestly drew insane crowds to the arena, and additional legends from the past and present have and do continually sell out the Garden's capacity, such as: Frank Sinatra, Simon & Garfunkel, Madonna, Dave Mathews Band and more.

MSG is known more for its amenities rather than its ambiance. The arena has the typical concourses encircling the arena with concessions and alcoholic beverages. Club suites, with 12 tickets each, are available to rent by groups or individuals on a single-day basis. State-of-the-art technology allows for flexible staging of concerts; musicians can choose to perform in the round, or have the deck placed at one end of the floor for a thrust stage setting, which creates the utility of a backstage area.

At MSG, patrons' expectations are always high; nothing short of the blood, sweat and tears of the performers are required to drive the energy in this colossal space. Whether it's a rockin' Led Zeppelin concert or a tied hockey game, a high-energy experience is what people pay for; and because of MSG's size and impressive technology, any event held here promises to be nothing short of epic.

MANHATTAN CENTER

311 W 34th St | New York, NY 10001 | 212-279-7740
Hours: Music times vary
Subway: A,C,E,1,2,3 to 34th St (Penn Station)
www.mcstudios.com

Photo by Eric Reichbaum   Written by: Laura Sherman

DRINKS: $$ FOOD: no	ATMOSPHERE Old World Charm	ADMISSION Varies	VENUE TYPE Concert Hall	MUSIC TYPE Various

The Hammerstein Ballroom holds an old world charm with a hand painted ceiling, elaborate wood work and three balcony areas. All tickets usually sell as general admission; with the ballroom's enormous standing room floor it is advised to arrive early to get a good spot in the front.

The allure of the ballroom, however, is held in the opera-house quality acoustics, which make every seat in the house sound like the best. Artists including Kylie Minogue, 311, Foo Fighters, Hanson, Backstreet Boys, Britney Spears, The Strokes, Moby, Smashing Pumpkins, Incubus, Katy Perry, Tool, Brand New, Good Charlotte, Matisyahu and many more have graced the stage.

Although the Manhattan Center is best known for the Hammerstein Ballroom, it also boasts The Grand, one of New York's best kept secrets. This 10,000 square foot space provides an amazing recording space for classical orchestras or intimate chamber ensembles.

HISTORY

Oscar Hammerstein built this extravagant venue in 1906, in an effort to bring opera to the people. Originally named Manhattan Opera House it quickly developed a reputation for its extraordinary acoustics, so much so that the Metropolitan Opera House offered $1.2 million for a ten-year moratorium on opera performances, which was happily accepted. The Shubert Brothers took over in 1911 and hosted vaudeville shows six nights a week, with concerts on Sunday nights.

Over the next few decades the venue went through several management changes. The Scottish Rite of Free Masonry purchased it in 1922 and Warner Bros leased the space from 1926, when history was made with the first ever musical soundtrack recording for commercial film. The vita phone sound-on-disc system captured the 107-piece New York Philharmonic orchestra performing for the film "Don Juan."

A name change in 1940 to Manhattan Center encouraged such diverse events as big bands, trade shows, union meetings, as well as large private and corporate events; and to this day the venue is a favored locale for live music concerts, awards and fashion shows, product launches, and more. In addition, the Manhattan Center Studios were formed in 1986 to allow for multimedia events. In 1997 the entire venue underwent a major face-lift and updated its equipment to state of the art technology. It has since become a popular place to record live performances; KoRn, All Time Low, and Coheed and Cambria have all recorded live DVDs.

GARMENT DISTRICT Between 8th Ave & 9th Ave

Midtown Manhattan

CARNEGIE HALL

881 7th Ave | New York, 10019 | 212-247-7800
Hours: Music times vary, Box Office: Mon–Sat 11a-6p
Sun 12p-6p, Summer Hours (July 1–August 23): Mon-Fri 11a-6p
Subway: N,Q,R to 57th St/7th Ave
www.carnegiehall.org

Written by: Nick D'Amore   Photo Credit: ©Jeff Goldberg/Esto; Courtesy of Carnegie Hall

MUSIC TYPE	VENUE TYPE	ADMISSION	ATMOSPHERE	* DINING & * INTERMISSION
Classical, World, Jazz, Pop	Concert Hall	$10 - $164	Inspirational	Gourmet Lite Fare, Premium Beverages

MIDTOWN
57th St & 7th Ave

Carnegie Hall has retained its reputation for excellence since its inception in 1891. From the wide spiraling staircase leading to the main hall, to the impeccably uniformed usher, who directs you to your seat, there is a whimsical, charming and earnest feeling remaining from the bygone era of the 19th century. The venue's name, the atmosphere and the respect it commands reverberates from past generations into the future.

The venue consists of three separate concert chambers, the largest of which is the Isaac Stern Auditorium/ Ronald O. Perelman Stage. World-class orchestras, conductors, and soloists perform in this hall. The intensity and vastness of the room does not overwhelm, but rather, points the listener's focus to the expansive stage, where the conductor moves the many musicians through stunning musical passages with dexterity and vigor. The concert chamber's breathtaking aural space provides startlingly clear and encompassing acoustics. Intense and beautiful sounds can swell up from the orchestra, or the room can be filled with merely a subtle string pluck. Audiences that are fortunate enough to see vocal pieces, hear the human voice as a true instrument. It can be staggering to hear how vocal performers can fill the space with their voices as intensely as the myriad of musicians behind them.

Carnegie Hall seeks to be as versatile and diverse as the performers within its space. For more intimate settings and events, there is the Joan and Sanford I. Weill Recital Hall, a 268-seat room that embraces a smaller audience. Not nearly as yawning and vast as the auditorium space, the tiny recital hall is still big on architectural flair. Initially built for chamber music performances, the hall now hosts events such as recitals, discussions, master's classes, as well as chamber music pieces.

Additionally, there is the Judy and Arthur Zankel Hall, which was renovated in September 2003. It houses performance and educational events, seating 599. From 1895 through the 1960s the hall was primarily leased to the American Academy of Dramatic Arts for theatrical performances. During the 1960s, the space became a venue for cinema, until renovations began in 1997.

Carnegie Hall is a friendly organization, striving to reach the full community. Don't hesitate to visit the venue and have a personal experience for yourself.

Carnegie Hall Tours

Mon-Fri: 11:30am, 12:30pm, 2pm, 3pm
Sat: 11:30am, 12:30pm
Sun: 12:30pm

TOUR TICKETS
$10 Adult, $8 Student/Senior, $4 Children under 12
Tour info: 212-903-9765 | tours@carnegiehall.org

Midtown Manhattan

MILES' CAFE

212 East 52nd St, 3rd Floor | New York, NY 10022
212-371-7657

Hours: Music times vary
Subway: E,V to 53rd St/Lexington | 6 to 51st St
www.milescafe.com/ny

Written by: Daniel Morrow

DRINKS: $-$$	ATMOSPHERE	ADMISSION	VENUE TYPE	MUSIC TYPE
$5+ FOOD: Full Menu	Minimalistic, Casual	$5 - $20	Small Club	Jazz

MIDTOWN EAST — Between 2nd Ave & 3rd Ave

A contender for most the unusual venue space is: Miles' Cafe, located on the 3rd floor of an office block. Upon exiting the elevator, it is pleasantly surreal to find a room decked out with acoustic treatment and a well-equipped stage, including the highly sought-after 1888 Steinway piano.

The small room is minimalistic, but carefully designed; white chairs and round tables are highlighted by caricature-style jazz sketches by Jonathan Glass. Once the music begins and the cocktails flow, a wonderful energy develops, as the warmth of the music permeates the room.

There are double performances every evening at 7:30 p.m. and 9:30 p.m., with an additional late-night show and two daytime shows every weekend. A straightforward $19.99 entrance fee ("No tax, no tip!") includes one performance, a cocktail and edamame popcorn. There's also a Japanese dinner menu available.
A perfect after-work midtown retreat, the club is gaining a reputation for its high quality jazz acts in a comfortable, informal setting.

HISTORY

The original Miles' Cafe in Tokyo has provided daily jazz entertainment for the last 10 years, in addition to being a renowned jazz school. One of its teachers, and the co-owner and sole booker of both the Tokyo and New York clubs, is, Satoru Miles Kobayashi. A virtuoso trumpet player and life-long ardent jazz fan, he has also conducted modern jazz research at the Tokyo University of Science. It was Satoru's love for New York jazz that led him to the city, where he books the club purely on quality of musicianship, not prestige or the size of a musician's following. He listens to each submission and chooses those that most excite him. With Satoru's specific favoring toward traditional, cool-style jazz—in the vein of his namesake the great Miles Davis—avante garde, freestyle or Dixieland jazz styles are not likely to be found here.

Sound Check
Sound Quality: Good
Stage Lighting: Good
Sightlines: Good
Eardrum Meter:
Green—Yellow

Tech Check
Mixer: Mackie 1642-VLZ3 16ch
Sound System: Yorkville YX15
Monitors: Yorkville YX12M
Backline: 1888 Steinway grand piano, Gretsch drums, Ampeg Micro bass amp

Midtown Manhattan

RADIO CITY MUSIC HALL

1260 Avenue of the Americas (6th Ave) | New York, NY 10020
212-247-3777
Hours: Music times vary
Subway: F,M to 50th St Rockefeller Center
www.radiocity.com

Written by: Emily Niewendorp

Photos provided courtesy of Radio City Music Hall

MUSIC TYPE	VENUE TYPE	ADMISSION	ATMOSPHERE	DRINKS: $$
Various	Concert Hall, Theater	Varies	Spectacular	Partial Bar FOOD: no

MIDTOWN Rockefeller Center

Radio City Music Hall is best known today for its live music and arts events, award shows and the ever-popular Christmas Spectacular.

The stage is the largest in the world; one hundred forty feet long, the length of a city block. The auditorium layout was influenced by Samuel Lionel "Roxy" Rothafel, who opened the venue and is credited for discovering the Rockettes. Roxy strove to recreate in Radio City's stage design the image of a sunrise—which he had witnessed at sea—via an enormous, golden stage curtain and ceiling lights which mimic a shimmering sunrise. The ceiling is a huge megaphone, which results in amazing acoustics. On the third mezzanine, speaking voices can be heard without amplification. Choral staircases with curtain entrances through the walls allow performers to reach closer to the audience. On each side of the stage, two alcoves house Mighty Wurlitzer organs. Four thousand organ pipes are hidden behind the house walls, with the wind to power the organs generated by sixty fans in the basement.

HISTORY

Radio City operated as a famous movie theater from its opening on December 27, 1932 until the late '70s. During this time, the venue also hosted live shows, famously including the dancing Rockettes, which drew more than three million visitors. Scheduled for demolition in 1978 because of film distribution changes, Radio City was saved by a public outcry and the Landmark Preservation Commission which recognized it as a city landmark.

An eight-month, seven million dollar restoration took place in 1989. The carpets and wall coverings were refreshed to their original lustrous condition, the seats were replaced in the original 1932 style (minus armrest ashtrays) and the technology was updated. One aspect of Radio City Music Hall that did not need upgrading is the stage's hydraulic system, which lifts and lowers the stage's movable parts, sometimes up to 40 feet. The original hydraulics system, invented by Peter Clark, has lived under the stage since 1932. This design was a U.S. Navy secret for many years. In fact, during its installation, a guard was on duty at all times protecting the secret.

As a live music venue, Radio City Music Hall has presented stellar entertainers over the years, including Frank Sinatra, Ella Fitzgerald, John Denver, Ray Charles, Bette Midler, Liza Minnelli, Sting and many more.

Midtown Manhattan

TERMINAL 5

610 West 56th St | New York, NY 10019 | 212-665-3832
Hours: Music times vary
Subway: 1,A,C,B,D to Columbus Circle
www.terminal5nyc.com

Written by: Ben Ramos

DRINKS: $$ $7+ FOOD: Asia Dog	ATMOSPHERE Industrial	ADMISSION $25+	VENUE TYPE Large Club Capacity 3,000	MUSIC TYPE All Modern Music

The main draw of the Terminal 5 is without a doubt the lineup. Night in, night out, the space books top level talent, from established bands with a solid fan base to up and coming new acts. The venue also doesn't distinguish between genres, scheduling a varying array of acts such as MIA, The Black Keys, Massive Attack, Of Montreal, The Raconteurs and Vampire Weekend.

During the daytime, the entrance to Terminal 5 looks like any of the several roll down garage doors that line the surrounding neighborhood. At night the doors open to a black and white tiled box office lined on each side by white walled hallways with rows of little chandeliers and helpful photo-colored maps of the venue to help you navigate between the floors.

Opened in 2007 and occupying the former space of the DEA raided Club Exit, the young club retains its gritty, fringe of town reputation with its simplistic design and standardized attributes. The main area contains a large elevated stage surrounded by three vertical mezzanines that wrap around the rectangular dance floor. The mezzanines put the viewer on top of the crowd, and nearly on stage, without joining the frantic main-floor action below. The elevated stage provides a large platform for performance, including space for a video board, full choreographed dance numbers as well as a fully organized and arranged lightshow set-up, to accompany the state of the art sound system.

Sound Check
Sound Quality: Great
Stage Lighting: Great
Sightlines: Good
Eardrum Meter: Red

Sound Check
Installed in Terminal 5 is a Clair Brothers Line Array sound system powered by Lab Gruppen amps—it doesn't get much better. Considering the 3 balcony levels and 40ft high ceilings, the sound clarity is mostly great. All bands that perform at Terminal 5 tour with experienced and seasoned sound engineers that can handle the challenge of providing fans with exceptional sound, some better than others.

MIDTOWN WEST Between 10th Ave & 11th Ave

Midtown Manhattan

93

TUTUMA SOCIAL CLUB

164 East 56th St | New York, NY 10022 | 646-300-0305
Hours: Thu-Fri 6p-1a, Sat 6p-2a
Subway: 4,5,6,N,R,W to 59th St/Lexington Ave
E,M to Lexington Ave/53rd St
www.tutumasocialclub.com

Written by: Daniel Morrow

MUSIC TYPE	VENUE TYPE	ADMISSION	ATMOSPHERE	DRINKS: $$-$$$
World: Afro-Peruvian Jazz	Small Club Restaurant & Music	Free	Simple, Intimate	Average $12 - $18 FOOD: Full Menu

MIDTOWN — Between Lexington Ave & 3rd Ave

Midtown Manhattan

The Tutuma Social Club is the only authentic Afro-Peruvian music venue in New York and it promises a fun and unique evening. This basement level venue is simple and intimate, keeping the focus on the music, dancing, and dining and all enveloped in a warm and friendly atmosphere.

Great effort is put forth by the venue to encourage the return of its customers and musicians. Audience members can enter daily raffle drawings and sign up for Tutuma's newsletter at their table. Membership is available with the incentive of 10% off all food and drink. The club also has structured deals for musicians: financial and promotional, including a free photo shoot.

The music here is invariably jazz, with a South American flavor. There is excellent acoustics and a full backline for musicians. Although the music is an integral part of the experience, there is never a cover charge or a drink minimum. The familial ambience, infused with Latin culture guarantees dancing and audience participation as the evening continues.

Internationally renowned Peruvian chefs Carlos Testino and Rodrigo Conroy have prepared a wonderful tapas-style menu of traditional plates. One dish, called *Causa*, allows diners to sample a medley of seafood in spices and sauces particular to Lima. Specialty cocktails are a big focus here too: the Pisco Sour is arguably the best in New York; the *chicha morada* is derived from a unique purple corn syrup recipe; and the *Algarrobina*, a traditional Peruvian drink, is made from the bark of a tree.

Santina, the owner of Tutuma toured Peru in 2008 with Gabriela Alegría and the Afro-Peruvian Sextets. After visiting Peruvian music clubs, also known as *Peñas*, and hearing traditional folkloric music, she was inspired to combine her love of restaurants with the sounds of Peru. Less than a year later in May 2009, Tutuma Social Club opened in NYC, with Gabriela Alegría and the Afro-Peruvian Sextets as its resident band.

Tech Check

The venue is small and requires minimal sound amplification. It's the perfect venue to hear the dynamics of a live performance. The sound system in place is primarily used to enhance the natural acoustics of the room.

B.B. KING

237 West 42nd St | New York, NY 10036 | 212-997-4144
Hours: Open daily, Music times vary
Subway: A,C,E,N,Q,R,1,2,3,7,S to 42nd St/Time Square
www.bbkingblues.com

Photo by Eric Reichbaum • Written by: Laura Sherman

DRINKS: $$	ATMOSPHERE	ADMISSION	VENUE TYPE	MUSIC TYPE
$6+	Casual	Free - $50	Supper Club	Various: Rock, Pop,
FOOD: Full Menu	Supper Club	$10 Table Minimum	Capacity 500 - 1000	Folk, Blues, Hip-Hop

THEATER DISTRICT — Between 7th Ave & 8th Ave — **Midtown Manhattan**

B.B. King Blues Club & Grill opened its doors in June of 2000 in the heart of Times Square, on bustling 42nd Street. Accessible from nearly all the city and regional train lines, the club draws the diversity of New York City and its tourists.

The club is devoted to creating a true blues experience, despite the sometimes harried environment of this tourist hotspot. It is known for its two unique performance spaces, the Showcase Room and Lucille's Grill.

Both of the music rooms provide a low-lit, high-energy atmosphere in a well-serviced space facing a large stage. The Showcase Room boasts a thirty-foot performance area, with two eight-foot video screens on either side that give musicians opportunities to enhance their show. Horse-shoe style seating leaves an open area before the stage for active listening and dancing, and the forty-foot bar adorned with signature saxophone beer taps further adds to the impressive aura. In an adjacent space of this downstairs club, is Lucille's Grill, one of the best kept secrets of the city. It has a one-of-a-kind lounge atmosphere, featuring live blues every night of the week, with no cover charge.

B.B. King Blues Club implies blues music and it has a deep connection to that genre, however the club caters to other tastes as well. The Showcase Room in particular hosts rock, metal, hip-hop and tribute bands. Other artists include George Clinton and the P-Funk All Stars, Macy Gray, Better Than Ezra, James Brown, The Beach Boys, The Roots, NOFX, Public Enemy, Rancid, Everclear and B.B. King himself.

The menu is as diverse as the Big Apple, with a hint of Southern flair. The weekends bring a different style of entertainment with special brunch performances on both Saturdays and Sundays. Starting at 11 a.m. on Saturday mornings you can partake in a fun-filled all-you-can-eat brunch with performances by the group, Strawberry Fields, featuring members from the hit musical on Broadway, *Beatlemania*. Sunday mornings bring uptown to midtown west, with the Harlem Gospel Choir and an all-you-can-eat soul food brunch.

Sound Check
Sound Quality: Great
Stage Lighting: Great
Sightlines: Great
Eardrum Meter: Yellow

Tech Check: Showcase Room
Sound System: Yamaha M7CL-48
Mains: 13 Stage Accompany C27, Subs: 4 Stage Accompany XB36 Subs, 4 L'Acoustics SB218's
Subs Delay: 6 Stage Accompany E24 2xSubs
Monitors: Yamaha M7CL-48
11 Wedges/8mixes: 8 Stage Accompany L27, 15" + Compact Driver, 2 Stage Accompany L24, 12" + Compact Driver, 1 Stage Accompany L26, 2-12" + Compact Driver, Drum Fill 1 Stage Accompany P17(s) : 2 x 18", Fly Fills, 2 B-52Pro SR-1515
Lighting: 1 NSI MC 7524, 1 NSI MLC 16
Backline: Full Backline (no cymbals)
Other: DJ setup, video projection, green room

BEST BUY THEATER

1515 Broadway | New York, 10036 | 212-930-1950
Hours: Box Office: Mon-Sat 12p-6p, Music times vary
Subway: N,Q,R,S,W,1,2,3 & 7 to 42nd St/Times Square
www.bestbuytheater.com

Written by: Daniel Morrow

Photos provided courtesy of Best Buy Theater

MUSIC TYPE	VENUE TYPE	ADMISSION	ATMOSPHERE	DRINKS: $$
Various: Rock, Pop, Folk, Blues, Hip-Hop	Large Concert Hall Capacity 2100	Varies	Quintessential Live Music Venue	Average $10 FOOD: Cafe

THEATER DISTRICT
44th St & Broadway

"Our house is your house," says Jeff Young, production manager of AEG's Best Buy Theater. Formerly known as the Nokia Theater, hospitality is indeed the name of the game at this venue, for it's obvious upon entry that the goal here is to provide music fans with a quality experience on all levels. It does not disappoint.

The venue sports a host of amenities for its patrons. Downstairs, you'll find a Cafe Europa that serves a generous fare of sandwiches, salads, snacks, and coffee. There are also three, full-service bars. Additionally, there are three coat rooms, a cocktail waitress inside the music hall to serve drinks during the show, copious bathrooms all around (so you'll never have to wait in a long line), and handicap facilities to boot. If you happen to be in the lobby area during show time, there's a 200" high-def LED screen, 9 high-def Plasma screens and numerous speakers for you to watch while you wait.

Inside the main hall, the 2100-seat venue is nothing short of spacious. The stage is immense and wide. The room is split into three, tiered sections, which allows for unobstructed views of the stage from every angle. The seats are comfortable and spaced far enough apart so that you never feel hemmed in. Four video monitors are strategically placed near the front and rear perimeters of the seating area, so that you won't miss a single detail of the performance.

All of the venue's features are outstanding, if not mind-blowing, but none more so than its sound and lighting system. Altogether, there are 46 amps and 275,000

Sound Check
by Daniel Morrow, Musician/Writer
While it may lack a little of the warmth and vibe of some of the older theater venues, the acoustics here are as good as any in the world. The room and stage have been treated so that there is no natural echo or sound anomalies. The engineer can therefore affect the overall sound with consistently precise results. The sound gives the impression of an arena venue and remains constant regardless of where you are seated in the house.

Midtown Manhattan

**Within walking distance to Port Authority, Penn Station and Grand Central Station
Cafe Europa offers sandwiches, wraps, salads, soft drinks**

watts of power at its disposal, making it a veritable "Carnegie Hall of rock rooms."

Sound quality at the theater is unparalleled. Approximately $3 million was invested into the facility's sound design to create state-of-the-art acoustics; the sound remains consistent, regardless of where you are in the hall. The sound is as close to perfect for a music venue as you are likely to hear, and celebrity musicians from around the world have attested to this fact. As Jeff proudly explains: "that is why bands play here, because they know they're gonna sound great and the reviews are always going to be great."

Many of the biggest names in mainstream music have performed on this stage: The Eagles, Steve Winwood, Bon Jovi, Rod Stewart, Jay Z, Rihanna, and Alicia Keys. Artists also receive top-notch hospitality; their VIP amenities include dressing rooms, a luxurious green room, showers, and catering.

The venue is also well equipped for recording and live streaming, which enables the theatre to host a plethora of events aside from music. For example, the Microsoft Vista launch was hosted live in this space, and simultaneously broadcasted on the LED screens of Times Square and on other mega-screens in 30 countries around the world.

But the live music experience is far and away the theatre's main focus. The extraordinary acoustics and high-caliber artists that the venue attracts, will continue to keep this, first and foremost, a premier music venue for years to come. As Jeff sums up: **"we're in New York; we should aim to be the best venue in the country, and we are the best."**

Tech Check
FOH Sound Engineer: Dave Brooks
Mixer: Midas Heritage 3000
Sound System: Mix Position 70' from Down Stage Center, Stage Dimensions 40'x 30'x 48", 12 JBL/Vertec VT4888 Mid-Size Format Line Array, 6 per side, 8 JBL/Vertec ASB6128V Subwoofer (under stage), 4-4880A long throw subs, 8 JBL/Vertec VT4887 Small Line Array format, 4 per side (mid delays), 4 JBL SRX-712M Low Profile Wedges Passive (rear delays), Crown power
Monitors: Midas XL-250
Clair Brothers 12am wedge package with 4-R4III side fills and 2-ML 18 Drum Subs, Crown power
Microphones: State of the industry
Lighting Control: Hog iPC Console W/ 2 Touch Screens, 4 Universes, Avolite Pearl 2004 Console W/ 2-17" Monitors
Other: Clearcom Communication, 2 Lycian M2 follow spots, 48 PA boxes acoustically placed around the room for a seemless sound experience
Comments: Best-in-class venue

Midtown Manhattan

INGLOT
TIMES SQUARE
NYC
AMERICAN EAGLE OUTFITTERS
2010
TOSHIBA
MERCURY FREE
LED BULB
TOSHIBA
TDK
W 48 St
OLIVE GARDEN
tkts
SONY
YAHOO!
ONE

DON'T TELL MAMA

343 West 46th Street | New York, NY 10036 | 212-757-0788

Hours: 4p-4a Daily
Subway: A,C,E to 42nd St/Port Authority | C,E to 50th St
N,R,S,1,2,3,7,9 to 42nd St/Times Sq
www.donttellmamanyc.com

Written by: Heather McCown

DRINKS: $$ Average $6 - $13 FOOD: Full Menu	ATMOSPHERE Fun!	ADMISSION Piano Bar - Free Theater, Free - $25	VENUE TYPE Piano Bar, Lounge, Theater	MUSIC TYPE Cabaret, Comedy, Musicals

THEATER DISTRICT — Between 8th Ave & 9th Ave

Don't Tell Mama opened in 1982, bringing a unique blend of karaoke and cabaret to the Theater District. Well-known on the performance circuit—Edie Falco, Rosie O'Donnell, or Eileen Fulton occasionally show up for a tune or two—it was also a location venue for sitcoms such as *Friends* and *Will & Grace*.

Nestled mid-block on 46th Street in Restaurant Row, DTM welcomes everyone, boasting a mixed crowd of singers and revelers. Entertaining and personable, DTM fills a gap; Jennifer Pace, one of the venue's celebrated bartenders, explains: "There are not a lot of Mom & Pop joints anymore."

Comprised of a main room and two private cabaret rooms, the club expanded in 1992 to include a restaurant serving New American Cuisine. When not dining, patrons can sit at black cocktail tables in the mirrored main room and enjoy the piano bar, or catch a dedicated act in one of the private rooms—a perfect spot to throw a party.

The burgundy walls are adorned with signed photographs of artists who have performed, such as: Eileen Fulton, Bea Arthur, Rue McLanahan, Jay Bradley, Kathy Griffin and Neil Patrick Harris. Jennifer relates a story of Tony Danza accidently burning a hole in her stockings one packed night, back when smoking was allowed.

DTM is unassuming, but holds its own. The booking director, Sidney Myer, clarifies that it is truly a performing arts center as it hosts acts from rock to opera, cabaret, gospel, and even magicians. He states, "Everyone has to start somewhere, and for many this is the place they began." Even the staff, which also performs, considers this a place to hone their craft.

While many of the performers have gone on to win Emmy and Grammy awards, and even the $100,000 Grand Prize on Star Search, don't be intimidated. If you choose to sing, DTM's friendly staff will guarantee you enjoy belting out a tune, whether it be a standard, or Lady Gaga's latest.

Midtown Manhattan

IRIDIUM

1650 Broadway | New York, 10020 | 212-582-2121
Hours: Sun-Thu 7p-11p, Fri-Sat 7p-1a
Subway: B,D,E to 7th Ave | N,R to 49th St
1 to 50th St
www.iridiumjazzclub.com
Written by: Aidan Levy

Sound Check
Sound Quality: Great
Stage Lighting: Great
Sightlines: Great
Eardrum Meter:
Green-Yellow

MUSIC TYPE	VENUE TYPE	ADMISSION	ATMOSPHERE	DRINKS: $$
Jazz	Supper Club / Capacity 180	$20 - $40 / Student Discounts	Dinner, Casual / Jazz Lounge	Average $7 - $12 / **FOOD:** Full Menu

THEATER DISTRICT — Between 50th St & 51st St
Midtown Manhattan

Since 1994, the Iridium has served as an incubator for numerous world-renowned jazz artists, among them James Carter, Ravi Coltrane, and Cyrus Chestnut. The impromptu nightly jam sessions in the subterranean 52nd Street throwback have led to myriad irreproducible "you had to be there" moments across a broad spectrum of styles, ranging from the time Lionel Hampton sat in with jazz icon Wynton Marsalis, to unexpected appearances by legendary guitarists Slash, Keith Richards and Jeff Beck. In its relatively short history, the Iridium has become one of the top-flight jazz venues in the city, an intimate performance space that attracts some of the biggest names in contemporary music. "You can never see Jeff Beck in such a small room," says Ron Sturm, Iridium general manager.

The Iridium is perhaps best known for its relationship with Les Paul, the father of the electric guitar, who made it his weekly home for more than 12 years, right up to August 2009, literally weeks before his passing.

To honor the memory of this unifying figure, the club continues to present upper-echelon guitarists in all genres with Les Paul Mondays, a weekly series featuring the Les Paul Trio—guitarist Lou Pallo, bassist Nicki Parrott, and pianist John Colianni—performing with different special guests, among them rock god Peter Frampton, journeyman guitarist Jeff Beck, and former Ozzy Osbourne lead guitarist Zakk Wylde.

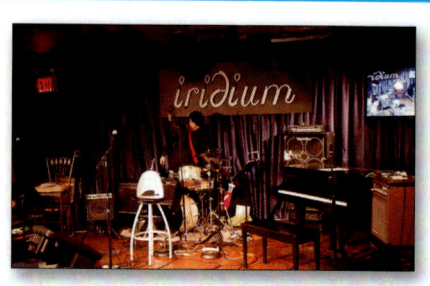

"Like Les Paul said, 'Music is music. What's good is good,'" says Ron. "So people play here who can shred guitar like Zakk Wylde, or they can play beautiful solo guitar like Martin Taylor or Stanley Jordan."

Continuing in this tradition, the Iridium stage has also featured a panoply of artists beyond category, including elder statesmen McCoy Tyner, Ahmad Jamal, and Max Roach, as well as young lions Kurt Rosenwinkel, Rudresh Mahanthappa, and John Medeski, a veritable who's-who of jazz greats. Rounded out by a gourmet menu and consummate wine list, the Iridium is that rare combination of jazz-age grit and insouciant class, all in an informal, freewheeling environment.

Tech Check
Sound System: Midas Venice 320, Meyer
Monitors: JBL EON, mixed from FOH
Stage Size: 12x16
Lighting: in process of updating
Other: Video projection, DJ setup, green room, dressing room

Sound Check
Sound Quality: Good
Stage Lighting: Good
Sightlines: Great
Eardrum Meter:
Green

SWING 46

349 W 46th St | New York, NY 10036
212-262-9554
Hours: Sun-Thu 5p-11:30p, Fri-Sat 5p-1a
Subway: A,C,E,1,9 to Times Square
www.swing46.com

Written by: Jasmine Lovell-Smith

DRINKS: $$-$$$	ATMOSPHERE	ADMISSION	VENUE TYPE	MUSIC TYPE
$7+ FOOD: Full Menu	Sophisticated, Casual to Dressy	$12 Sun-Thu $15 Fri & Sat	Supper Club	Big Band, Swing

Entering Swing 46 is like stepping back into 1940s New York. The lettering on the awning reads "dining dancing cocktails." With live dance music seven nights a week, this polished, sophisticated venue provides the perfect atmosphere for all three offerings.

The cozy red-walled interior is outfitted with dark wood furnishings, mellow lighting, crisp white tablecloths and red carnations in glass vases. The relaxed yet attentive staff and mixed clientele lend the place an approachable, friendly quality that avoids being stuffy or overly formal.

The front room presents a long, elegant wooden bar, with mini chandeliers overhead and a mirrored wall behind covered in rows and rows of sparkling glasses. Ample table seating is provided in this room for those preferring a quieter dining experience. The venue has an extensive drinks list and a full menu, specializing in classic American cuisine such as steak and seafood.

Past the bar is the entrance to the back room, where the music and dancing take place. The intimate wooden dance floor is right in front of the stage. The stage, complete with grand piano, is surrounded by both formal table seating and more casual areas to perch for drinks. Music from the ten-piece dance band is tight and swinging, and perfectly in sync with the period atmosphere.

Swing 46 is the last remaining swing supper club on the east coast, and a perfect spot for parties and special events. It was recently voted the number one place to dance in New York City by MSN, and free dance lessons are provided as part of the entertainment. Conveniently located in midtown Manhattan's theater district, the venue draws a diverse crowd and is particularly popular with tourists looking to experience the New York of a bygone era.

THEATER DISTRICT
Between 51st St & 52nd St

Midtown Manhattan

ADDITIONAL VENUES

Birdland
315 West 44th St | New York, NY 10036 | 212-581-3080
www.birdlandjazz.com

Birdland's history dates back to 1949 and the hay-days of jazz, when Charlie Parker and other famous musicians drew intense crowds. Over the years, Birdland lived at several different locations, even uptown, until it moved back to midtown in '96, where today you can appreciate the best jazz in the world in a classy supper club.

Guantanamera
939 8th Ave | New York, NY 10019 | 212-262-5354
www.guantanameranyc.com

Guantanamera is a traditional Cuban joint with daily live music. It appears more like a restaurant than a music venue, but the bands are dynamic and riveting, and probably most representative of Cuban culture—a part of daily life and activities. Enjoy a Mojito or sangria, choose a hand rolled cigar and dance the rumba or the mamba with the regulars.

Hard Rock Cafe
1501 Broadway | New York, 10036 | 212-343-3355
www.hardrock.com

Hard Rock Cafe started as a single diner in London ran by two fun-loving Americans. Musician Eric Clapton developed an affinity to the place and after a whimsical request by one of the owners, Eric offered up his guitar. More instruments and memorabilia found their place on the cafe's walls and the rest is history. In New York, Hard Rock has built a rockin' large stage below Times Square.

Hiro Ballroom in the Maritime Hotel
88 9th Ave | New York, NY 10011 | 212-727-0212
www.hiroballroom.com

Hiro Ballroom is a gorgeous space peppered with ornate Chinese lanterns hanging from a barrel-vaulted ceiling. Double staircases lead to the balcony, which overlooks the dance floor, table seating and a full bar. Spectacular stage lighting and audio systems round out the potential for an exceptional music experience. Hiro is open weekends for ongoing DJ parties and weekdays per event.

Gramercy Theater
127 East 23rd St | New York, NY 10010 | 212-777-6800
www.livenation.com

Gramercy Theater is a historic building opened in 1937 that existed as a movie theater hosting various genres, until it was renovated into an Off Broadway theater house in 1998. In 2006, Live Nation turned the space into a concert hall drawing A-list performers to crowds of enthusiastic New Yorkers. Under Blender Magazine's sponsorship since 2006 the venue is known as Blender Theater.

Irving Plaza
17 Irving Place | New York | 212-777-6800
www.livenation.com

Irving Plaza has championed the arts since 1860, albeit under various names and through several interior and exterior changes. Its uses included: concerts, balls, lectures, Yiddish theater, burlesque, cinema, a community center, and finally a music venue for punk rock, new wave, reggae, alternative rock, ethnic music and more. Young people today dig the old, funky decor and the inclusive, concert-hall vibe.

Roseland Ballroom
239 West 52nd St | New York, NY 10019 | 212-247-0200
www.livenation.com

Located in New York City's Theater District, the Roseland Ballroom has been in its current location since 1956. This flexible venue hosts standing-room only and supper club style shows, and has various stage configuration capabilities. It is one of NYC's more intimate venues for big-name, high-energy events, while still holding a large capacity of people (800 – 3,200). As a multi-purpose hall, expect events such as musical acts (Madonna, Dropkick Murphy, Ke$ha) Hillary Clinton's birthday party, movie premieres, conventions, fashion shows, the annual Broadway Bares/Equity Fights AID dance benefit, and more.

Photo by Jasna Boudard

MANHATTAN UPTOWN

UPPER WEST SIDE

	GENRE	PAGE
Beacon Theatre	VARIOUS	106
Dizzy's Club Coca Cola	JAZZ	107
P&G Bar	ROCK, POP, BLUES, JAM	108
Smoke	JAZZ	109

UPPER EAST SIDE

Bar East	ROCK, POP, FOLK, SINGER-SONGWRITER	110

SPANISH HARLEM

Camaradas	LATIN JAZZ, WORLD	111
FB Lounge	LATIN JAZZ, WORLD	112

HARLEM

Showmans	JAZZ	113
Shrine	WORLD, ROCK, POP, REGGAE, AFROBEAT	114
St. Nick's Jazz Pub	JAZZ	115

ADDITIONAL VENUES

	NEIGHBORHOOD	116
Apollo	Harlem	
Cleopatra's Needle	Upprer West Side	
Cotton Club	Harlem	
Feinstein's	Upper East Side	
Lenox Lounge	Harlem	

Uptown Manhattan

BEACON THEATRE

2124 Broadway | New York, NY 10023 212-465-6500
Hours: Music times vary
Subway: 1,2,3 to 72nd St
www.beacontheatre.com

Written by: Emily Niewendorp

MUSIC TYPE	VENUE TYPE	ADMISSION	ATMOSPHERE	DRINKS: $$
Various	Concert Hall/Theater Capacity 2,894	Varies	Extravagant	Partial Bar, $8+ FOOD: no

UPPER WEST SIDE — Between 74th St & 75th St

Beacon Theater's near-perfect acoustics, grandiose auditorium and extravagant Art Deco designs place it in the upper echelon of New York City music venues.

Its recent restoration returned the worn-down structure into a feast for the eyes and heart, an affect that was similarly received by the theater's original attendees as well—those enduring the Great Depression. The auditorium is a medley of Greek, Roman, Renaissance, Rococo and Moorish styles, displayed in flat gold-painted ornaments and sculptures. A double balcony with red rows of seating and the vibrant colors on the proscenium, combine with riveting stage performances and events to create an unforgettable experience.

The most famous bands have played Beacon Theater over the years: the Rolling Stones, Jerry Garcia, Aerosmith, Michael Jackson, James Taylor, Radiohead and Queen. Since 1989, the Allman Brothers have performed 173 shows at the Beacon. For many years they played each spring in a weekend event that became known as "The Beacon Run."

Other types of events are also popular at the Beacon; Bill Clinton celebrated his 60th birthday at the venue with a private Rolling Stones concert, and His Holiness the Dalai Lama chose the Beacon Theatre as the site of his teaching classes in August of 1999.

HISTORY

The Beacon is known as the "older sister" to Radio City Music Hall, opened a few years beforehand in 1929 by the same man, Samuel "Roxy" Rothafel, widely known as a theatrical impresario. He considered Beacon a masterpiece of its time with stylish Art Deco designs by Walter Ahlschlager, and elegant marble entryways. Roxy's vision of an international entertainment and cultural events destination has awed crowds through the decades, spanning both silent film/vaudeville and talking picture eras.

The venue's 2008 restoration revealed a surprise: two architectural firms, each with their own set of plans, designed the theater in 1929. The second set of plans was applied when Warner Bros. took over the lease and construction of the theater, before the building was ever completed. In order to honor the building's preservation as a national landmark as of 1979, the company overseeing the restoration painstakingly studied both sets of original plans, as well as black and white photos, in order to restore the space to its original designs and image that are so beautifully presented today.

Uptown Manhattan

Sound Check
Sound Quality: Great
Stage Lighting: Great
Sightlines: Great
Eardrum Meter:
Green–Yellow

DIZZY'S CLUB COCA COLA

33 West 60th St | New York, NY 10023
212-253-0036
Hours: Mon-Thu, Sun 6p-1a, Fri-Sat 6p-2:30a
Subway: A,C,E,D to Columbus Circle
www.jalc.org

Written by: Robbie Gonzalez & Paula Pahnke

Photo Credit: Daryl Long

DRINKS: $-$$$	ATMOSPHERE	ADMISSION	VENUE TYPE	MUSIC TYPE
$5+ FOOD: Full Menu	Elegant Jazz Club	$20 - $30 $5 - $10 Students	Supper Club Capacity 140	Jazz

UPPER WEST SIDE
Columbus Circle

"Take care of the music and the music will take care of you;" that is the motto of Todd Barkan, the legendary record producer and current programming director of Dizzy's Club Coca-Cola, one of the three main performance venues that make up Jazz at Lincoln Center. From the moment you approach the entrance to this elegant jazz club, you are greeted with the gracious familiarity of a guest whose arrival has been eagerly anticipated. That is the heart and charm of Dizzy's. The lush and spacious layout complements an intimate atmosphere that combines unrestricted luxury with the relaxed sensation of a personal musical experience.

Housed on the 5th floor of the Time Warner Center at Columbus Circle, the club boasts an illustrious view of the New York City skyline, which shimmers through the floor to ceiling window as the stage's backdrop. Named for jazz great Dizzy Gillespie, the club conserves the classic vibe of jazz club anchors, The Blue Note and The Iridium, which have played host to music legends from Sarah Vaughn, to Les Paul. Uniquely shaping a contemporary jazz experience, under the direction of the club's managers, Roland Chassagne and Todd Barkan, Dizzy's showcases notable jazz talents and up-and-coming musicians, providing an accessible experience to both jazz enthusiasts and novice guests. In the tradition of the Jazz at

Credit: Julie Skarratt

Lincoln Center organization, Dizzy's is promoting the next generation of jazz performers and listeners, alike, by endorsing young artists during their after hour sets and offering discounts to students for all performances.

As soulful as the music, the menu boasts an array of Creole favorites like Southern Fried Catfish Po' Boy sandwiches and entrees that include Miss Mamie's Fried Chicken and Low Country Shrimp and Grits. Dizzy's Club Coca-Cola creates a state-of-the-art atmosphere for both traditional jazz lovers as well as the next generation to come.

Credit: Courtney Spencer

Tech Check
Sound System: Amek BB 100 console with up to 18 inputs. JBL AM6340/95 Left and Right (2 Total), JBL AM6200/95 Center Fill Controlled Left/Right; Subwoofers: JBL S121 Custom Sub with 8" drivers
Monitors: 5 monitor mixes
Lighting: ETC Smartfade 1248 Console
Backline: Steinway Concert B Piano tuned to A440, full backline

Uptown Manhattan

107

P&G BAR

380 Columbus Ave | New York, NY 10024
212-874-8568
Hours: Mon-Sat 11a-4a, Sun 12p-4a
Subway: 1 to 79th St | B,C to 81 St
http://www.pandgbar.com

Written by: Emily Niewendorp

Sound Check
Sound Quality: So-So
Stage Lighting: So-So
Sightlines: Good
Eardrum Meter: Yellow

MUSIC TYPE	VENUE TYPE	ADMISSION	ATMOSPHERE	DRINKS: $$
Rock, Pop, Blues, Jam	Basement Club	Free	Neighborhood Bar	FOOD: no

UPPER WEST SIDE
Corner of West 78th St & Columbus Ave

P&G Cafe and its famous neon sign occupied the corner of West 73rd Street and Amsterdam Avenue for 67 years until it was pushed out by the landlord in a 2008 public fight. Still a gritty and friendly "real person's bar," P&G now occupies the corner basement of a sleek, red stone building a few streets away from its original spot.

An outdoor staircase leads down to the venue, where flat-stone columns create a loose border between the bar and stage area; folks at the bar can converse freely and the music spreads throughout the multi-roomed venue. The music room's small stage is enclosed on three sides, creating an intimate setting with a variety of seating in booths and high and low tables. P&G also offers pool tables, a jukebox, flat-screen TVs and darts, with plans to develop the kitchen area.

P&G's fourth-generation proprietor, Steve Chahalis, has added daily live music to this new location because: "I love music, I love musicians."

A musician himself, he books the bands, while his wife, Holiday, runs operations and tends bar. P&G regulars are thankful—there are not many music venues on the Upper West Side. There is no cover at P&G, yet Steve gives the bands a percentage of the bar. Two to three bands play per night, each normally for two-hour sets. On Monday nights, musicians get lengthy 45-minute sets at the open mic, and every Tuesday, vocalist Jonny Rosch, best known from the Blues Brothers Band, plays along with various guests.

Prominent musicians have come through the doors of P&G such as Steely Dan and drummer Shawn Pelton. Blues Brothers Band has played there, as has Aerosmith legend Steven Tyler, who stopped by one night to have a drink and jumped on stage to sing with the band.

Pictured: Mary Gatchell

Tech Check
Sound System: Unavailable

Uptown Manhattan

Sound Check
Sound Quality: Great
Stage Lighting: Great
Sightlines: Good
Eardrum Meter:
Green–Yellow

SMOKE

2751 Broadway | New York, NY 10025
212-864-6662
Hours: Mon-Fri 2p-3a, Fri-Sat 11:30a-3a
Subway: 1 to 103rd St
www.smokejazz.com

Jazz Brunch Sat & Sun 11:30a - 3p

Written by: Laura Sherman & Monica U. Garcia

DRINKS: $$-$$$ FOOD: Full Menu	ATMOSPHERE Supper Club Lounge	ADMISSION Free - $35	VENUE TYPE Small Club Capacity 60	MUSIC TYPE Jazz

UPPER WEST SIDE Between 105th St & 106th St

Uptown Manhattan

Intimate and welcoming, the Smoke Jazz and Supper Club was a favorite of jazz singer Etta James, who performed there every Valentine's Day. With plush red leather seating for just over 50, the glow of antique chandeliers and candle light on exposed brick walls sets the mood for a trip to a place where time doesn't exist. Sensuous, heavy draping does more than help create the intimate mood—it raises the acoustic quality of the room. The sound is impeccable in every seat in the house.

Smoke attracts some of the world's best jazz performers including Wynton Marsalis, Bill Charlap, Ron Carter, Kenny Washington, Neal Smith, Jimmy Cobb, Eve Cornelius and many more. Smoke hosts a variety of music including funk, soul jazz, Latin jazz, Afro-Cuban, and a 16-piece jazz band.

Co-owners Paul Stache and Frank Christopher work to ensure that Smoke offers its patrons the complete experience. The club offers dinner with every show, and even has the option of a prix fixe or á la carte menu. Three hours of jazz also accompanies the Saturday and Sunday jazz brunch.

The greatest element of Smoke is the diversity of the  crowd. "One of the truly magical things about Smoke is that it transcends generations—that whenever you walk through the door at Smoke, no matter how old you are, you become ageless," says a regular customer of the club.

Smoke is described as "magical" time and time again, and it isn't only about the music. Smoke Jazz and Supper Club offers an ethereal experience, transporting you to a setting you hoped existed, and to which you will return.

HISTORY

Since 1999, Smoke has continued the legacy of the club formerly known as Augie's. The author Paul Auster, a regular at Augie's, is said to have based one of his characters from his screen play *Smoke* on the real life Augie. In the movie, Harvey Keitel plays protagonist Auggie, the owner of a Brooklyn smoke shop. In turn, Smoke Jazz and Supper Club was so-named in tribute to Paul Auster.

Tech Check
Sound System: Allen+Heath, EAW Speakers, QSC Power, Lexicon Verbs

BAR EAST

1733 1st Ave | New York, NY 10128
212-876-0203
Hours: Wed-Sat 7p-2a | Upstairs 6p-4a
Subway: 4,5,6 to 86th St | 6 to 96th St
www.bareast.com

Written by: Emily Niewendorp

Sound Check
Sound Quality: So-So
Stage Lighting: So-So
Sightlines: Good
Eardrum Meter:
Yellow—Red

MUSIC TYPE	VENUE TYPE	ADMISSION	ATMOSPHERE	DRINKS: $-$$
Various: Rock, Pop, Folk, Sing-Songwriter	Small Club Capacity 200	$5 - $10	Neighborhood Bar	Happy Hour $2+ FOOD: no

UPPER EAST SIDE — Between 89th St & 90th St

Bar East Ale House is a beacon of light on the Upper East Side. Far away from the downtown music scenes, it is the only venue in the neighborhood that keeps a regular performance schedule.

Bar East has two levels, each accessed by its own door from the street. The music room, downstairs, is long and wide with a large, rainbow-shaped bar and a small stage. Originally known as Underscore, the venue's name was recently discarded and now goes by the name of the upstairs bar. The Ale House, upstairs, opened in 1998 and is a neighborhood hang-out. There is a long list of micro brews and craft ales that are brought in weekly from Defiant Brewery, 25 miles outside the city.

Musically, anything from ska to salsa can be heard at the venue, though its mainstay is rock. The club recently started directing focus towards the musical integrity of its shows by taking control of the booking, which it had outsourced in the past. This change will show the venue's true colors, as it loves to seek out and support up-and-coming bands. Once, it discovered an Alabama band online that was coincidently planning a tour through NYC. The band agreed to play a show at Bar East and a surprisingly large NYC crowd with Alabama roots showed up in support.

HISTORY

Co-owner Paul Wilson describes the early days of starting the venue as "a blessing and a curse" but says that "providing something [live music] that everyone loves is a wonderful way to make a living." Although a life-long music lover, he confesses that creating this venue was more of an accident. His musician friends talked him into it after he'd initially proposed putting in a bowling alley. The music venue took off with several bands playing nightly and local kids playing matinee shows for their families and friends.

Miles Robbins, son of Tim Robbins and Susan Sarandon, decided he wanted to have his first show at Bar East. The three showed up, with friends Sean Penn and Eddie Vedder; Vedder ended up getting on stage to play. Other well-known musicians have also played there including Michael Grey from The Misfits and Chris Baron from The Spin Doctors.

Sound Check
By Daniel Morrow, Musician/Writer

This venue is planning a much welcomed makeover. Currently the room feels a little cold and lifeless with acoustics to match. There is great potential for good sound here; the stage is slightly elevated, there's a sound booth ideally situated at the back of the room and a dedicated sound engineer. With this room, the vibe is what you make it; being the only venue in the area, certain crowds are already giving the room a good feel. The rebranding should provide additional appeal to musicians and their fans.

Uptown Manhattan

Sound Check
Sound Quality: Good
Stage Lighting: So-So
Sightlines: So-So
Eardrum Meter: Yellow

CAMARADAS
2241 1st Ave | New York, NY 10029
212-348-2703
Hours: Open daily 3p, Sat 4p
Subway: 6 to 116th St
www.camaradaselbarrio.com
Written by: Emily Niewendorp

DRINKS: $-$$	ATMOSPHERE	ADMISSION	VENUE TYPE	MUSIC TYPE
$5+ FOOD: Full Menu	Latin infused, Working-class Pub	$5+	Restaurant, Bar Capacity 79	Latin Jazz, World

Culture, history, camaraderie and home; the night these aspects of Camaradas el Barrio came together Afro-Puerto Rican roots music was pulsating, the bar was packed and owner Orlando Plaza's mother's recipes were streaming out of the kitchen. Orlando and his fellow partners, Raúl Rivera and Jay Zhao, learned then that their patrons were calling Camaradas 'church.' Deeply rooted in Puerto Rican traditions and the local community, their crystal-clear vision of a public home for all people had finally come to fruition.

Camaradas is one long, narrow room, with a bar and wooden tables for dining. The stage is very small, but that does not stop live bands from playing regularly, and dancers quickly filling up the space. Traditional Puerta Rican tapas are served, while the bar boasts an international and island selection of beers and large tasty sangria pitchers. Art work is displayed on the rustic brick and corrugated tin walls as a rotating gallery.

Camaradas is known in New York City for its Latin music, drawing an array of skin colors and age groups. The spirited music and dancing may take first-timers by surprise, but everyone quickly embraces the music as wholeheartedly as the regulars. Nearing its sixth year of business, Camaradas routinely hosts Navegante, self-described as "electro-land funk." Camaradas and Navegante's partnership—based on mutual trust—supports both parties and adds a vibe of creative freedom. The weekly calendar is chock full of Afro-Caribbean bands from Cuba, the Dominican Republic, Haiti and Colombia; DJs; Ladies Night; and various fusion bands.

HISTORY
In Camaradas, Orlando and his partners are producing a feeling. Orlando mentions courageous family businessmen, his work as a historian, a Puerto Rican bookstore on Avenue B, the Nuyorican Poets Cafe and tales of the Palladium days from the '40s and '50s as his inspiration. In those days, musicians from the Barrio (Spanish Harlem) proudly played in the Barrio. Setbacks from poverty and crime over the years dampened some of the neighborhood's culture, but Puerto Ricans and locals in el Barrio have fought to preserve their culture through social programs, clinics and museums such as El Museo del Barrio. Camaradas has become another vital establishment, where the neighborhood can celebrate their heritage.

Tech Check
Sound System: BYOS—Bring Your Own Sound. DJ Setup only.

SPANISH HARLEM Between 115th St & 116th St

Uptown Manhattan

FB LOUNGE

172 E 106th St | New York, NY 10029 | 212-348-3929

Hours: Music Wed-Sat, Music times vary, Open Tue-Sun 6p
Subway: 6 to 103rd St
www.fondaboricua.com

Written by: Danny Garcia

MUSIC TYPE	VENUE TYPE	ADMISSION	ATMOSPHERE	DRINKS: $-$$
Latin Jazz, Salsa, Afro-Cuban, Jazz	Small Club Capacity 130	Free - $20	'Place of Excellence'	Average $5 - $12 **FOOD:** Full Menu

SPANISH HARLEM — Between 3rd Ave & Lexington Ave

Uptown Manhattan

Proud of their Latino heritage, FB Lounge is described by its owners, brothers Jorge and Roberto Ayala, as a 'cultural center.' "There is no better place to hear the sound of Latin American music, than FB Lounge," says Roberto Ayala. The venue caters to traditional Afro-Cuban, Latin jazz, salsa, charanga, rumba and more. Opened in 2008, FB Lounge is located in the neighborhood known as El Barrio (or Spanish Harlem), directly across the street from the brothers' well-known Puerto Rican restaurant of 14 years, La Fonda Boricua.

FB Lounge is a bar, venue, and restaurant designed with class. "This is a place of excellence. There is no 2nd chance to make a good first impression." says Roberto Ayala. Natural wood-stained horizontal wooden boards line the lounge area. The comfort of the plush red leather couches and the coffee table at the entrance are inviting, but the sounds from the stage direct you past the long narrow bar to the performance space where table service is available.

In the performance area, the raised stage covers the entire length of the back wall. Spacious and large enough to accommodate a 7 foot baby grand piano, it still offers plenty of room for traditional Latin ensembles. Wooden beams cross section the ceiling and walls and Latin artwork lightly decorate the walls. Legendary and world-class musicians have performed at FB Lounge, such as Alfredo Chocolate Armenteros, Bobby Sanabria, Ron Carter, Louis Hayes, Mulgrew Miller, Steve Nelson, and The Mambo Legends Orchestra. Recently, Wynton Marsalis stopped in to perform with his friend Papo Vazquez.

La Fonda Boricua, the lauded neighborhood restaurant that FB Lounge takes its name from, provides a full menu of traditional Latin American favorites. World-renowned chef, Bobby Flay challenged La Fonda Boricua to an arroz con pollo Throwdown, on the popular Food Network show. The Ayala brothers won the battle.

Sound Check
Sound Quality: Great
Stage Lighting: Good
Sightlines: Good
Eardrum Meter:
Green–Yellow

SHOWMANS

375 W 125th St | New York, NY 10027 | 212-864-8941
Showtime Hours: Mon-Thu 8:30p, 10p, 11:30p
Fri-Sat 9:30p, 11:30p, 1:30a
Subway: A,C,B,D to 125th St
www.myspace.com/showmansjazz

Written by: Mark Osborne

DRINKS: $-$$	ATMOSPHERE	ADMISSION	VENUE TYPE	MUSIC TYPE
Average $6 - $12 FOOD: no	Friendly Neighborhood Bar	Free 2 Drink Minimum	Small Room Capacity 75	Jazz

HARLEM — Between St Nicholas Ave & Morningside Ave

Uptown Manhattan

Located in the heart of Harlem, Showmans honors the age-old structures of jazz: hospitality, respect and great music. Once a next-door hangout for performers at the Apollo Theater, Showmans has moved several times since it opened in 1942. Folks continue to frequent the small joint for its long-standing values and sense of community.

Step off the street and into a time warp. This is the Harlem of Coleman Hawkins, T.S. Monk, and Sonny Rollins. The wood paneling and exposed brick give the impression the place has not been updated for decades, and frankly why should it? Loyal customers frequent Showmans, yet they refrain from conducting themselves proprietarily. This interesting mix of older locals is extremely welcoming; seemingly proud to introduce tourists and first-time visitors to their slice of life, seldom found now in the city. The crowd interacts, drinking and dancing together in reflection of the multicultural 'new' Harlem.

Showmans is a long narrow room, with the bar and seating filling up one entire side. The stage is located at the back of the room, and is raised enough for decent visibility throughout the bar. The sound, like the atmosphere, is very warm, and not overpowering.

Mona, Showmans manager and part owner, has been booking the bands since 1978; and not just any bands: saxophone great, Jerry Weldon, performs there every Wednesday. Mona is the consummate hostess, offering anecdotes, and appetizers for free. Within the first few minutes of arriving you can see that Showmans is her labor of love and one of the reasons people return.

Take a rendezvous uptown and check out this jazz jewel; you will meet good people, and hear great jazz, with enough money left over for a cab fare home.

Sound Check
Sound Quality: Good
Stage Lighting: Good
Sightlines: So-So
Eardrum Meter:
Green–Yellow

SHRINE

2271 Adam Clayton Powell Jr Blvd | NY 10030
212-690-7807
Hours: 4p-4a Daily
Subway: B,2,3 to 135th St
www.shrinenyc.com

Written by: Rachel Antonio

Sound Check
Sound Quality: Great
Stage Lighting: Great
Sightlines: Good
Eardrum Meter:
Yellow—Red

MUSIC TYPE	VENUE TYPE	ADMISSION	ATMOSPHERE	DRINKS: $-$$
World, Rock, Pop, Reggae, Afrobeat	Small Club Capacity 74	Varies	Robust Diversity	Average $5 - $13 FOOD: Full Menu

HARLEM — Between 133rd St & 134th St

Shrine is a live music venue, bar and restaurant known for years only to a hip cognoscenti due to the club's decision to not advertise its name on the building's façade, until recently.

The venue exhibits a lot of history for a place that has only been open since 2007. The West African artifacts and native tapestries are part of the owner's roots, while the club's decor belies a passion for western pop music. Album covers and vinyl records ranging from Diana Ross to the Beatles to Michael Jackson act as wallpaper, while the high ceiling is plastered with posters. Musically, the venue embraces music from around the world: jazz, rock, Afrobeat, reggae and more. Dancing is encouraged, wherever there is room, and after hours Shrine is a club with guest DJs.

Shrine's owner, Abdel, explains how the venue came about: "The Shrine is a realization of a lifelong dream. Music has always been the focus of my life. I grew up in Burkina Faso surrounded by music; I moved to New York to work in music. The Shrine is my home. It's everything I believe a live music venue should be. We are known for having one of the best PA systems in the city; we are also known for being a great place for musicians and music lovers to come together. I'm proud of that."

The crowd is mixed and hails from all over the city. Young and old, glam and casual, Shrine is part of a newer Harlem where diversity is robust. The area is gentrified and non-locals are among the regulars.

In Abdel's own words: **"Harlem is the best neighborhood in New York! There's been a lot of talk recently about a new Harlem Renaissance, but Harlem has always been a center of music and culture—the difference is that now downtown is taking notice! Harlem is one of the most diverse places in the world… celebrating the music, the neighborhood, life!"**

Tech Check
Sound System: Midas Venice 320, Meyer Sound UPA-1P, USW-1P Sub
Monitors: 4 mixes, EV ZX4 wedges
Backline: Full backline provided
Microphones: 5 Shure Beta 58, 10 Sennheiser
Stage Size: 10'x20'
Lighting: Yes
Recording capabilities: Audio/Video
Other: Video projection, DJ setup

Uptown Manhattan

ST. NICK'S JAZZ PUB

773 St Nicholas Ave | New York, NY 10031 | 212-283-9728
Hours: Mon-Thu 1p-3a, Fri-Sat 4p-4a | Shows at 7p
Subway: A,C,D,B to 145th St
www.stnicksjazzpub.net

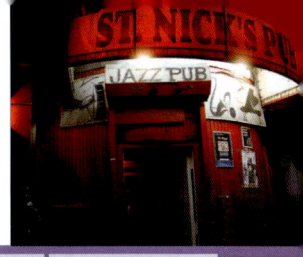

Written by: Rachel Antonio

DRINKS: $-$$ Average $7+ FOOD: no	ATMOSPHERE Magical	ADMISSION Free - $5	VENUE TYPE Small Club	MUSIC TYPE Jazz

HARLEM Between 148th St & 149th St

Uptown Manhattan

In the heirarchy of Harlem jazz clubs, St. Nick's Jazz Pub is one of the elder statesman. Under its present name, St. Nick's is at least 50 years old. However, its roots go back to the 1940s, born of the Jazz artistry of previous clubs in the Sugar Hill neighborhood. St. Nick's is welcoming, and the crowd is diverse and full of life. The environment is lively and the music is of a serious jazz nature played by seasoned jazz musicians.

St. Nick's street sides unassuming red marquee sits on an architecturally-conformed block of curved building fronts. A step into the venue is like crossing the threshold into another world. Inside, string lights crisscross overhead, a lighted star tops the stage, and the bar is festooned with a Happy Birthday banner. Every night is a celebration at St. Nick's. In contrast, the room setup is informal and has the feel of a makeshift recreation room that saw its better days 20 years ago, but nobody goes to St. Nick's for its furnishings. Here we see evidence of the social changes that have taken place in Harlem during the past decade. A tangle of cultures and socioeconomic groups come together united by the love the music.

The cool finesse that characterizes St. Nick's music is exemplified by Atiba Wilson's B4 Quartet. The lead of the Quartet wears sunglasses, a tie-dyed shirt and a Jamaican hat. As he switches from the drums to the flute, his colleagues follow seamlessly. He hypes up the crowd and in unison listeners clap, whistle, tap their toes and cheer. Effortlessly, the B4 Quartet commands the audience's attention. The band's sound is also smooth enough that it blends into the bar's background atmosphere when conversations levels raise a notch.

St. Nick's Jazz Pub is open every night of the week. Saturday is a special night when West African music is showcased beginning at midnight. St. Nick's is here to stay and jazz aficionados have no complaints.

Sound Check
Sound Quality: Good
Stage Lighting: So-So
Sightlines: So-So
Eardrum Meter:
Green-Yellow

Tech Check
Sound System: Basic PA used for vocals, primarily an acoustic venue.

ADDITIONAL VENUES

Apollo
53 West 125th St | New York, NY 10027 | 212-531-5305
www.apollotheater.org

One of the most famous music halls in the USA, Harlem's Apollo Theater is the cathedral of traditional African American music. Its name evokes an era of great jazz musicians; Ella Fitzgerald made her singing debut here at age 17, and the theater has carried this tradition to the present day. Long known for it's support of new artists, the Apollo emphasizes new talent with its weekly Amateur Night. The Apollo music cafe located upstairs, is a new lounge-style environment that features music genres from the Apollos heritage, as well as contemporary genres.

Cleopatra's Needle
2485 Broadway | New York, NY 10025 | 212-769-6969
www.cleopatrasneedleny.com

In a cozy restaurant setting Cleopatra's Needle proffers some of NYC's best jazz music and jam sessions. An appealing interior of wood-framed windows, exposed brick, simple designs and well-placed lighting set the tone for jovial nightly tunes. The owner, Maher Hussein, honors his Egyptian roots, as well as nearby Central Park's ancient re-erected obelisk: Cleopatra's Needle.

Cotton Club
656 West 125th St | New York, NY 10027 | 212-663-7980
www.cottonclub-newyork.com

In an oblong white stucco building, the Cotton Club carries on a legacy dating back to 1923, a time when upscale cliental came uptown to hob-nob with their peers and enjoy fine entertainment from across the country. Tourists from around the country head uptown today to mingle with the regulars who sing with The Cotton Club All Stars—a thirteen-piece swing band and a seven-piece blues and jazz band—and dance the night away.

Feinstein's
540 Park Ave | New York, NY 10065 | 212-339-4095
www.feinsteinsattheregency.com

Feinstein's at Loews Regency Hotel, is a fine-dining supper club in a warm, richly-decorated room; a modern-day parlor for musical gatherings and entertainment.

Lenox Lounge
288 Lenox Ave | New York, NY 10027 | 212-427-0253
www.lenoxlounge.com

Lenox Lounge has the advantage of built-in character—evident in its sleek Art Deco designs, and historically from its legendary lineups of Miles Davis, John Coltrane, "Lady Day" herself (Billie Holiday) and more. Since its opening in 1939, this mecca of jazz has continually featured all-time greats, and contemporary high-end acts today vie for their chance to play the hallowed Zebra Room, a magnificent performance space.

BUSHWICK AV
GRAND ST
ATTENTION DRIVERS
YIELD
TO
SW-621
DEPT OF TRANSPORTATION
GRAND ST
BUSHWICK AV

BROOKLYN NORTHSIDE

WILLIAMSBURG

Venue	GENRE	PAGE
Brooklyn Bowl	ALL: ROCK, POP, FOLK, R&B, BURLESQUE, DJ	120
Bruar Falls	INDIE, UNDERGROUND, EXPERIMENTAL	122
Glasslands	INDIE, EXPERIMENTAL, AMBIENT, DJ	123
Knitting Factory	ROCK, POP, INDIE, HIP-HOP, PUNK	124
Music Hall of Williamsburg	VARIOUS: ROCK, POP, FOLK, INDIE	125
Lovin' Cup Cafe & Cameo Gallery	INDIE, FOLK, EXPERIMENTAL	126
Pete's Candy Store	FOLK, COUNTRY, SINGER-SONGWRITER	128
Public Assembly	ROCK, INDIE, DJ	130
Spike Hill	ROCK, FOLK, INDIE, BLUES, SINGER-SONGWRITER	131
The Trash Bar	ROCK, INDIE, PUNK, METAL	132
Union Pool	FOLK, ALT COUNTRY, GOSPEL, INDIE	134
Zebulon	JAZZ, WORLD, COUNTRY, EXPERIMENTAL	136

GREENPOINT

Venue	GENRE	PAGE
Matchless	VARIOUS: INDIE, ELECTRONIC, METAL, DJ	137

BUSHWICK

Venue	GENRE	PAGE
Goodbye Blue Monday	ALL GENRES	138
Pine Box Rock Shop	ROCK, INDIE, FOLK, EXPERIMENTAL	139

ADDITIONAL VENUES

Venue	NEIGHBORHOOD	140
The Charleston	Williamsburg	
Coco66	Greenpoint	
Europa	Greenpoint	
The Gutter	Williamsburg	
Tommy's Tavern	Greenpoint	

Brooklyn: Northside

119

BROOKLYN BOWL

61 Wythe Avenue | Brooklyn, NY 11211
718-963-3369
Hours: Open Mon-Fri 6p, Sat-Sun 12p
Subway: L to Bedford, G to Nassau
www.brooklynbowl.com

Written by: Emily Niewendorp

Sound Check
Sound Quality: Great
Stage Lighting: Great
Sightlines: Great
Eardrum Meter: Yellow

Photographer Adam Macchia

MUSIC TYPE	VENUE TYPE	ADMISSION	ATMOSPHERE	DRINKS: $-$$
All Genres & Burlesque, Circus, DJ, Jazz Brunch	Mid-Size Club Capacity 600	Free - $30 Most Shows $5	Quintessential Live Music Venue	Average $4 - $9 FOOD: Full Menu

WILLIAMSBURG Between North 11th St & North 12 St

Brooklyn: Northside

Brooklyn Bowl, is a carnival in a stately barn. Its bright red entrance, in an alley between the venue and neighboring Brooklyn Brewery, gives a hint of the atmosphere inside. The venue is one gigantic space—its performance area, Blue Ribbon restaurant and bowling alley partitioned off by countless half-walls and walkways.

The venue is a luxurious playground and a brilliant addition to Williamsburg's scene. In the large foyer/lounge, patrons relax and dine in the company of a towering shelf of old-fashioned punch down dolls from carnival games. A fortune teller hovering over the ATM and carnival hands painted on the darkly, stained walls that point to in-venue destinations add a fun, eerie vibe. The main bar around the corner replicates a water-shooting gallery.

When you step down onto the performance floor, the live show grabs your attention. This area is enclosed by half-walls separating it from the 16-lane bowling alley. Its tall stage and light show become the main focus. To top it off, video feeds project the performance onto large screens that hang throughout the venue.

Many music genres are presented at Brooklyn Bowl. DJs play after the shows and there are party and DJ nights; Questlove, from The Roots, spins weekly. After performing, musicians can relax in a new private deck built above the green room or enjoy a meal and go bowling.

Brooklyn Bowl is a certified green venue, containing the first green bowling alley in the world. Beers are available only on tap—from local breweries—and bike racks outside have room for 30+ capacity. Many other aspects contribute to the green business as well. The owner, Peter Shapiro, says, "It all was a pretty big gamble, but it looks like it has worked."

The restaurant is open until 2 a.m. weekdays and 4 a.m. weekends. The Blue Ribbon "bowling alley" style menu offers salads, fried chicken, burgers, sandwiches, entrees and shakes.

Bowling: 16 lane bowling alley
$20 – $25 a 1/2 hour per lane

Food by Blue Ribbon Restaurant

Family Days, Sat & Sun
12pm-6pm, All Ages

HISTORY

Peter Shapiro was bitten by the live music bug during his proprietorship of legendary Wetlands Preserve rock venue, from 1996 – 2001. Peter says, "After it closed I was really eager…, but wanted to let Wetlands rest and do a venue a little differently."

For years he looked around Manhattan and Brooklyn with new partner and former Wetlands manager, Charley Ryan. Wanting a venue that was different than the typical rectangular-shaped room, the men took a gamble on a combo of 3 things: music, food and bowling. A large space was needed for these ideas, which they discovered in 61 Wythe Ave. when they were walking the streets one day. This building, an iron works foundry dating back to 1881, was now a gutted warehouse with no electricity or plumbing, but an amazing shell and bones. The endeavor developed and the space evolved into the impressive performance venue, bowling alley and restaurant that it is now.

Brooklyn Bowl opened in July 2009 with several key events putting the club on the music scene radar. A Jelly pool party with Dan Deacon, Deerhunter & No Age was rained out and moved to Brooklyn Bowl weeks before the venue was even planning to have shows. Additionally, numerous artists came out to support and promote the venue; artists that got their start at Wetlands, such as Blues Travelers, Rage Against the Machine, Pearl Jam, The Roots and Dave Mathews Band. SoulLive, an acid band, had a 10-night run, with many guests.

There is a panorama of activity going on upon entering 23,000-sq. ft. Brooklyn Bowl. **"The vertigo of so much going on can hopefully make you forget about your real life,"** says owner Peter Shapiro.

> "…the good ideas come at a show. Go to a show and escape from normal life…it doesn't get old for me. That's where I go and enter another world; you're not in real-life world." Peter Shapiro, Co-owner

Tech Check
Sound System: Digidesign Venue Profile Main PA (10) JBL Vertec 4888DPAN (5/side) (4) JBL Vertec 4880A (2/side) (1) JBL VP7221/95DPAN VIP lanes fill; Fill Speakers (throughout); (24) JBL 12" coaxial (13) JBL 8" coaxial, Crown XTi & CDi Power
Monitors: Stage Monitors (12) JBL VRX915M (floor wedges) (1) JBL VRX 915SP (drum monitor sub) (2) JBL SRX 738F (sidefills)
STAGE LIGHTING: ETC Ion, ETC Universal Fader
DJ BOOTH GEAR: (2) Pioneer DVJ1000 DVD/CD turntables (1) Pioneer SVM1000 Audio/Video mixer. (2) Technics 1200s Vinyl turntables (1) DJM800 Audio, (1) 20" iMac for audio/video
Other: Projection/LCD, Digital HD Matrix System, green room, dressing room
Backline: Full backline
Stage Size: 35' x 20'

Brooklyn: Northside

BRUAR FALLS

245 Grand St | Brooklyn, NY 11221
347-529-6610
Hours: 11a-4a Daily
Subway: L to Bedford
www.bruarfalls.com

Written by: Sarah Oramas

Sound Check
Sound Quality: So-So
Stage Lighting: So-So
Sightlines: So-So
Eardrum Meter:
Yellow-Red

MUSIC TYPE	VENUE TYPE	ADMISSION	ATMOSPHERE	DRINKS: $-$$
Indie, Underground, Experimental	Small Club Capacity 160	Free	Neighborhood Dive Bar	$3+ FOOD: no

WILLIAMSBURG — Between Driggs Ave & Roebling St

Brooklyn: Northside

Bruar Falls is a dive music-bar, well-liked for its cheap beers, laid-back vibe and calendar of local, music acts. The small stage is raised up one step and back-dropped with a kaleidoscope-colored sheet. The sound could be a little better, but the bands are great: indie, raw, eclectic and experimental.

Bruar Falls is a new home to a specific, Brooklyn vibe. Williamsburg bands tend to have their own rhythm and, although there is a lot of competition venue-wise in the area, owner Andy Bodor felt that opening Bruar Falls would fulfill a certain niche. Owner of established Cakeshop on Ludlow as well, Andy wanted to venture into another neighborhood and offer a performance space to the overflow of bands that he could not book at the Manhattan venue.

Andy is focused on heightening the live music experience. He chooses bands that fit in at Bruar Falls: **"I only book the most engaging acts...hot, electric, alive and pulsating throughout your being."** Bands that have played the venue include Bobby Conn, German Measles, Surfer Blood, The xx, Dum Dum Girls, Veronica Falls and Smith Westerns.

There are ideas for other small venues in the future. "I really wouldn't know what to do with a large one," says Andy. He is also working toward a steadier release rate for his record label, Capeshok.

Is there an actual Bruar Falls and where is it? The venue's wall-size photo hints to an actual place. Judy, co-owner of the venue and Andy's sister-in-law, is from the Highlands of Scotland, where the real Bruar Falls are located. The attraction was formed by glaciers millions of years ago. The spot is beloved by many, includin Judy's parents, who would "meet and canoodle" there. There is even a poem written about it by Robert Burns, asking the provincial duke to plant trees on the barren landscape. The Duke eventually did, hence the lush forest surrounding the falls.

The music venue, Bruar Falls, manages to translate an essence of the real Bruar Fall's ambience into an urban setting. **It's about "mist and mystery of being lost in this area at 3 in the morning, but not caring because you are with a love," says Andy.** A little bit of the Scottish Highlands in Williamsburg. Must be why there is a decent house ale for $4 on tap.

Sound Check
Sound Quality: Good
Stage Lighting: Good
Sightlines: Good
Eardrum Meter:
Red

GLASSLANDS

289 Kent Ave | Brooklyn, New York 11211
718-599-1450
Hours: Tue-Sun 9p-4a
Subway: L to Bedford | J,M to Marcy
http://glasslands.blogspot.com

Written by: Sarah Oramas

DRINKS: $-$$	ATMOSPHERE	ADMISSION	VENUE TYPE	MUSIC TYPE
Average $5 - $12 FOOD: no	Warehouse Utopia	Free - $10	Warehouse, Art Gallery, Capacity 250	Indie, Experimental, Ambient, DJ

The Glasslands Gallery is an oasis found in industrial Williamsburg on a street lined mostly by warehouses and the old Domino Sugar Refinery. With a strong sound system, a full bar and carefully crafted decor, the well put-together Glasslands Gallery offers a contrast to the area's other warehouse venues.

"The whole place feels holly hobby—'do-it-yourself.' Like the people who put this together did it with their own two hands, literally, they built their bathroom," says a patron, Theresa Galeani. The space is decorated with rotating art installations, the current being a semi-permanent cloud ceiling above the stage and a tree house balcony. "The cloud installation is made entirely of tissue paper and was done by artists Cameron Michel and Vashti Windish, who run the art gallery Live With Animals in the Secret Project Robot space, which is right down the street from Glasslands," according to Abbey Ley, who assists the owners in operations. The design for the space was developed by owners Rolyn Hu and Brooke Baxter, but comprised of creations by different artists working in concert around a common theme, such as the current "Futuristic Forrest."

Any seat or standing point in Glasslands provides excellent views of the stage. Bands are close enough to the audience for interaction, even from the balcony, making every spot in the room feel connected to the show. Some notable performers that have graced the stage include Moby, Yeah Yeah Yeahs, The Blow, MGMT, and Vampire Weekend, and others like Neon Indian, who in particular, return to perform. With shows every night of the week (except Mondays) this venue has a lot to offer. In addition to live music, The Glasslands Gallery also hosts dance parties, special events, and ongoing interactive art projects.

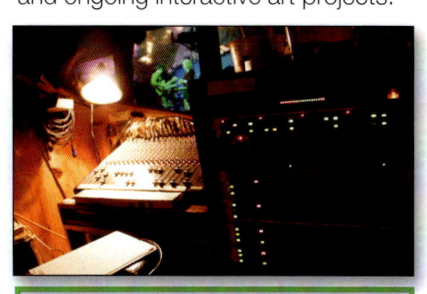

Sound Check
by Drew Henkels, Musician/Sound Engineer
The sound has improved exponentially in the last year. We went from a barely functioning beer-splattered buggy speakers to a brand new 16 channel Allen & Heath mixing console, two 18" subwoofers, two monitor stage mixes, two 15" full range and two full range EAW three-way speakers.

WILLIAMSBURG
Corner of South 2nd St & Kent Ave

Brooklyn: Northside

123

KNITTING FACTORY

361 Metropolitan Ave | Brooklyn, NY 11211
347-529-6696
Hours: Mon-Fri 5p-4a, Sat-Sun 12p-4a
Subway: L,G to Lorimer/Metropolitan | L to Bedford
www.bk.knittingfactory.com

Written by: Daniel Morrow

Sound Check
Sound Quality: Great
Stage Lighting: Great
Sightlines: Great
Eardrum Meter:
Yellow-Red

MUSIC TYPE	VENUE TYPE	ADMISSION	ATMOSPHERE	DRINKS: $-$$
Various: Rock, Pop, Indie, Hip Hop, Punk	Small Club Capacity 275	Varies All Shows Ticketed	Quintessential Live Music Venue	$6+, Happy Hr 5-7p FOOD: no

WILLIAMSBURG
Between Havemeyer St & Roebling St

Brooklyn: Northside

The newly re-opened Knitting Factory in Williamsburg is a big change from its previous incarnations in Manhattan. Still extremely band friendly, broad in its tastes, and partial to quality acts, this club is sleeker with advanced technical equipment in the live room and a seperate bar area with additional programming. In Williamsburg the club is imbedded in the community by offering all-age activities and collaborating with public organizations.

There's a hint of a possible new order for music venues here with a heavier emphasis placed on a comfortable and larger bar area, which allows for a dynamic social atmosphere. The front bar has two large TV monitors geared toward sporting events programming. A small stage for DJs, comedians, poetry readings, karaoke and small acoustic set-ups, is discreetly carved into the sidewall. Just as you're wondering where the music room is, a superb surprise reveals itself. Behind the bar, where you might expect to see a blank wall, or mirrored reflections of liquor bottles, there stands a gloriously large window to the main music venue.

HISTORY

Knitting Factory has a long history and an ever-expanding presence today. It opened on Houston St. in 1987, later moving to Leonard St., and finally re-locating in 2009 to Williamsburg. Around 2005, the club invested in several clubs in northwest America, only to buy them outright a year later, which expanded the Knitting Factory into an entertainment company. The company is currently re-igniting its record division, growing as a management company, streaming live shows online, working on a live TV show, *and* writing a book.

Sound Check
Daniel Morrow, Musician/Writer

A lot of time and money was invested into the acoustics of the space, built to the same specs as a professional recording studio. The room size is generous and the stage has room for 10 to 15 musicians. The space is perfect for up-and-coming bands and singers from huge bands, who perform solo acts. This luxury of space can sometimes seem to be a problem—an audience of 30 or so can leave the room feeling empty. On the other hand, with the state-of-the-art sound equipment and acoustics to rival its counterparts, the listening experience is excellent, whatever the act.

Sound Check
Sound Quality: Great
Stage Lighting: Great
Sightlines: Great
Eardrum Meter:
Yellow-Red

MUSIC HALL OF WILLIAMSBURG

66 N 6th St | Brooklyn, NY 11211
718-486-5400
Hours: Music times vary
Subway: L to Bedford
www.musichallofwilliamsburg.com

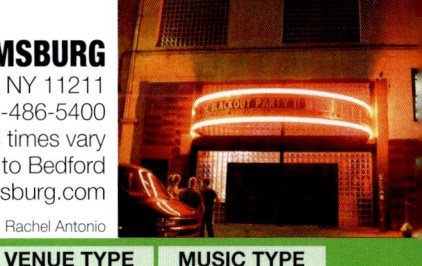

Written by: Rachel Antonio

DRINKS: $-$$	ATMOSPHERE	ADMISSION	VENUE TYPE	MUSIC TYPE
Average $7+ FOOD: no	Quintessential Live Music Venue	Varies	Mid-Size Room	Various: Rock, Pop, Folk, Indie

In 2007, the former North 6 music venue followed in the footsteps of its surrounding neighbors and experienced a major transition. From a low-key local music space attracting surprisingly notorious musicians, the new Bowery Presents Music Hall of Williamsburg has become a premier music venue and a major Brooklyn hot spot.

Don't let the trendy kids standing outside distract you; the crowds here are eclectic, casual, and respectful. Patrons whoop and scream at their favorite artists and dance in their allotted space, all the while somehow holding onto their beer without spilling a drop.

The venue's interior maintains a fresh look and feel, with its high ceiling, exposed-brick walls, hardwood floors, and wrought iron barricades. Although the space reads as cool and modern, it is nonetheless welcoming and comforting. It features two bars, a main standing room with elevated sides and a mezzanine with a few circular tables and chairs.

It is a venue for national acts, which often have great local talent opening for them. Indie bands grace the stage often. One headline tour consisted of Harper Blynn, Cray Brothers, and Greg Laswell, however, many other genres fill the venue's calendar: Mates of State, Kelis, Deer Tick, Elizabeth & The Catapult, The Honey Brothers, Aimee Mann, Dan Zanes and Friends, Matisyahu and more.

Williamsburg has always been characterized by its free-for-all vibe, hence quirky, fun moments are a part of the culture at Music Hall of Williamsburg. Pete Harper, musician and founder of the local Brooklyn band Harper Blynn, once taunted the crowd right before the band broke out in an all-male rendition of Beyonce's "Halo," by saying: "If you can't dance to this, you're never going to have sex again!"

WILLIAMSBURG
Between Wythe Ave & Kent Ave

Brooklyn: Northside

Tech Check
Sound System: YAMAHA PM5D-RH 48ch
16 L'Acoustics dV-DOSC flown (8 per side)
4- L'Acoustics dV-DOSC SUB (3x15" per cabinet) 4- L'Acoustics V-DOSC SB-218 SUB (2x18" per cabinet) 2- L'Acoustic ARC (for front fill or sidefill application)
L'Acoustics Power; LA48a All Crossovers XTA DP448, Radial 56 Channel Active split with record split
Monitors: YAMAHA M7CL-48 ch
8 x 115xt L'Acoustic floor monitors, 2 x 112xt L'Acoustics floor monitors, Drumfill: 1 L'Acoustic dV-DOSC sub/1 L'Acoustic ARC; L'Acoustics Power LA48a All Crossovers XTA DP448

LOVIN' CUP CAFE & CAMEO GALLERY

93 N 6th St | Brooklyn, NY 11211 | 718-302-1180
Hours: 6p-Late Daily
Subway: L to Bedford
http://www.myspace.com/cameogallery

Written by: Emily Niewendorp

MUSIC TYPE	VENUE TYPE	ADMISSION	ATMOSPHERE	DRINKS: $-$$
Indie, Folk Experimental	Mixed Media Art & Music Gallery	Cameo $5 - $20 Lovin' Cup Free (Tips)	Honest, Warm, Fun	House-made Elixers FOOD: Full Menu

WILLIAMSBURG
Between Berry St & Wythe Ave

Brooklyn: Northside

The year following Cameo's opening was 2009, a period of gathering momentum, when word flitted from person to person in Williamsburg that Cameo was, "so cool! It's behind Lovin' Cup. You walk past the kitchen and a maze of hallways. Then it opens up—like, two stories high—and there is this awesome chandelier."

> "We like to think we contribute to the community by offering creative people a stomping ground to meet new friends, rehearse with their band, throw an art show, get nourished in body and mind, and catch a buzz without dropping a lot of money."
> — Nicolette Sampson, Co-owner

Lovin' Cup Cafe is a piano bar built from recycled wood and antique fixtures. Its programming emphasizes more subdued music sounds complimentary to a social bar and cafe—acoustic versions of rock acts, singer-songwriters, folk, jazz, soul, reggae, ragtime and blues. It is a laid-back, neighborhood favorite, and a gathering place before Cameo Gallery opens.

Under its dancing chandelier, Cameo Gallery is an art space with a large, raised stage that was recently expanded into a more spacious, less boxy, room. The chandelier, designed out of fabric, was an installation piece by Adam Keller for The Albertan's music residency in spring 2009. Cameo was a surprise to the owners, Josh and Nicolette Sampson, because it evolved after Lovin' Cup's opening. The room had been operating as a small recording studio, but it morphed into something more: a recording/rehearsal studio by day, and an art gallery and performance venue by night. Josh and Nicolette think of it as, "recording sessions with an audience." The couple took this course and ran with it, throwing their personal interests into the business. Josh formed his current band from Lovin' Cup and Cameo Gallery regulars, and Nic's background in the visual arts supported the formation of a vibrant home for local artists. In Cameo, sometimes the art gallery is a background for the music and at other times, the music accompanies the art.

Cameo's booking used to be outsourced, but Revtone, Josh's booking company and digital music boutique, now heads up the programming. Cameo offers nights of varying genres, especially music that is new to Williamsburg. A few bands that have played there are: Boy Crisis, Derek Trucks, Hank and Cupcakes, Asa Ransom, Surfer Blood, Alberta

Cross, The Governors, Suckers, Mumford and Sons, Weird Owl, Littlans, London Souls, Earl Greyhound and Ben Sollee.

In Lovin' Cup Cafe and Cameo Gallery, the Sampsons have struck gold, as locals herald the spot as their new favorite music venue.

HISTORY

Fair prices, top-notch food and music, and a nurturing environment for its artistic-minded patrons helped Lovin' Cup Cafe and Cameo Gallery through the 2008 recession. This uncomplicated standard continues to help the venue weather unsettled financial times. Josh and Nicolette explain, "Fortunately we never were going to rely on a Wall Street clientele to sustain our business."

Josh and Nicolette moved to Williamsburg from Manhattan to participate in the neighborhood's lively scene, without any intention of opening a venue themselves. While many club owners in Manhattan have been anxious about the spread of the live music scene to Brooklyn, Josh and Nic have successfully capitalized on the shift. The couple was apartment hunting, when they came upon the building that had previously been Anytime Cafe. Seeing potential in the space for music and art, and a project to work on together, Josh and Nic decided to open a bar on the spot. Lovin' Cup Cafe—named after the Rolling Stones song—opened after 2 ½ days of construction and redesigning, with a little help from their friends. They envisioned Lovin' Cup as a cafe and bar for musicians and friends to hang out and "throw down an acoustic set in the restaurant for appreciative customers," which has become exactly the case.

Sound Check: Lovin' Cup
Sound Quality: Good
Stage Lighting: Minimal
Sightlines: So-So
Eardrum Meter:
Green-Yellow

Sound Check: Cameo
Sound Quality: So-So
Stage Lighting: Minimal
Sightlines: Great
Eardrum Meter:
Yellow-Red

Tech Check
Sound System: Midas Venice 320, EAW
Monitors: 3 wedges mixes, 3 JBL 12 inch speakers, 1 large drum monitor
Backline: Partial
Recording: 6 mic room recording or Protools from board
DJ: MK II Technique turn tables and mixer
Comments: The Lovin' Cup stage is as warm and personal as it gets. Cameo Gallery has the best sightlines for a small club and plenty of PA for 'cutting edge art rockers.' All that's needed is some creative acoustic treatment to take this room to another sonic level.

PETE'S CANDY STORE

709 Lorimer St | Brooklyn, NY 11211 | 718-302-3770
Hours: Open 5p Daily
Subway: L,G to Lorimer/Metropolitan
http://www.petescandystore.net

Written by: Emily Niewendorp

MUSIC TYPE	VENUE TYPE	ADMISSION	ATMOSPHERE	DRINKS: $-$$
Folk, Country, Singer-songwriter	Small Club Music Rm Capacity 40	Free	Neighborhood Bar	Average $3 - $10 FOOD: Partial Menu

WILLIAMSBURG — Between Meeker Ave & Richardson St

Pete's Candy Store is an affable bar and live music room. The bar is small, and maze-like. Discovering the different rooms and hallways can recall memories of exploring an old house as a kid. The space is made up of real wood wainscoting, mellow-yellow walls and old-fashioned pieces—the vintage, red refrigerator behind the bar was installed by the strength of six men. There is a beautiful back patio and garden, and the kitchen sells grilled ciabatta sandwiches.

"The driving motive behind the performance room was to make the performers feel good. It's intimate. People that come to see a special musician and get a decent seat usually have a memorable experience," the owner, Andy, says. A long and narrow room, with no cover, it is a good idea to arrive early to get a good seat. Latecomers often sit on the floor or stand in the back to absorb a performance. Successful musicians, such as Norah Jones, still play the venue often, but these shows are never posted or even leaked. Andy sums up the ethos of these secret shows best: "It's a wonderful experience for those who just happen to be there—an intimate show that everyone enjoys. It gives freedom for the artist to mess around, workshop and experiment in a live setting, while they are 'hiding from the public at large.'"

The music style at Pete's Candy Store has been consistently wide open to anything that musically fits the small space, which is perfectly suited for singer-songwriters, alternative and antifolk musicians, and experimental performers, as well as a haven for side projects of bigger rock bands. **Devendra Banhart, Will Oldham from the Palace Brothers, Joanna Newsom, Akron/Family, Sufjan Stevens, the Wainwrights—Loudon, Martha and Rufus, Deer Tick and Beth Orton have all graced the stage.**

HISTORY

Pete's Candy Store serviced the local sweet-toothed in Williamsburg from the early 1920s all the way to the '70s. The business then changed to a greasy spoon and most recently a cover diner for a mob-operated business that was more often closed than open. All the time, the old-fashioned 'Pete's Candy Store' sign hung above the entrance. In spring of 1999, Andy took over the space. He fixed up

Brooklyn: Northside

> "Oh, I mean there is nothing like it. It's nothing like listening to recorded music. If you want to go see people playing music you have to go there and see them. When it's good it's totally thrilling."
>
> Andy, Owner

portions that had fallen into disrepair, and added and knocked out walls and doorways to improve the atmosphere. He kept the storefront intact, and after much thought kept the original name—no other name suited the place.

The news of a music venue at Pete's Candy Store spread quickly. It was the first nightly live music venue in Williamsburg and the discovery was significant for people, even though it was off the beaten track. An out-of-the-way music venue at that time was a phenomenon and it became an exciting destination. The energy at night was stimulating, opening everyone's senses.

Andy recalls that, "Those memories are special to those who were around during the hay-day of the venue's first few years."

Non-music-oriented locals express their sentiments about Pete's Candy Store as well. Over the years, many folks have enlightened Andy about their personal experiences at the candy store. Neighborhood ladies spoke of their employment there in the '70s and standing on ladders to paint the words, 'Pete's Candy Store.' Others remember doing their homework there after school when they were kids, and folks who have moved away are amazed to hear the store is still there, except it is a bar and music venue—adult candy.

Sound Check
Sound Quality: Great
Stage Lighting: Good
Sightlines: So-So
Eardrum Meter:
Green–Yellow

Sound Check
by Daniel Morrow, Musician/Writer

It is a tiny room with the mixer on stage so performers get the luxury of adjusting their own sound. Speakers are at the front and the back of room. The stage is slightly elevated. This small, rectangular room defies all the laws of acoustics and sounds great. It is ideal for 2 or 3 piece acoustic set ups, but can also work for electric set ups if the sound is effectively controlled (i.e. not too loud!).

Brooklyn: Northside

PUBLIC ASSEMBLY

70 North 6th St | Brooklyn, NY 11211
718-384-4586
Hours: Sun-Thu 7p-2a, Fri-Sat 7p-4a
Subway: L to Bedford
www.publicassemblynyc.com

Written by: Sarah Oramas

Sound Check
Sound Quality: Good
Stage Lighting: Good
Sightlines: Great
Eardrum Meter:
RED

MUSIC TYPE	VENUE TYPE	ADMISSION	ATMOSPHERE	DRINKS: $-$$
Rock, Indie, DJ	Front Rm Capacity 140 Back Rm Capacity 74	Free - $20 2 rooms–seperate $	Renovated Industrial Warehouse	Average $4 - $7 FOOD: no

WILLIAMSBURG — Between Wythe Ave & Kent Ave

Occupying a large industrial space in a renovated warehouse, Public Assembly boasts two separate rooms and two stages for live shows, and offers a variety of performances making Public Assembly popular for Brooklyn locals. Between the live music shows, rave parties and hosting the biggest regularly scheduled techno party in New York, the club appeals to the masses.

The main room extends, from the towering stage in the rear of the venue, all the way to street side. This main room is essentially two open spaces: the bar and standing area closest to the stage; and an open gallery/lounge with a garage-style glass door, which exists solely for atmospheric measure.

The second live room is much smaller and darker, and has a limited bar. With a capacity of just 74, it provides a standing room only live music experience that's up close and personal with the performers. A particularly nice feature of the back room is that between sets, music is piped in from the front, allowing patrons to sample the front room's experience.

What makes this venue special, according to employee Lisa Hsu, is its malleability. "You can do anything you want to it, everything from comedy nights, rock shows to huge techno parties."

Public Assembly stages live shows or special events in both rooms nearly every night of the week. Highlights include its Monday night burlesque show, regularly scheduled hip-hop nights, and their "Play It Loud" techno parties.

Sound Check
by Daniel Morrow, Musician/Writer

For a club of its size, the stage is awesome; large and elevated. The FOH sound is loud and clear but as a musician this can be a problematic venue; the monitors on stage need a little upgrade. Everything is mic'd up so we recommend keeping those guitar amps low and playing the drums lightly for overall audibility on stage.

Brooklyn: Northside

Sound Check
Sound Quality: Good
Stage Lighting: Good
Sightlines: Good
Eardrum Meter:
Yellow-RED

SPIKE HILL

184 & 186 Bedford Ave
Brooklyn, NY 11211 | 718-218-9637
Hours: 11:30a-2a Daily
Subway: L to Beford
www.spikehill.com

Written by: Sarah Oramas

DRINKS: $-$$	ATMOSPHERE	ADMISSION	VENUE TYPE	MUSIC TYPE
Average $6+ FOOD: Full Menu	Chill, Relaxed	Free - $8	Small Room Capacity Music/Bar 200	Rock, Folk, Indie, Blues, Sing-Songwriter

Spike Hill caters to a slightly older, hip crowd, creating an atmosphere that has a relaxed, upscale edge. Spike Hill's ties to the community run deep; the venue opened on Williamsburg's main drag—Bedford Avenue—before it was a main drag. Owner Joe Schmitz explains, "We didn't come in to take advantage of the music scene. We kinda grew up here."

The venue hosts a variety of local Brooklyn indie rock bands and singer-songwriters. It is also known among established musicians as an ideal place to hold unannounced shows. Corin Bailey Rae played after a nearby, larger performance. She went to Spike Hill and performed for a few lucky patrons. "We do a lot of unannounced and under the radar shows where bigger bands, who want to play for fun and not be bombarded by fans, play," Joe says.

Spike Hill schedules nightly shows and a weekly open mic. The room has a high-quality sound system and excellent ambient lighting. With a large bar and a reasonably-sized standing room, the club is intimate without feeling overly crowded, even during a packed show. For those who prefer to take a seat while they watch a performance, the bar stretches from the back of the dance floor to the front door, offering a lot of seating. Even near the front door one does not feel too far away from the action. The bar is notable for its extensive whiskey, wine and beer selection and menus are available to order from the restaurant next door.

Pictured: Lowry

Tech Check
Mixer: Soundcraft GB2 - 24ch
PA/Mains: Meyer UPA-1P, USW-1P
Monitors: JBL JRX112,115
Lighting: Leprecon LP 612-MPX-D/A
Backline: Full Backline provided

Sound Check
by Daniel Morrow, Musician/Writer
Four monitors on stage are quite exceptional (many venues twice the size of spike hill make-do with one) The sound is nicely absorbed by a thick red curtain on stage and ceiling treatment throughout the room. The lighting is very professional with different colored washes providing the appropriate ambience. There is video capability, and sound recording is available for a mere $10 (2 room mics in addition to the sound coming from the desk).

WILLIAMSBURG
Between North 6th St & North 7th St

Brooklyn: Northside

THE TRASH BAR

256 Grand Street | Brooklyn, NY 11222 | 718-387-2222
Hours: 5p-4a Daily
Subway: L to Beford | G to Metropolitan | J,M to Marcy Ave
www.thetrashbar.com

Written by: Emily Niewendorp

MUSIC TYPE	VENUE TYPE	ADMISSION	ATMOSPHERE	DRINKS: $-$$
Rock, Indie, Punk, Metal	Small Club Capacity 175	$6 - $10	Gritty Rock Club	$3+ FOOD: Snacks

WILLIAMSBURG — Between Driggs Ave & Roebling St

The Trash Bar has become a favorite neighborhood bar for rock 'n' roll and punk rock music in Williamsburg. People dig the happy hour specials and either love or tolerate its trashed state because simply put: they have a really great time there.

The Trash Bar is trailer-world-meets-grandma's-living-room. The floorboards show in spots and over time antiques, band stickers, Polaroid photos and personal albums have been attached to the walls. Once, a hammered troubadour came in and swung his guitar at the bartender for not giving him a free beer. His guitar was confiscated and nailed to the wall in front of him. In this beat-up, second- or third-hand rock 'n' roll dive, there are no attitudes or fronts. The bartenders are friendly 'smarty-pants' artists, who bartend to make ends meet.

It's usually free to enter the front bar area, where tattered car seats provide seating. Shoot a game of pool, play the juke box or a variety of games. The curtained hallway leads to the music room—a large open space with a huge, sand-filled stage. It has its own bar in the corner, and looks much like the front room.

The Trash Bar hosts long-time NYC, hard-core, punk band, Murphy's Law four times a year. On those nights the place fills up with a high-energy hard-drinking crowd that is also oddly respectful—even in the mosh pit. It is "a super-cool, different breed," owner Aaron Pierce says. TV on the Radio played at The Trash Bar, drawing a line down the block, as well as Kevin Kinney from Driving and Crying.

The bar has a good wine list, cheap beer and free tater tots with a drink purchase. Paying the music room cover from 8 p.m. to 9 p.m. guarantees free PBR and well drinks for that hour. In the live room there are occasional sporting events, films and comedians—even a non-denominational church service on Sundays from 5 p.m. to 7 p.m.

Sound Check
By Daniel Morrow, Musician/Writer

There's a huge difference between front of house and stage sound, so beware. The engineers tend to mix very loud in this room and the monitors on stage cannot currently compete with the P.A. system and drums. But the good news is the sound is much better front of house than you could ever imagine on stage.

Brooklyn: Northside

Walt, former Continental booker and lead guitarist for The Bullys, fills Trash Bar's music programming with rock 'n' roll, ranging from alternative to aggressive, with variations such as speed, classical and even jazz. Five bands play a night from 8 p.m. to 1 a.m.

HISTORY

In 2004 Aaron Pierce imported car seats ripped out of vehicles from his favorite junk yard in upstate NY to his new venue in Williamsburg—the former Club LUXX. He trashed up the place, added the dividing wall to separate the music room from the front bar, called it The Trash Bar and opened for business. Williamsburg had been continually developing as an artistic neighborhood at the time. Fast forward six years, The Trash Bar now sits surrounded by high-end restaurants and towering condos. Some of the fortunate artists with affordable or rent-controlled apartments have stayed, but many have been pushed out to neighboring areas. Trash Bar stands out as being completely different, yet this extreme works—people like diversity in New York City.

Trash Bar is a composite of Aaron's favorite bars: 1) CBGBs 2) Motor City 3) Mercury Lounge and 4) BBQ Bar from Orlando, FL—a vision from Terry Gilliam's film, "Brazil." He says the venue "…just worked out. It filled a niche and a void that was very much missing at the time."

"Trash Bar has always been the place to go where no one gives a shit what kind of shoes you're wearing," Aaron says. "As the neighborhood tax bracket goes through the roof and the baby carriages start strolling down the block… that is all well and good, it increases the safety and cleanliness of the neighborhood, but this [Trash Bar] will continue to be a relief watering hole from that idea."

Sound Check
Sound Quality: Good
Stage Lighting: Good
Sightlines: Good
Eardrum Meter: Yellow—Red

Tech Check
Sound System: 24ch Allen&Heath, JBL/EV
Monitors: 4 mixes, 3 Turbosound wedges, 1 JBL drum monitor
Backline: Full Backline (no cymbals)
Comments: 2-Track and multitrack audio recording available, DJ ready, stage size is 16'x20'

Brooklyn: Northside

133

UNION POOL

484 Union Avenue | Brooklyn, NY 11211 | 718-609-0484
Hours: Mon-Fri 5p-4a, Sat-Sun 1p-4a
Subway: L,G to Lorimer/Metropolitan
http://www.myspace.com/unionpool
http://unionpool.blogspot.com/

Written by: Emily Niewendorp

MUSIC TYPE	VENUE TYPE	ADMISSION	ATMOSPHERE	DRINKS: $-$$
Folk, Alt Country, Gospel, Indie	Small Club Capacity 180	$8 - $10 Not More Than $15	Neighborhood Bar	Average $7 FOOD: Taco Truck

WILLIAMSBURG
Corner of Union Ave & Meeker Ave

Union Pool is a long-time popular, neighborhood bar that buzzes with humanity without feeling crowded. Small-looking from its exterior, it actually provides several areas for hanging out, a beautiful music room, and well-thought-out music scheduling.

The stage is an attractive jewel-box style theater, fronted by a large dance floor of which people do not hesitate to take advantage. Union Pool's other spaces include: a main bar with aqua-colored walls and a DJ booth, and the patio area, which is outfitted with benches, lounge chairs and a little botanical pool and water fountain. A taco truck from which tasty midnight snacks are dispensed sells amazing tamales and more.

Union Pool has always nurtured community and band relations. Its long-time employees and bartenders are also artists and musicians who promote and connect the venue with great musicians. Bands at Union Pool are fed by the house, and the cover at the music room's door and band merchandise sales go to the musicians and sound person. Maintaining these standards is important to Union Pool management under the philosophy: "The band has a hard enough time as it is."

The room draws bands who are on the verge of playing larger Brooklyn and Manhattan rooms; acoustic musicians, indie bands, touring national acts, secret shows, private one-offs and tapings. Well-known bands that have played at Union Pool are Cat Power and TV on the Radio. Shows at Union Pool are often at-capacity, signaling one of the final, intimate-sized shows for the band on its way up. The venue does not try to follow trends, but strives to provide stimulating, original, quality music.

> "I have always been involved in music. I moved to New York 5 years ago when I took this job. I've run bars before, this is the first venue I've run. I used to promote when I was 20 in California where I grew up. I used to do a bunch of hard core shows. Did a lot of promotion, playing in bands, touring in bands. There is always music around. So it's great, it's been really fun."
>
> Sage, Manager

Brooklyn: Northside

Union Pool offers music five to seven nights a week. Reverend Vince Anderson plays two sets for his devotees at 11 p.m. every Monday. Free shows are usually offered every other Tuesday. On Friday and Saturday nights DJs play after the bands—there are occasional DJ parties as well; and summer-time brings Sunday evening shows, as well as free Saturday afternoon shows on the patio, from 3 – 8 p.m.

HISTORY

Back in the '70s, Union Pool was a concrete warehouse for pool and exterminator supplies. The building went dormant for 15 years, until it opened as a bar in 2000. Music came to Union Pool still a few years later. On the outskirts of the Bedford Avenue art scene at that time, the venue's first shows were raw and punk in nature, and could only offer performers a ramshackle stage and PA system.

Around 2006, the space was upgraded, adding a back patio, the music room's bar and a proper sound system. The venue began to focus on low-key, local country and folk music, with the occasional trendy show brought in by outside promoters, such as Todd P. When current manager, Sage, came on board he expanded the music program beyond two or three shows a week. The venue also experimented with more music styles, and built on what worked best sonically within the space. In the spring of 2010, the music room was sound-proofed to heighten sound quality and counter noise complaints from neighbors. The Brooklyn Queens Expressway runs right past the venue, but the traffic noise does nothing to disrupt enjoyment of the music—it actually helps buffer the noise impact, as well as provide an easy access for patrons.

As Williamsburg has developed, Union Pool has become the epicenter of the area. It is between two major train stops and train lines and in a thriving young, artistic neighborhood.

> *"From when I grew up all we ever did was go to shows and skateboard… it was my first experience with a true community…indie music or punk music wasn't cool, it was an outscast kind of thing and we did things to feel comfortable with our peers…high school sucks. We want to be around people that feel that way we feel."*
> Sage, Manager

Sound Check
Sound Quality: Good
Stage Lighting: Good
Sightlines: Good
Eardrum Meter:
Yellow

Tech Check
Sound System: Not Available

ZEBULON

258 Wythe Ave | Brooklyn, NY 11211
718-218-6934
Hours: Open 4p Daily
Subway: L to Bedford
www.zebuloncafeconcert.com

Written by: Emily Niewendorp

Sound Check
Sound Quality: Good
Stage Lighting: So-So
Sightlines: Good
Eardrum Meter:
Green–Yellow

MUSIC TYPE	VENUE TYPE	ADMISSION	ATMOSPHERE	DRINKS: $-$$
Jazz, Experimental, World, Country	Small Room	Free	Quaint, Bohemian	Average $3 - $10 FOOD: Small Menu

WILLIAMSBURG — Between Metropolitan Ave & North 3rd St

Zebulon brings to mind the sort of quaint workingman's pub you might come across in a French coastal village. It is dignified in its dark wood Old World persona, yet casual in its cafe-style layout and low lighting punctuated by the glow of opaque white, glass globes overhead. Near the East River in Williamsburg, Zebulon sits on a quiet street offering a romantic setting that gathers momentum later in the evening.

The stage that runs along the back wall is small, but still a focal point. An earthy color scheme and ceiling fans add a Casablanca touch, and, while a French vibe is evident in the many inlayed wall mirrors, the 90-year old wooden bar, found in an old warehouse when the owners, Guillaume Blestel and Jef Soubiran, were building Zebulon's interior, is all-American. Bob Marley, Frank Zappa and Jimi Hendrix album covers sheath the beam along the ceiling, with many more LPs showcased on a shelf near the doorway.

Zebulon was opened in 2004 by Jef and Guillaume, inspired by their passion for music and food, respectively. The full bar offers sandwiches, appetizers and snacks. Music performances take place almost daily and are free. Musically, Zebulon crosses many genres: ethnic, progressive, jazz and avant garde, to alternative and folk, and combinations thereof. The venue also schedules theatrical productions and film screenings.

Zebulon has the settled, welcoming feel of a place with a long history. Early evening shows offer a mellow experience, while late evening and weekend shows pack the room—a caution to those who value their personal space.

Tech Check
Sound System: Mackie 1402 Mixer, JBL EON main speakers
Monitors: EON Stage Monitor
Backline: Full Backline including Fender Rhodes 88 key, Sonor Vintage Drums
Comments: Most bands need very little in terms of sound reinforcement. Stage volume seems to work perfectly for this room.

Brooklyn: Northside

Sound Check
Sound Quality: Good
Stage Lighting: Good
Sightlines: Good
Eardrum Meter:
Yellow–Red

MATCHLESS
557 Manhattan Ave
Brooklyn, NY 11222 | 718-383-5333
Hours: Open 5p Daily
Subway: L to Beford | G to Nassau
www.barmatchless.com

Written by: Jen Meola

DRINKS: $-$$	ATMOSPHERE	ADMISSION	VENUE TYPE	MUSIC TYPE
2 for 1, 5-8pm FOOD: Full Menu	Neighborhood Bar	Free - $10	Small Club	Indie, Electronic, DJ, Acoustic, Metal

From the signage outside you would think you were entering an auto body shop, but inside Bar Matchless you'll discover a cool indie rock bar where the locals hang out and emerging bands from all over New York play.

Bar Matchless is a live music venue that supports the Brooklyn music scene. On any given night you can wander in off the streets of Greenpoint to check out a live show in the back room. The stage is high, allowing you to see the band performing wherever you're standing in the narrow room. A small bar is conveniently located in the back corner.

Upon entering the front bar you're enveloped in a chill atmosphere with low lighting and comfy red booths. The DJ mixes it up on the turntables and bodies responds in rhythm. If you need fresh air after dancing, step outside onto the patio and cool down. Additional activities include: working your way down the 16-tap beer list during Tuesdays' two-for-one drink special, or rocking out during "Heavy Metal Parking Lot Karaoke" on Wednesday nights.

Bar Matchless is a great neighborhood place to grab a few drinks and a casual bite. The full kitchen offers a variety of dishes and is open until 3 a.m.

Sound Check
by Justin Hosek, Sound Engineer

Needless to say, I was very worried showing up at this club and seeing a half broken Mackie 1604! Boy was I surprised when I fired it up and the system had plenty of headroom. In-ear monitors helped to supplement the 2 EV powered monitor speakers on stage. I doubled up on light duty and manned the small pin spots as well as a projector to really make this show look very slick.

GREENPOINT
Corner of Manhattan Ave & Driggs Ave

Brooklyn: Northside

GOODBYE BLUE MONDAY

1087 Broadway | Brooklyn, NY 11221
718-453-6343
Hours: Sun-Thu 11a-2a, Fri-Sat 11a-3a
Subway: J to Kosciusko | J,M,Z to Myrtle
www.goodbye-blue-monday.com

Written by: Sarah Oramas

Sound Check
Sound Quality: Good
Stage Lighting: Good
Sightlines: Good
Eardrum Meter:
Green–Yellow

BUSHWICK
Between Malcolm X Blvd & DeKalb

Brooklyn: Northside

MUSIC TYPE	VENUE TYPE	ADMISSION	ATMOSPHERE	DRINKS: $
Everything	Small Club Capacity 100	Free (Pass the Bucket)	Junk Shop meets Cafe	Beer & Wine FOOD: Snacks

Coffee shop by day, live music venue by night and junk store at all times, Goodbye Blue Monday embodies artists, hipsters and the budget conscious. Vampire Weekend and other popular acts credit this unique little venue as the place where they got their start.

Each night eight or more sets are divided between the venue's two stages, ranging from indie rock and singer-songwriter, to experimental, reggae and more. The inclusiveness and acceptance for diversity projected by the owner, Steve Trimboli, allows unknown artists time on stage. "I don't book shows, I confirm," said Steve. This lack of filter warrants music that may not always be to your liking, however, GBM *does* attract talented performers that pack the house and the venue is well-known on the touring circuit.

The club's entrance is guarded by junk-art figurines. Inside, every inch of wall space is covered by kitschy collections and crammed with remnants of the former junk shop from which this venue sprung. The makeshift bar sells cheap beer and wine; Frankenstein-style bar stools, and tables and chairs offer cafe-style seating. In the backyard the second stage sits in a ramshackle sculpture garden.

Several staple events have sprung up on Goodbye Blue Monday's calendar: monthly poetry readings, Wednesday open mic comedy nights, and The Bushwick Book Club—performances on the first Tuesday of every month.

HISTORY

When GBM opened in 2005 Steve had just acquired a massive assortment of stuff from cleaning out a house. He opened shop and started selling many of the items on eBay. Within the first year he started serving coffee and booking shows—as he had done at his former venue, Scrap Bar in Greenwich Village, which closed in 1995. Steve soon acquired a beer and wine license and this junk shop turned into a true-blue live music venue.

Sound Check
by Daniel Morrow, Musician/Writer

One of the few venues to have live video and audio streaming of every show, the recordings do not pretend to be of professional quality but are an excellent bonus. The room has a great vibe and for a non-purpose built D.I.Y venue the sound is surprisingly good both on stage and out front. There's also a piano and a large storage space behind the stage for instruments.

PINE BOX ROCK SHOP

12 Grattan St | Brooklyn, NY 11206 | 718 366-6311
Hours: Mon-Fri Open 4p, Sat-Sun Open 2p
Subway: L to Morgan
www.pineboxrockshop.com

Written by: Emily Niewendorp

DRINKS: $-$$	ATMOSPHERE	ADMISSION	VENUE TYPE	MUSIC TYPE
Happy Hour 'til 8pm FOOD: Snacks	Neighborhood Bar	Free - $10	Small Club	Rock, Indie, Folk, Experimental

BUSHWICK
Between Morgan Ave & Bogart St

The October 2010 opening of Pine Box Rock Shop, by proprietors Heather and Jeff Rush, is a welcoming addition to the Morgan stop on the L train. This cluster of warehouses, and cobblestone streets is a playground for artists and entrepreneurs. It lacks the cliche trends and commercialism you see in Williamsburg, and is removed from the frenzy of Manhattan.

Pine Box is a former casket factoy, lined partially floor to ceiling with stained pallet boards, creating a signature look that is clean and unassuming. The long wooden bar incases ticket stubs in its clear top and provides seating along the entire length of the room. Seating for groups is nestled in the back, where a nearby ramp leads up to the live music room.

The music room is under construction with plans to present a full schedule in Spring/Summer. Heather and Jeff, both long-time musicians claim, "We'll be the first band to play on our stage." Heather and Jeff are prioritizing the details, such as: the room's layout for attractive visual and sonic experiences, live recordings, quality gear, an elevated platform, and for the drummers: Jeff says, "We are probably going to have a fairly pimped out house drum-set." Count on discovering music that sounds good in the room, with a focus on local acts. Heather rounds their intentions out well: "What I hope will happen is that people will be willing to come here even though it's a smaller showroom and expect to see better shows."

Heather and Jeff, who relocated from Seattle several years ago, have added many personal touches to the bar. The tap beer list is excellent for those who love flavorful microbrews, ales and stouts. Pinebox is also a vegan bar; Jeff clarifies: "I don't think it means much of anything to most people, but to vegans it's awesome that it exists."

> "We are so excited. I love this neighborhood [Bushwick]. I love how positive [it is]…everybody was like, 'I'm so glad you're here, I love your bar.' Our neighbors love us. Even the people who aren't bar-people love us. My neighbor across the street, she doesn't even drink, she's just happy there is more traffic and light on the block."
>
> Heather, Co-owner

Brooklyn: Northside

ADDITIONAL VENUES

THE CHARLESTON
174 Bedford Ave | Brooklyn, NY 11211 | 718-782-8717
www.thecharlestonbar.com

Williamsburg's oldest bar—The Charleston—invites with its large retro-styled bar room. Hang out, have some drinks and enjoy the southern kitchen. Past graffiti sprayed brick walls and 1950s diner booths the bar leads you to its musical heart: the basement space, which houses great live rock, metal and indie-rock music, six days a week.

COCO66
66 Greenpoint Avenue | Brooklyn, NY 11222 | 718-389-7392
www.coco66.com

A big neon red "BAR" sign marks the entrance to Coco 66, a huge, atmospheric and trendy live music bar. A well-equipped sound system is a perfect base for the numerous metal, pop, rock, '80s music and alternative live bands that play there. Regulars enjoy the music, food, pool and dart games in this stylish venue.

EUROPA
98 Meserole Ave | Brooklyn, New York 11222 | 718-383-5723
www.europaclub.com

Club Europa unifies opposites: rock music and livestream club sounds; baggy pants and sneakers next to high heels and minis; and cold beer along with vodka on ice. Live music acts, framed in red velvet curtains open the night at this large Eastern European venue that later turns into a night club.

THE GUTTER
200 North 14th St | Brooklyn, New York 11211 | 718-387-3585
www.thegutterbrooklyn.com

'The Gutter' in Brooklyn's Williamsburg neighborhood is so-named for its 8 bowling lanes, not for its clientele (although it does give off a faux dive-bar vibe). The large bar area is sandwiched by the bowling lanes on one side, and the 'Backroom' on the other. The Backroom is a performance area, but is also available for private functions. The bar has a wide variety of beers on tap and all priced very reasonably.

TOMMY'S TAVERN
1041 Manhattan Ave | New York, NY 11222 | 718-383-9699
www.tommystavern.com

Tommy's Tavern is a live music bar with inexpensive drinks and a 'do it yourself' vibe. A big pool table, pinball machine and live music acts of local rock, cover and metal bands entertain the locals. Bands play three to four nights a week in the small stage-less back room.

Photo by Eric Reichbaum

BROOKLYN CENTRAL

PARK SLOPE	GENRE	PAGE
Barbes	WORLD	143
Puppets Jazz Bar	JAZZ	144
The Rock Shop	ROCK, POP, FOLK, JAZZ, BLUES, HIP-HOP, DJ	145
Southpaw	ROCK, POP, FOLK, JAZZ, BLUES, HIP-HOP, DJ	146
Union Hall	INDIE, ROCK, POP, FOLK, COMEDY	148

GOWANUS		
The Bell House	ALL MODERN MUSIC PLUS WORLD, COMEDY, DJ	150
Littlefield	ROCK, POP, FOLK, INDIE, HIP-HOP, REGGAE, DJ	152

RED HOOK		
Bait & Tackle	ROCK, FOLK, SINGER-SONGWRITER	154
Jalopy	WORLD, FOLK: BLUEGRASS, ROOTS	155
Rocky Sullivan's	TRADITIONAL IRISH, CELTIC HIP-HOP/ROCK	156
Sunny's Bar	FOLK, BLUEGRASS	157

DUMBO		
Galapagos	PERFORMANCE ART, DANCE, THEATER	158

ADDITIONAL VENUES	NEIGHBORHOOD	159
BAM (Brooklyn Academy of Music)	Fort Greene	
Douglass Street Music Collective	Gowanus	
Fifth Estate	Park Slope	
Hank's Saloon	Boerum Hill	
Ibeam	Gowanus	
Sycamore	Ditmas Park	
Tea Lounge	Park Slope	

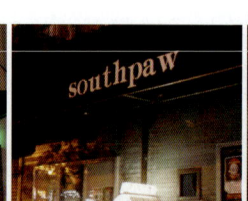

Brooklyn: Central

Sound Check
Sound Quality: Good
Stage Lighting: Good
Sightlines: Good
Eardrum Meter:
Green–Yellow

BARBES

376 9th Street | Brooklyn, NY 11215
347-422-0248
Hours: Open 5p Daily
Subway: F to 7th Ave
www.barbesbrooklyn.com

Written by: Dmitry Iyudin

DRINKS: $-$$	ATMOSPHERE	ADMISSION	VENUE TYPE	MUSIC TYPE
Average $6+ FOOD: no	Neighborhood Bar	$10 Suggested	Small Room	World

Alexis Cuadrado

PARK SLOPE
Corner of 6th Ave & 9th St

In an intimate back room at Barbès a globe-spanning blend of eclectic music is set amongst French flair. The live music varies from ragtime and opera to Eastern European Gypsy flavored funk. This bare-bones neighborhood bar located in the heart of Park Slope is owned by two Brooklyn musicians—both originally from France—and draws a lovely, literate crowd.

Inside the venue, tin-ceilings and low light create perfect ambiance for a romantic rendezvous or a stimulating evening out with friends. A great selection of reasonably priced wines adds to the experience. Proximity to bustling 5th and 7th Avenues, and local culinary favorites such as Sidecar and Blue Ribbon, make this a perfect spot for an aperitif or a night cap.

Every first Sunday of the month Barbès features readings by prominent authors such as Paul Auster and Chuck Klosterman. On Monday the performance area is turned into a makeshift movie theater for screenings of independent features, animation and classics from around the world. Admission is free to both.

> "We try to provide music that cannot easily be heard in other places. We don't just provide specific genres, but tend to present a lot of artists from a cross-section of world music—personal compositions and classical—all sorts of things that you don't usually find in a very, very small performance space. And we try to make it as assessable and democratic as possible. It's a space to see both high and low brow music in a bar setting.
>
> Music is always live, real music is live. I love records. That's where it starts. I am a musician also. I play music, I listen to music. It's a part of my daily life. I can't imagine a world without it.
>
> Recorded music fulfills a very different part, a very different need. We can listen to recorded music in our house but when it comes to performing music and sharing it, it has to be live."
>
> Olivier Conan, Co-owner

Sound Check
There is no proper stage but the playing area is highlighted by a kitschy Hotel D'Orsay sign.

Brooklyn: Central

143

PUPPETS JAZZ BAR

481 5th Ave | Brooklyn, NY 11215 | 718-499-2622

Hours: Set times: Mon-Sat 6p & 9p, Sat 12a
Sunday Jazz Brunch 12p-3p
Subway: F,M,R to 9th St/4th Ave
www.puppetsjazz.com

Vegan & Vegetarian Cuisine

Written by: Sarah Oramas

MUSIC TYPE	VENUE TYPE	ADMISSION	ATMOSPHERE	DRINKS: $-$$
Jazz	Small Room Capacity 48 - 70	Free - $12 2 Drink Minimum	Intimate Neighborhood Bar	Average $5 - $12 FOOD: Full Menu

PARK SLOPE — Between 11th St & 12th St

Brooklyn: Central

Puppets Jazz Bar is dedicated to Brooklyn and New York jazz musicians and offers live music seven days a week. It is new to its second location on 5th Avenue and is becoming a beloved neighborhood haunt for artists and jazz enthusiasts. Puppets Jazz has a lot to offer: anywhere from two to five performances per day in a variety of styles within this broad musical genre, and boasts some notable established performers as well.

Owner Jaime Affoumado has been a jazz musician for over 20 years, in addition to: a vegan chef; a child actor; and a professional skateboarder nicknamed "Puppethead," from which he named his venue. Jaime's commitment to the music shows up in the array and quality of performers showcased at this little bar: Grammy award winning pianist Arturo O'Farrill plays regularly at Puppets Jazz, but the stage is also graced by many lesser-known, but incredibly talented locals.

The staff is welcoming in this intimate room; any passerby might pop in and enjoy the music without feeling the slightest bit out of place, which is precisely the goal. Co-owner Martin Fagin, who came on board at this second location says, "We try to expose people to jazz because once they hear it, they want to come back."

The space is minimal and appealing to the senses, with dim lighting, black leather bench-seating lining the walls and small round tables perfect for small groups of listeners. At the rear of the room the curved stage brushes up close to the seats leaving minimal room between the tables and the musicians.

This small space offers a lot for its size with its full, mostly vegan and all vegetarian menu, a standard bar with a selection of bottled beers, and a spacious backyard patio. Indoors there is seating for just 48 and the backyard can accommodate at least 30 more. For anyone looking to hear high quality jazz in a relaxed and friendly atmosphere, this is a great destination.

Sound Check
Sound Quality: Good
Stage Lighting: Good
Sightlines: Good
Eardrum Meter: Yellow

Tech Check
Sound System: Acoustic Venue, Vocal PA, Mackie mixer, Behringer acitve speakers
Backline: Drums, Bass amp, Yamaha C2 Baby Grand piano

THE ROCK SHOP

249 4th Avenue | Brooklyn, New York 11215 | 718-230-5740
Hours: Sun-Wed 5p-2a, Thu-Sat 5p-4a
Subway: D,N,R to Union St
www.therockshopny.com

Written by: Daniel Morrow

DRINKS: $-$$	ATMOSPHERE	ADMISSION	VENUE TYPE	MUSIC TYPE
Average $7 - $9 FOOD: Bar Menu	Neighborhood Bar	$7 - $20	Small Club	Various: Rock, Pop, Folk, Jazz, Hip-Hop, DJ

"No frills, no product placement, just good sounding music," says The Rock Shop's manager, Brian Hakenrider. This ethos is establishing The Rock Shop as quite the local hot spot. The venue is run by people with an established pedigree in the New York music environment, who have worked at well-known clubs in Manhattan.

The Rock Shop has smartly created its own Brooklyn personalilty. A look at the ground floor performance room reveals an intimate space, with a tall stage and comfortable sofas surrounding a large standing area. Its intimate confines give the venue a real, palpable energy. The room has also been acoustically treated so that, for sound and vibe, it is a quality place for up-and-coming bands to play and build a following.

Although national touring acts and regionally renowned bands play here, it is local bands that fill the majority of the evening slots, giving the venue a distinct neighborhood flavor. The community spirit is adding greatly to The Rock Shop's appeal, but the venue's popularity can also be attributed to the many other attractions it has to offer. **Brian describes the place as "a one-stop shop: music, sports and a great place to hang out."**

There are 10 flat-screen TVs mounted around the venue and a quality jukebox. The upstairs is equipped with a pool table, dartboard and non-stop televised sports. There is also a wonderful roof-top deck encased by bamboo shoots. Bands are already claiming this area as the venue's green room!

Indie rock music is The Rock Shop's mainstay. There are plans for occasional jazz shows and even comedy acts. The versatility of the venue allows it to morph naturally from sports bar to music venue to comedy club to late night hang-out. It is this fresh and open approach that makes The Rock Shop both a cool place to hang out and a respected music venue for local and touring bands.

PARK SLOPE
Between Carroll St & President St

Sound Check
Sound Quality: Good
Stage Lighting: Good
Sightlines: Good
Eardrum Meter: Yellow

Sound Check
by Daniel Morrow, Musician/Writer
The acoustics and sound system are excellent. The walls are brick with large acoustic panels and there's extensive lighting all around. The stage is at least 3 feet high and there's plenty of mics and channels on the mixing desk to accommodate large group set ups. The room is small but there's a very lively vibe.

Brooklyn: Central

SOUTHPAW

125 5th Ave | Brooklyn, NY 11217 | 718-230-0236
Hours: 8p-4a Daily
Subway: D,N,R to Union St | 2,3,4 to Bergen St
www.spsounds.com

Written by: Emily Niewendorp

MUSIC TYPE	VENUE TYPE	ADMISSION	ATMOSPHERE	DRINKS: $-$$
Various: Rock, Pop, Folk, Jazz, Hip-Hop, DJ	Mid-Size Club Capacity 350 - 500	Free - $25	Respected, Relaxed, Unpretentious	Average $6+ FOOD: no

PARK SLOPE
Between St Johns Pl & Sterling Pl

Brooklyn: Central

Southpaw is a diamond in the rough. Housed in monochrome gates and a black awning, the music venue sits inconspicuously on commercial Fifth Avenue in northern Park Slope, Brooklyn.

People flock to experience the eclectic music that takes stage in the club's large, wide-open, album-decorated walls. Some larger-named musicians that have graced Southpaw's stage are Cat Power, Brazilian Girls, Devendra Banhart and Deer Tick. International bands appear regularly, and the music ranges from hip-hop to indie rock and rockabilly. Events include country festivals, monthly or quarterly series for unsigned talent, supervised sessions for kids to work on their music, disco parties, family parties, children's shows, fundraisers and the occasional theatrical production. Many of these events are not for Southpaw's profit, but to break even, so everybody in the community is encompassed.

There is high energy in Southpaw. There is unabashed individualism in both the employees and the patrons; they really love their music. At a time when the music industry may be oversaturated and not paying financially, talented musicians and artists are touring the country, playing at Southpaw, experimenting, crafting, and sharing their gifts with live audiences. It is a great time to hear and be a part of living, diverse music and Southpaw recognizes that. **[And if you were wondering: the folks at Southpaw *are* lefties.]**

HISTORY

Southpaw was founded in 2002 by big-hearted, music-loving Brooklyn boys: Michael Palms and Matthew Roth. Combined, they brought extensive, indirect experience to their venture. Michael's passion for music started in his youth. As a kid, he combed the West Village record stores, regularly trekked out to Maxwell's music venue in Hoboken and bravely stood up against the norm of pop culture. He followed The Clash and rockabilly and punk music. In his 20s, Michael worked at the Brooklyn Brewery in Williamsburg in accounting and also watched as the Brewery's distribution spread to new, large-sized bars with cool names. He and Mathew went bar-hopping often and saw an opportunity to market on a small-martini/DJ-bar idea. Matthew at the time was gaining practical experience working in construction management and dealing with city permits, hurdles and bureaucracy.

Pictured above: DJ setup, Navegante, Hank & Cupcakes

Michael and Mathew initially looked at spaces in Williamsburg; however they discovered large-capacity spots in surrounding—questionably-safe—neighborhoods with affordable prices. Michael also realized that a large-capacity spot would be perfect as a live music venue, so he persuaded Mathew into opening a music venue instead. As Southpaw came together, Michael and Mathew honored their roots in Brooklyn culture and community by working toward good relations with other club owners, the city and their new neighbors in Park Slope.

Southpaw quietly eased into Park Slope opting for neutral colors from the street-view and keeping its gate down during the day. Fifth Avenue at the time was a sparse strip, but the venue was conscious of potential noise complaints and the general distaste of gentrification and rent increases in the mouths of locals. The basic difficulties of securing paperwork, licenses and permits to open the venue were immense. After opening, the club managed to keep its momentum over such hurdles as: the aftermath of 9/11, the 2004 smoking ban, and neighborhood changes, and continues to operate as a well-run, popular live music venue.

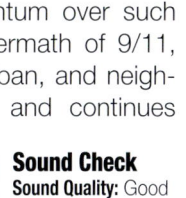

Pictured: Hank & Cupcakes

> "I'm [Southpaw] not just an indie rock, college educated, white, fresh to NYC, you-have-to-play-there kind of venue. I'm an everybody kind of person. I'm an everybody kind of venue. As long as it's relatively safe and everyone is respectful, I will host a show. Hi to everybody out there. Keep working hard, let's do this!"
> — Mikey Palms, Owner

Sound Check
Sound Quality: Good
Stage Lighting: Good
Sightlines: Good
Eardrum Meter: Yellow

Tech Check
Sound System: Allen & Heath 4000 32 ch, 10,000 watt tri-amped FOH rig
Monitors: 5 mix bi-amped monitor rig, including a tri-amped drum fill w/ sub
Backline: Full Backline (no cymbals)
Lighting: 12 channel Leprechaun 2 scene programmable board running 22 instruments
DJ: Full DJ setup
Recording: 32 track digital recording
Hospitality: Soundheck for all bands, 2 guests per band member, 2 drinks per band member after 25 or 30 paid or 1/2 price drinks/drink special
Comments: 12'x15' stage, 6'x4' projection, theatrical curtain, video projection

Brooklyn: Central

UNION HALL

702 Union Street | Brooklyn, NY 11215 | 718-638-4400
Hours: Music: 8p-12mid, Bar: Sun-Thu Open 4p Fri-Sat Open 12p
Subway: R to Union St | F to 4th Ave
www.unionhallny.com

Written by: Emily Niewendorp

MUSIC TYPE	VENUE TYPE	ADMISSION	ATMOSPHERE	DRINKS: $-$$
Indie, Rock, Pop, Folk, Punk, Comedy	Small Club Capacity 120	$5 - $12	Eccentric Social Club	Average $5+ FOOD: Bar Menu

PARK SLOPE — Corner of 5th Ave & Union St

Brooklyn: Central

Union Hall goes above and beyond the call of duty in the personality category. The venue's secret, social-club feel permeates the upstairs bar/lounge and extends downstairs to the glassed-in stuffed bird display in the music room. The ground floor bar is decked out in large bookshelves, dark woodworking, rich-colored furniture, and textured wallpaper. Furniture arrangements section off the room, creating a cozy, sink-yourself-in ambience.

The venue is both a curious destination place for people all over the city and a neighborhood hang-out for loyal customers. Indie music is most common, from rock to singer-songwriter, although the venue is open to all kinds of music. Downstairs the crowd gives special attention to the music, which is sometimes a nice surprise for both musicians and newcomers. This energy is even more prevalent because of the small size of the room. Union Hall highlights musicians that believe in the craft and are making a name for themselves, but also those that enjoy sharing an incredible experience with the audience.

Musicians take notice of Union Hall's appreciation toward musicians. The general manager Kevin says: "We happened to be lucky enough to get an artist named Andrew Bird to play and it was kind of a secret show. I think he was coming into town to do something much bigger and I think Jack [booker at the time] knew him or his management. And he came to play kind of a practice show to a small audience...stage wise he is very talented, he's got a lot going on. And he really enjoyed the venue himself, so it was nice to have...he became a fan of us."

The bar serves burgers and small dishes. There are two popular bocce ball courts, multi-level corners where groups settle, and a large pull-down screen for sports and films.

> "It's the best way to hear music. A lot of times you hear a record...you can tell there is some production going on. And when you hear the live music, fresh, coming at you - the musicians are just playing and its a super practiced song or maybe its not, maybe they are improvising and you get all that fresh, good stuff at a moment's notice...I like that raw sound."
>
> Kevin Avanzato, Manager

HISTORY

Union Hall was developed to provide something specific and new for the surrounding community. The space had been vacant for quite some time before the building's owner found the folks at Union Hall, who agreed it was important to impact the community in a positive way. Favorable word spread quickly on the street attesting to the venue's musical success. This has given the impression of a venue established long before 2007, but such is not the case.

In 2007, Union Hall was opened, inspired by the venue's sister bar, Floyd, NY, a neighborhood bar in Brooklyn Heights. Kevin Avanzato was hired to help build Union Hall and being music lovers, the owners and Kevin decided to utilize the new two-floor space by including live music. A cabinet shop beforehand, the entire interior was renovated and designed to represent Union Hall's private club feel. The bookshelves and bocce ball courts were built and the walls were plaster finished. Time was spent in antique stores salvaging and picking out particularly large paintings. Books were bought by the foot from The Strand Bookstore in Manhattan and some were donated as well: one woman gifted her entire 1960s edition of Encyclopedia Britannica to Union Hall instead of throwing it away.

Through the opening process, relationships were developed and Kevin was asked to stay on as general manager of the venue. Musically, Kevin and the owners had not developed a vision for Union Hall. For the first three years, Jack MacFadden was hired to program the room full time. Through his connections, Jack drew great talent, understood how to best use the space and its assets and from there, the venue blew up to the popular, well-supported place it is today.

Sound Check
Sound Quality: Good
Stage Lighting: Good
Sightlines: Good
Eardrum Meter: Yellow

Tech Check
Sound System: Yamaha MG 24/14FX, 24ch
Monitors: 2 Mackie C300's, JBL JRX112M
Backline: Drums (no cymbals), Ampeg 115 combo bass amp, Roland keyboard amp
Lighting: Basic lighting package
Comments: Stage size 10.5' x 14', Dell Digital Projector, 7' x 5' Projection Screen DVD/VCR Player

THE BELL HOUSE

149 7th Street | Brooklyn, NY 11215 | 718-643-6510
Hours: Mon-Fri 5p-4a, Sat-Sun 5p-4a
Subway: F,G,R to 4th Ave
www.thebellhouseny.com

Written by: Nick D'Amore

MUSIC TYPE	VENUE TYPE	ADMISSION	ATMOSPHERE	DRINKS: $-$$
All Modern Music, Dance, World, Comedy	Lounge Capacity 150 Main Rm Capacity 350	Front Lounge, Free Main Space, $5 - $25	Spacious, Multi-room Lodge	Average $6+ **FOOD:** Dub Pies

Set amid the boxy utilitarian buildings at the end of a block in the Gowanus section of Park Slope, is perhaps the brightest spot of the borough's burgeoning music scene: The Bell House. Converted from a 1920s printing press warehouse to a spacious and welcoming venue, this hot spot has retained its antique charm, while using a sparse decor to mimic its surroundings.

The Bell House was conceived by the same folks who established the great Union Hall in Park Slope and Floyd, NY in Brooklyn Heights. It is easily one of the top music venues in Brooklyn and, perhaps, the entire city. The music room, located in the back of the venue, is well suited as a multi-purpose space and a glance at the venue's calendar of events is evidence of the venue's versatility and the disparate groups of people who can enjoy events there together.

Keep an eye out for nights of large-scale trivia, burlesque shows, ping-pong tournaments or a viewing of the television season finale of *Mad Men*. Whisk away the tables and chairs and there is ample standing room for rock shows, DJ dance parties and shows featuring established artists that inevitable pack the place, such as: Jonathan Richmond, Roky Erickson, Nick Lowe, or John Oates—of Hall & Oates. Some of the more memorable events in The Bell House's brief history include The Thermals' performance, the many *LOST* viewing parties of NBC's hit TV show, the reunion of New York hardcore legends, Agnostic Front, and a fundraiser for Haiti, following its disastrous earthquake. Heather Dunsmoor, who books the club, says she focuses on events that can fill the spacious room, but, "We're open to anything as long as there is public interest in it."

Music events at the The Bell House are particularly satisfying, due in part to the room's good acoustics. The 25-foot wooden arched ceiling guarantees stellar live sound. Excellent sightlines also play an integral role in

Interior photos provided courtesy of The Bell House

the appeal. Contrary to most music venues, where the stage is positioned at the far end of a rectangular space, the 450 square-foot stage at the The Bell House is along a side wall, creating a room more wide than long. This allows for an intimacy between the audience and the performer, despite the room's large size.

The Bell House staff is also focused on providing the performers themselves with an optimum experience at the venue. They work to make each event as fun and stress-free as possible for the acts booked, whether by providing great sound or fulfilling a rider request. "We've always been very aware of artists needs and we try every day to make sure performers walk away with a great experience. As long as they're happy, we're happy," Heather says.

The front bar is a laidback area where patrons can enjoy a break from the crowd, a quality pint or cocktail, and relax and converse on comfortable couches and chairs. Both the music room and the front bar/lounge serve primarily local and independent beers and interesting cocktail creations, such as: Surfer Rosa, Pinkerton and Mellow Gold. Also, there is a limited, but intriguing food selection at the Bell House, such as cheeses, and various meat and vegetarian pies.

Similar to the complementary venues that have sprung up around Brooklyn in the recent years, The Bell House strives to be an active and positive component to their surrounding neighborhood.

Sound Check
Sound Quality: Good
Stage Lighting: Good
Sightlines: Good
Eardrum Meter: Yellow

"It changes every day, but we try to keep our fingers on the pulse of what people want to see and do and we try to bring them that. If we're going to expect people to go out of their way to come out here, we want to make sure it's a special experience for everyone, which includes the performers, the guests, and our staff."

Heather Dunsmoor, Booker

Tech Check
Sound System: Allen & Heath GL2400-32 FOH Speakers: EAW LA460 (x4), EAW FR159z (x2), EAW SB250z SUBs (x2)
Monitors: EV ZX5 (x3), EAW SM159zi Amplification: Crown Xti 4000 (X6)
Backline: Full Backline (no cymbals)
DJ: Pioneer DJM 400 mixer, Pioneer CDJ 1000MK3 CD players (x2), Stanton STR8-100 Digital Turntables (x2)
Lighting: High End Systems HOG500 lighting board, 20 gelled par cans
Comments: Stage Size 16'4" x 24', Video Projection, 13 ft screen behind stage, BenQ MP771 short throw projector

Brooklyn: Central

LITTLEFIELD

622 Degraw Street | Brooklyn, NY 11217
Hours: Open for Events, Sun-Thu 8p-12a | Fri-Sat 8p-4a
Subway: 2,3,4,5,B,D,N,Q to Atlantic/Pacific St
R to Union St
www.littlefieldnyc.com

Written by: Emily Niewendorp

Courtyard photo by: Patrick Parault

MUSIC TYPE	VENUE TYPE	ADMISSION	ATMOSPHERE	DRINKS: $-$$
Rock, Pop, Folk, Indie, Hip-Hop, Reggae, DJ	Warehouse Capacity 406	Varies	Industrial Art Space	Average $3 - $10 FOOD: no

GOWANUS — Between 4th Ave & 3rd Ave

Littlefield's beginnings embody life in the 21st century: an eco-friendly, live-music venture purchases a warehouse from an out-of-business plastic bag distributor, with the transaction initiated over Craigslist. Meet Littlefield, an oasis destination in Gowanus, the industrial, up-and-coming Brooklyn neighborhood situated between Park Slope and Carroll Gardens.

As an eco-friendly venue creatively transformed out of a warehouse environment, everything in Littlefield was chosen for its recyclable and aesthetic qualities. Green ivy along its outside walls greets patrons as they enter the front patio. This patio area was cut out of the building to create outdoor space between the street and the venue. The storefront of glass and steel leads into the bar and art gallery, which is sometimes separated from the music room beyond by a large rolling wall. This massive wall contains collections of rotating art. Most pieces in the venue are salvaged; the bar and tabletops were fashioned from old bowling alley lanes from an Elks Lodge. The bar is lined with reclaimed stainless steel, and light fixtures from Build It Green in Long Island City, Queens add further ambience by creating a starry-night effect. One of the coolest alterations from the warehouse's original structure is the scalloped walls, made from recycled truck tires. Not only do these walls add personality, but they improve the room's sound quality as well.

Part of the challenge for Littlefield is attracting patrons from the minimal amount of foot traffic on the block and establishing the venue as a neighborhood hangout. Julie and Scott work to nurture the local community by reciprocating business with their neighboring proprietors. Local arts, music and cultural centers are flourishing and many are getting involved in Littlefield's music programming. Neighborhood bands and individuals can curate their own shows, creating one-genre bills.

Currently, Littlefield is open only on days that have a show scheduled. **Performance types in this warehouse space include: indie rock; hip-hop; reggae; dance parties—with the large wall rolled back; film screenings; art exhibits; opera; fashion shows and comedy.**

Brooklyn: Central

Photo by: Rob Hazel

Photo by: Eric Michael Pearson

Occasional All Age Shows | Art Exhibits | Fashion Shows

"The feel is so different from night to night, and the crowds are so different, but, you see people come back when a genre comes back." says Julie, Littlefield's co-owner.

Catering to both the art and the music world, Littlefield is finding its niche in Brooklyn. With its dedicated owners and staff, and an ongoing effort to provide consistent sound quality, Littlefield can truly be a multi-functioning and multi-genre venue.

The bar encourages imbibers to try new concoctions. Check out Littlefield's specialty cocktails list, the high-end national microbrews and the bio-dynamic wines.

Photo by: Patrick Parault

HISTORY

In May 2009, owners Julie and Scott opened Littlefield after years of involvement in various music scenes across the country and one fateful trip to Oslo, Norway. Julie says:

"...we took a trip to Oslo to visit Scott's relatives and we heard this music. We followed it into this industrial neighborhood, where warehouses were tagged with beautiful artwork and we found this tiny club called Blå. It was on the canal, with an outdoor bar and we thought, 'How wonderful to have found this little gem just by passing and hearing the music.'"

Despite opening Littlefield in the aftermath of the 2008 recession, Julie and Scott believe that their excitement is worth the risks and stress involved. "We try to put all the positive things into our place. Basically, if you build something you should love every part of it," Julie says.

Sound Check
Sound Quality: Good
Stage Lighting: Good
Sightlines: Good
Eardrum Meter: Yellow

Tech Check
Sound System: Mackie Onyx 32, EAW 3-way loudspeaker array, QSC power
Monitors: 4 mixes, 4 JBL JRX 100
Backline: Full Backline
Lighting: 4 Leco lights 20 Par lights
DJ setup: 2 Technics 1200, 2 Pioneer CDJ 800 Numark, 2 Channel DJ Mixer
Comments: Stage size 24' x12', video projection ceiling mounts in both rooms but no in-house projector, green room, dressing room, backstage area

Brooklyn: Central

BAIT & TACKLE

320 Van Brunt St | Brooklyn, NY 11231 | 718-797-4892
Hours: Mon-Fri 4p-4a, Sat-Sun 2p-4a
Transportation: A,C,F to Jay St/Borough Hall—then Bus B61 to Red Hook | F,G to Carroll St—then, $6 Cab
www.redhookbaitandtackle.com

Written by: Heather McCown

MUSIC TYPE	VENUE TYPE	ADMISSION	ATMOSPHERE	DRINKS: $
Rock, Folk, Singer-songwriter	Neighborhood Bar	Free	Unapologetically Quirky	Cheap Beer/Full Bar FOOD: no

RED HOOK — Corner of Van Brunt St & Pioneer St

Brooklyn: Central

Tired of staring at the pigeons on your fire escape? Then head down to Bait & Tackle to enjoy the natural, and not so natural, fauna of Brooklyn. Opened around 2004, this bar took up residence where a real bait shop operated for years. The current owners assimilated the prior identity of the space to create a live music venue that is truly comfortable and unique.

From the stuffed game, antler horns and assorted fishing and hunting paraphernalia hanging from the walls, to the beautiful natural wood bar top, B & T gives no apology for its character. "They don't try to be hip—they don't have to...it just is what it is," says Erin, a former bartender who trims a friend's hair with a straight-edge between sips of beer.

There are plenty of places to hide in the bar's camouflage decor, yet Bait & Tackle is also a great place to meet friendly neighbors, discuss local events and commiserate underneath the bucket lamps hanging above the bar. Positioned in Red Hook, where residential blocks meet industrial buildings, the bar feels like a no-man's land. "People come here to hideout from other areas of Brooklyn," Erin, states, as she explains how the venue has become a refuge from the hipster scene in other neighborhoods.

The stage area consists of a small space in the center of the room, and lends itself to an ideal setup for acoustic or small acts that don't mind a stuffed billy goat peering over their shoulders while they are playing. With a full PA system, mixer, and speakers, Bait & Tackle is a great venue to plug-in and play.

This is a come as you are kind of place. Grab a seat on one of the vinyl sofas with a friend, play a game of Buck Hunter, or just rest your feet on the railroad tie at the bar and enjoy the warmth of a good conversation and the sounds of live music.

JALOPY

315 Columbia St | Brooklyn, NY 11231 | 718-395-3214
Hours: Tue-Fri 2p-2a, Sat-Sun 12p-2a
Subway: F,G to Carroll St
www.jalopy.biz

Written by: Heather McCown

DRINKS: $	ATMOSPHERE	ADMISSION	VENUE TYPE	MUSIC TYPE
Coffee/Beer	Workshop by Day,	Free - $10	Small Room	Folk, Bluegrass,
FOOD: Snacks	Vaudeville by Night		Cafe	Roots, World

In 2005, Geoff and Lynette Wiley turned a storefront into a live music venue. The business is additionally a school, workshop, and theater. It carries the look and feel of a century-old instrument that has been carefully maintained and continues to emit beautiful melodies. Off the beaten path, Jalopy is a music oasis for music enthusiasts.

Located just off the entrance to the Brooklyn-Battery Tunnel, Jalopy attracts music lovers who want to listen to something different. "We focus on traditional roots music, old time bluegrass and world music," states Lynette. In Jalopy, she and Geoff have realized a long-term dream by providing not only a live music venue, but also a home for lessons on guitar, ukulele, fiddle, mandolin and banjo. Geoff leads a staff of six permanent instructors and arranges visiting artist workshops.

"This is the only place to pick up mandolin," explains Steve, a dedicated student of Jalopy. "And there is no childish or competitive behavior." Indeed, the vibe is inclusion, bringing people together for a common goal of making and enjoying music; musicians—young and old, beginners to advanced—play together and build confidence in their craft. Due to a resurgence in folk/roots music in Brooklyn, Jalopy's patrons range from 22 to 75 years old.

This friendly joint is Geoff and Lynette's home and they happily invite everyone to take part in its activities. Antique and gently used instruments hang in the front room, all reconditioned by Geoff and available for sale. Within moments of setting foot inside, expect to be greeted and enticed into a friendly conversation over a ball jar mug of draft beer or a hot tea. Patrons mingle inside the foyer, on the front stoop, or settle into one of the chairs to listen to the music. There is always a lively banter gently accompanying the twang of strings. Performances take place on a raised stage in the rear of the venue and old church pews and mismatched chairs are scattered around. Geoff handles the sound system and assists the musicians attentively.

Although visiting Jalopy involves a bit of a hike, it is well worth the effort. Come early, stay late, but enjoy the atmosphere, stories, and camaraderie that Jalopy represents.

Sound Check
Sound Quality: Good
Stage Lighting: Good
Sightlines: Good
Eardrum Meter: Yellow

RED HOOK
Between Hamilton Ave & Woodhull St

Brooklyn: Central

ROCKY SULLIVAN'S

34 Van Dyke St | Brooklyn, NY 11231 | 718-246-8050
Hours: Open 11a Daily
Transportation: A,C,F to Jay St/Borough Hall—then Bus B61 to Red Hook | F,G to Carroll St—then, $6 Cab
www.rockysullivans.com

Written by: Bill Nevins

MUSIC TYPE	VENUE TYPE	ADMISSION	ATMOSPHERE	DRINKS: $-$$
Traditional Irish, Celtic Hip-Hop/Rock	Small Club	Free - $10	Celtic Spirited Restaurant/Pub	Full Bar / FOOD: Pub Menu

Brooklyn: Central — RED HOOK — Corner of Dwight St & Van Dyke St

Rocky Sullivan's is an authentic Irish pub, whose bartenders know "how to pour a real Irish pint!" Celtic-spirited folks, off duty police officers, artists, movie actors, Irish visitors and folks with left-leaning politics all favor Rocky's, resulting in an interesting social and cultural mix. The juke box is an eclectic joy and the live music shows are varied. You're as likely to hear the Unity Squad playing there as traditional fiddle music or old style Irish *sean nós* singing.

The entertainment also includes regular quiz and comedy nights, darts tournaments, open mics and readings; giving Rocky's a fun feel and a literary flare that is lacking in other "Irish-themed" establishments.

There's also fresh Sixpoint Ale, brewed right next door, brick-oven pizza, frequent fresh-lobster dinners and a wonderful deck on the roof of Rocky's, where patrons can enjoy a view of the waterfront and the lower Manhattan skyline.

HISTORY

Chris Byrne and Derek Curtis established their new Brooklyn location after sky rocketing rent hikes forced them to leave the midtown Manhattan location, which had been an anomalous and beloved fixture since 1996. Many the midtowner's heart was broken when Rocky's shut down, but since then plenty of patrons have navigated the rather challenging, but interesting route to the new cobble-stoned, art gallery-friendly Red Hook—by subway and bus, car, cab, or the free water taxi from Wall Street in Manhattan.

Brooklyn-born Chris "Seanchai" Byrne (pronounced *shan-a-kee*, Gaelic for "story teller") was for a decade the bagpipe, tin whistle and Irish bodhran-drum wielding front man and rapper for that Celtic band, the Irish-flavored punk-reggae-hip hop aggregation Black 47. Black 47 had an MTV hit with "Funky Ceilidh," toured America and Ireland, made the cover of *Time* and played in films and on late night talk shows. Chris left the group amicably in the early 2000s, preferring to concentrate on his own musical career with Seanchai and the Unity Squad, the Irish trad/hip hop/rock act that he leads with his partner, Rachel Fitzgerald.

And here comes the curve-ball: Chris also spent ten years as a member of the NYPD. "I was more radical than many of the people who would see me on the street," recalls Chris, "But I doubt they knew that." It's a tribute to Chris's skills as a pub keeper and to the comfortable atmosphere at Rocky's that everyone somehow gets along.

Sound Check
Sound Quality: Good
Stage Lighting: Good
Sightlines: Good
Eardrum Meter: Yellow

SUNNY'S BAR

253 Conover St | Brooklyn, NY 11231-1022 | 718-625-8211
Hours: Wed, Fri, Sat 8p-4a
Transportation: A,C,F to Jay St/Borough Hall—then Bus B61 to Red Hook | F, G to Carroll St—then, $6 Cab
www.sunnysredhook.com
Written by: Paula Pahnke

DRINKS: $	ATMOSPHERE	ADMISSION	VENUE TYPE	MUSIC TYPE
Cash Only	It's a trip – literally!	Free	Small Room	Folk, Bluegrass
FOOD: no	Slightly Mysterious			

The mystique of Sunny's Bar is rooted in its old world ambience. The bar nestles itself on a quiet, cobblestone street right off the Pier 41 waterfront, in Red Hook, Brooklyn. Housed within a vintage landscape, this once watering hole for long-shore fishermen, has become a neighborhood institution, playing host to a variety of American folk talent and performers within the Brooklyn roots music scene.

Owned and operated by the Balzano family for over three generations, artist and proprietor Sunny Balzano and his wife, Tone, have created an off-the-grid oasis that caters to an eclectic crowd who doesn't mind a fifteen minute walk from the nearest train station. "People like the idea of going to a place where they feel like they could almost get lost and they'd be proud to get lost; they'd be proud the cab driver got lost," says Tim Sultan, a bartender, who's worked at Sunny's for over fifteen years.

The front room is rustic and adorned with maritime antiquities, quirky strings of Christmas lights and abstract canvases painted by Sunny, himself. The long, mahogany bar houses an impressive selection of beer and hot cider, served with a splash of whiskey or rum—the house favorite during the winter months—however, Tone clarifies,

"I believe people would still come even if all we served was Budweiser."

A makeshift stage allows for audience and band interaction. "There's a human connection when you play for people sitting right in front of you," Tone explains. Patrons can be seen attempting to two-step, especially on Wednesday nights, which feature Smokey Hormel of Smokey's Roundup, who's played with everyone from Beck to Johnny Cash. On Friday and Saturday nights performers like John Pinamonti can be heard paying homage to Brooklyn natives with songs like "The Ballad of Biggies Smalls" (referencing the late Bed-Stuy Rapper, The Notorious B.I.G.), accompanied by a mandolin.

The back room is a refined parlor and often the scene for impromptu jam sessions. Anyone within arm's reach of an instrument is encouraged to join. The walls exhibit local artists' work that rotates throughout the year, and once a month authors are invited to read excerpts from their work during the Sunday at Sunny's reading series.

RED HOOK
Between Reed St & Beard St

Brooklyn: Central

GALAPAGOS ART SPACE

16 Main St | Brooklyn, NY 11201 | 718-222-8500
Hours: Music times vary
Subway: F to York St | A to HIgh St 2,3 to Clark St
www. galapagosartspace.com

Written by: Emily Niewendorp

Sound Check
Sound Quality: Good
Stage Lighting: Goo
Sightlines: Good
Eardrum Meter: Yel

MUSIC TYPE	VENUE TYPE	ADMISSION	ATMOSPHERE	DRINKS: $$
Performance Art, Dance, Theater	Theater Mid-Size Club	Free - $20+	Innovative, Refined, Eccentric	Average $8 FOOD: no

Galapagos Art Space, known for its nurturing impact on Brooklyn's artistic and cultural communities and its 1600 square foot indoor lake, grew out of the first wave of artists that migrated to Brooklyn from Manhattan right before the stock market crash in '87. After the crash, artists and entrepreneurs interested in Williamsburg immediately withdrew back to Manhattan. Galapagos' director, Robert Elmes explains, "Williamsburg was left on its own to evolve separately from the City. A bunch of people had moved out there and now there was almost no connection to the City." In this 'isolation' a small, inclusive community of pioneering artists developed a strong identity amongst gatherings, events and shows, ultimately creating appealing prospects for real estate and housing interests when the market bounced back.

In the early '90s, Robert was involved in big warehouse events that climaxed in a show called Organism, for which a building was rented. That venue operated as Mustard for one year. At that point, in 1995, Robert realized he wanted a "very focused and very designed" venue and spent the next three years opening Galapagos Art Space on N 6th St in Williamsburg. Robert says of Galapagos: "it really grew out of the DIY (do it yourself) movement; interesting, fun shows that you could be a part of if you help clear out the warehouse, or drag the old car out, clean it, etc. And so the neighborhood got known for that sort of spirit and quality."

For the next ten years Galapagos gathered accolades by staging an unprecedented range of poignant artistry in its exotic atmosphere of medieval stone highlighted by an indoor water pool. By 2008 the real estate bubble that brought the artists, young people and businesses to Williamsburg in the '90s and early '00s pushed many out with rising rents. Galapagos opted to relocate to DUMBO, where it expanded in size, added Kunsthalle Gallery and was able to financially maintain its mission of a reciprocal relationship to those within its cultural ecosystem.

Inspired by New York artists, Robert says, "we have refined and honed the dream venue that we really wanted to build—a sort of listening room." For emerging and mid-career artists, Galapagos is a gorgeous, modern space, full of possibilities.

> "In any city in any one moment there is only five good bands. Everybody argues about what band should be on that list, but we want to find that list for ourselves and present those artists."
>
> Robert Elmes, Director

ADDITIONAL VENUES

BAM
30 Lafayette Ave | Brooklyn, New York 11243 | 718-636-4100 | www.bam.org

Brooklyn Academy of Music is Brooklyn's oldest center for the arts, dating back to 1861. It is a leading New York City institution in the fields of visual art, dance, music, film, theater and more. BAMcafe Live offers free weekend shows, highlighting burgeoning rock, jazz, R&B, pop musicians and more.

DOUGLASS STREET MUSIC COLLECTIVE
295 Douglass St | Brooklyn, NY 11217 | www.295douglass.org

Douglass Street Music Collective is a music rehearsal and performance space run by 15 member-artists whose areas of expertise range from classical to world music. The members perform regularly and shows are open to the public. Non-member musicians can perform by submitting collaborative proposals to specific members.

FIFTH ESTATE
506 5th Ave | Brooklyn, NY 11215 | 718-840-0089 | www.fifthestatebar.com

The Fifth Estate engages the non-conformists and proclaims itself as a haven for those who don't identify or fit into traditional social groups. A laid-back, intimate spot, the venue nurtures a grassroots community and offers a back room where developing and touring bands can play.

HANK'S SALOON
46 3rd Ave | Brooklyn, NY 11217 | 718-625-8003 | www.hankssaloon.com

The old-time landmark boasts country karaoke with live bands on Monday night, honky-tonk with Sean Kershaw and the New Jack Ramblers on Sunday night, as well as various music acts throughout the week. The length of the bar runs the size of a double-wide, with a cutout stage in the back.

IBEAM
168 7th St | Brooklyn, NY 11215 | www.ibeambrooklyn.com

Ibeam Music Studio's classes and events offer instruction for students and professional musicians, rehearsal and recital rental space, membership opportunities, and an informal performance space—perfect for small gatherings. Performance proposals are accepted, as well as, submissions for the many performance series curated by the staff.

SYCAMORE
1118 Cortelyou Rd | New York, NY 11218 | 347-240-5850
www.sycamorebrooklyn.com

Sycamore features red and white tiled floors and blue painted metal chairs—including an excellent selection of American whiskey. The venue is multi-functioning; a specialty flower shop, private event rental and live music venue, focusing on acoustic local and touring talent.

TEA LOUNGE
837 Union St | Brooklyn, NY 11217 | 718-789-2762 | www.tealoungeny.com

Tea Lounge is a large cafe and lounge serving eco-friendly coffee, tea, sandwiches and wifi by day, and a full bar at night with live music, open mics, movies, and all-age events. The live music shows include jazz, orchestral, rock, folk and more.

Map Key

DOWNTOWN MANHATTAN
MAP 1
TRIBECA
SOHO
NOHO
CHINATOWN

MAP 2
LOWER EAST SIDE
EAST VILLAGE

MAP 3
GREENWICH VILLAGE
WEST VILLAGE

MIDTOWN MANHATTAN
MAP 4
CHELSEA
GARMENT DISTRICT
HELL'S KITCHEN
THEATER DISTRICT
MIDTOWN

MAP 5
GRAMERCY
CHELSEA
MURRAY HILL
MIDTOWN EAST

UPTOWN MANHATTAN
MAP 6
UPPER WEST SIDE

MAP 7
UPPER EAST SIDE
SPANISH HARLEM

MAP 8
HARLEM

BROOKLYN NORTHSIDE
MAP 9
WILLIAMSBURG
GREENPOINT
BUSHWICK

BROOKLYN CENTRAL
MAP 10
DUMBO
RED HOOK
CARROLL GARDENS
BOERUM HILL
FORT GREENE

MAP 11
GOWANUS
PARK SLOPE
DITMAS PARK

Map 1: Downtown

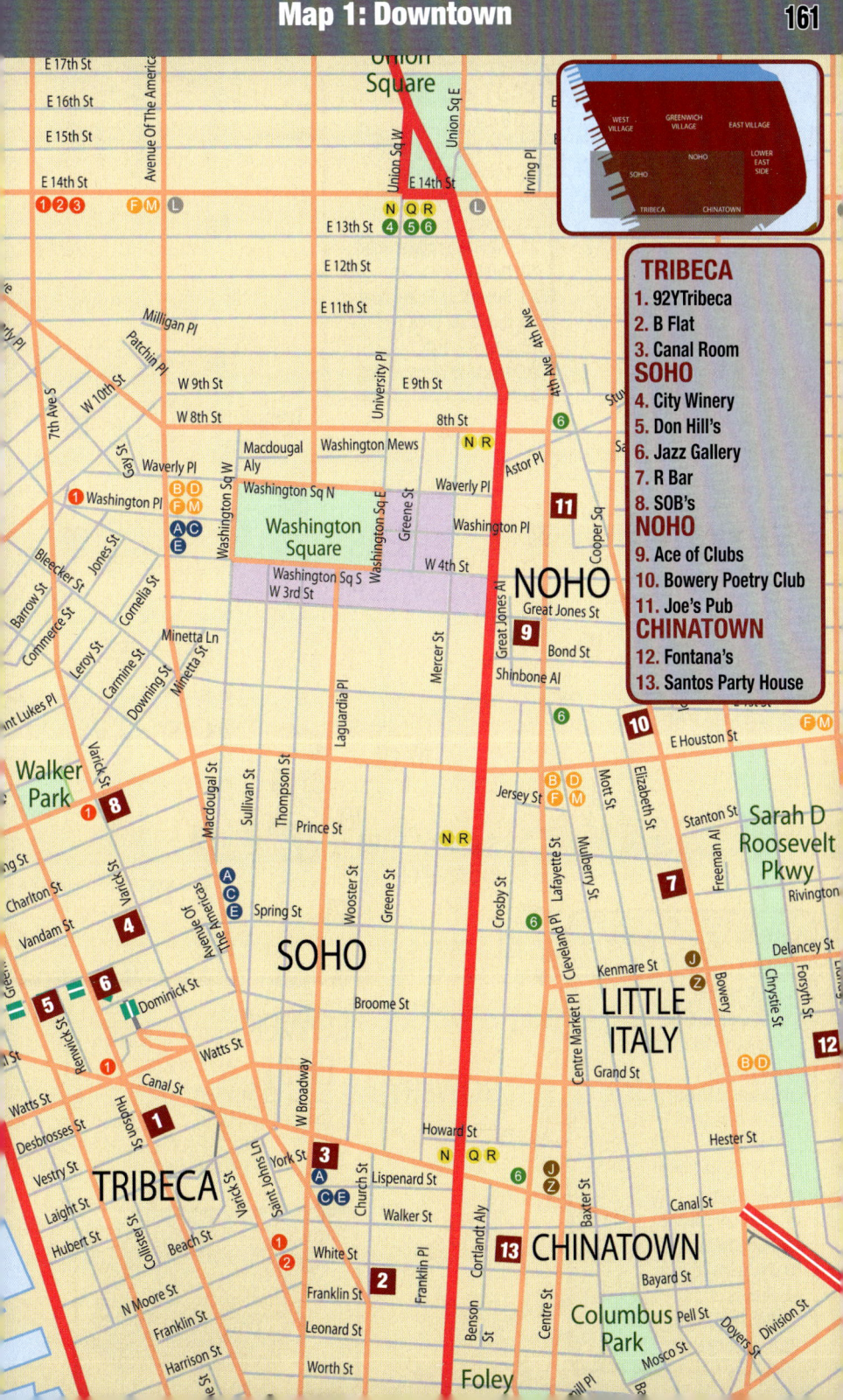

TRIBECA
1. 92YTribeca
2. B Flat
3. Canal Room

SOHO
4. City Winery
5. Don Hill's
6. Jazz Gallery
7. R Bar
8. SOB's

NOHO
9. Ace of Clubs
10. Bowery Poetry Club
11. Joe's Pub

CHINATOWN
12. Fontana's
13. Santos Party House

Map 2: Downtown

EAST VILLAGE
16. Banjo Jim's
17. The Bowery Electric
18. Lakeside Lounge
19. Lit Lounge
20. Jules
21. Otto's Shrunken Head
22. Nublu
23. Nuyerican Poets Cafe
24. Sidewalk Cafe
25. Webster Hall
26. Studio@ Webster Hall

LOWER EAST SIDE
1. The Local 269
2. ABC No Rio
3. Arlene's Grocery
4. Bowery Ballroom
5. Cakeshop
6. Crash Mansion
7. The Delancey
8. Fat Baby
9. The Living Room
10. Mehanata
11. Mercury Lounge
12. National Underground
13. Parkside Lounge
14. Pianos
15. Rockwood Music Hall
16. Tammany Hall

Map 3: Downtown

163

WEST VILLAGE
13. 55 Bar
14. Arthur's Tavern
15. Caffe Vivaldi
16. Cornelia St. Cafe
17. Duplex
18. Fat Cat
19. Garage
20. Marie's Crisis
21. Smalls
22. Village Vanguard

GREENWICH VILLAGE
1. Bar Next Door
2. The Bitter End
3. Blue Note
4. Cafe Wha?
5. Groove
6. Kenny's Castaways
7. Les Poisson Rouge
8. Red Lion
9. Sullivan Hall
10. Terra Blues
11. Village Underground
12. Zinc Bar

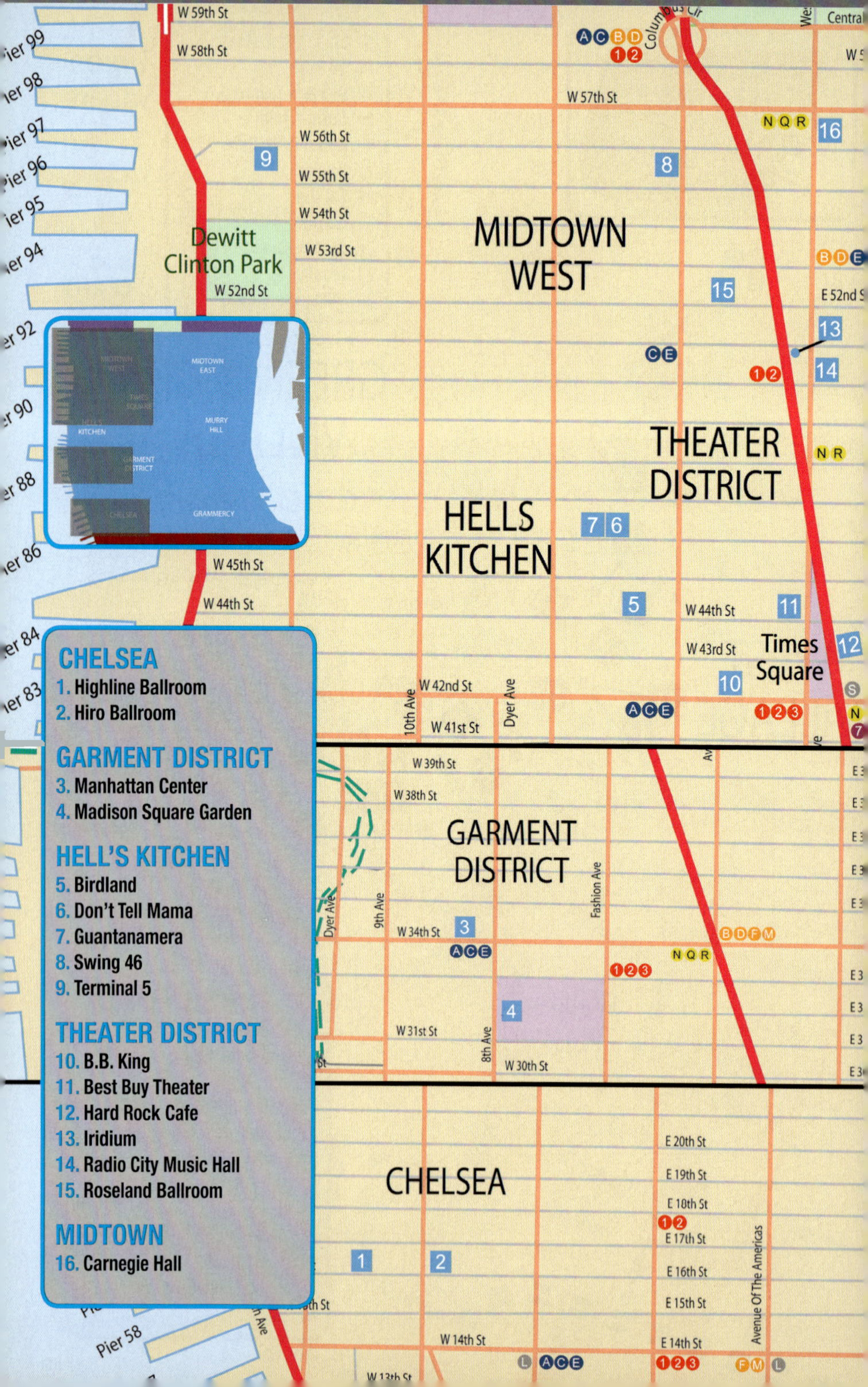

Map 4: Midtown

CHELSEA
1. Highline Ballroom
2. Hiro Ballroom

GARMENT DISTRICT
3. Manhattan Center
4. Madison Square Garden

HELL'S KITCHEN
5. Birdland
6. Don't Tell Mama
7. Guantanamera
8. Swing 46
9. Terminal 5

THEATER DISTRICT
10. B.B. King
11. Best Buy Theater
12. Hard Rock Cafe
13. Iridium
14. Radio City Music Hall
15. Roseland Ballroom

MIDTOWN
16. Carnegie Hall

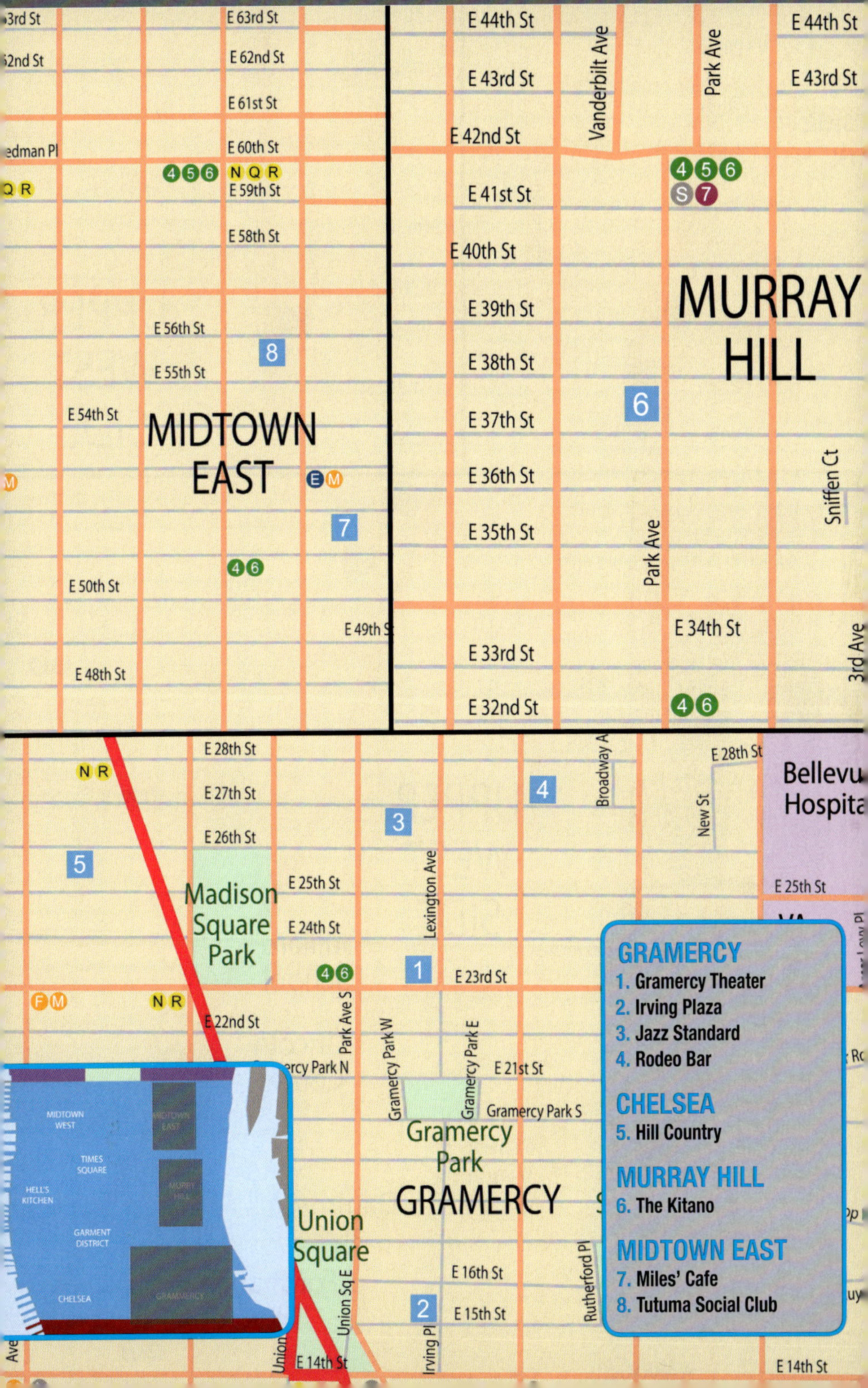
E 63rd St
E 62nd St
E 61st St
E 60th St
E 59th St
E 58th St
E 56th St
E 55th St
E 54th St
MIDTOWN EAST
E 50th St
E 49th St
E 48th St
E 44th St
E 43rd St
E 42nd St
E 41st St
E 40th St
E 39th St
E 38th St
E 37th St
E 36th St
E 35th St
E 34th St
E 33rd St
E 32nd St
Vanderbilt Ave
Park Ave
MURRAY HILL
Sniffen Ct
3rd Ave
E 28th St
E 27th St
E 26th St
E 25th St
E 24th St
E 23rd St
E 22nd St
E 21st St
E 16th St
E 15th St
E 14th St
Broadway
New St
Bellevue Hospital
Madison Square Park
Lexington Ave
Park Ave S
Gramercy Park N
Gramercy Park W
Gramercy Park E
Gramercy Park S
Gramercy Park
GRAMERCY
Union Square
Union Sq E
Irving Pl
Rutherford Pl
GRAMERCY
1. Gramercy Theater
2. Irving Plaza
3. Jazz Standard
4. Rodeo Bar
CHELSEA
5. Hill Country
MURRAY HILL
6. The Kitano
MIDTOWN EAST
7. Miles' Cafe
8. Tutuma Social Club

Map 6: Uptown West

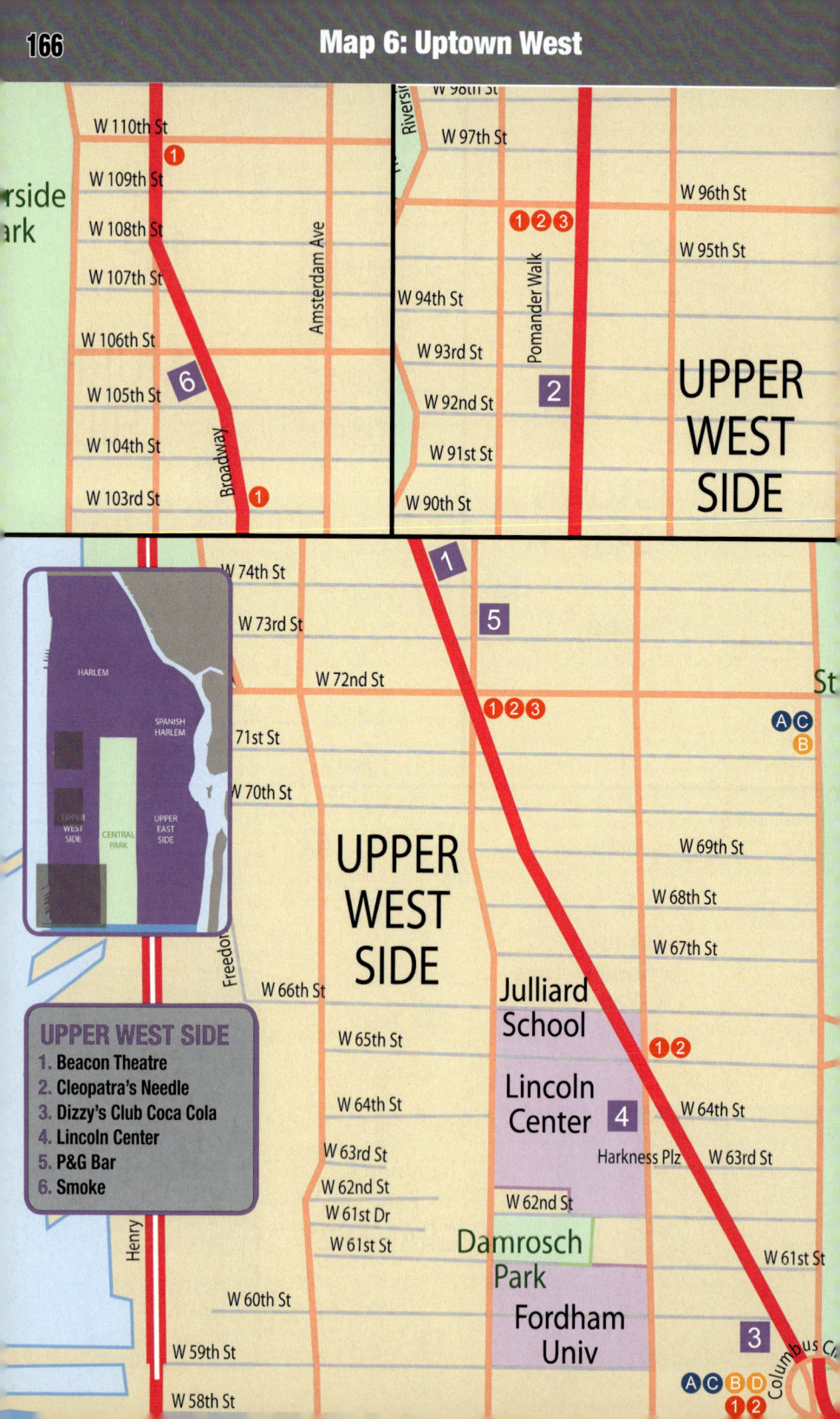

UPPER WEST SIDE

1. Beacon Theatre
2. Cleopatra's Needle
3. Dizzy's Club Coca Cola
4. Lincoln Center
5. P&G Bar
6. Smoke

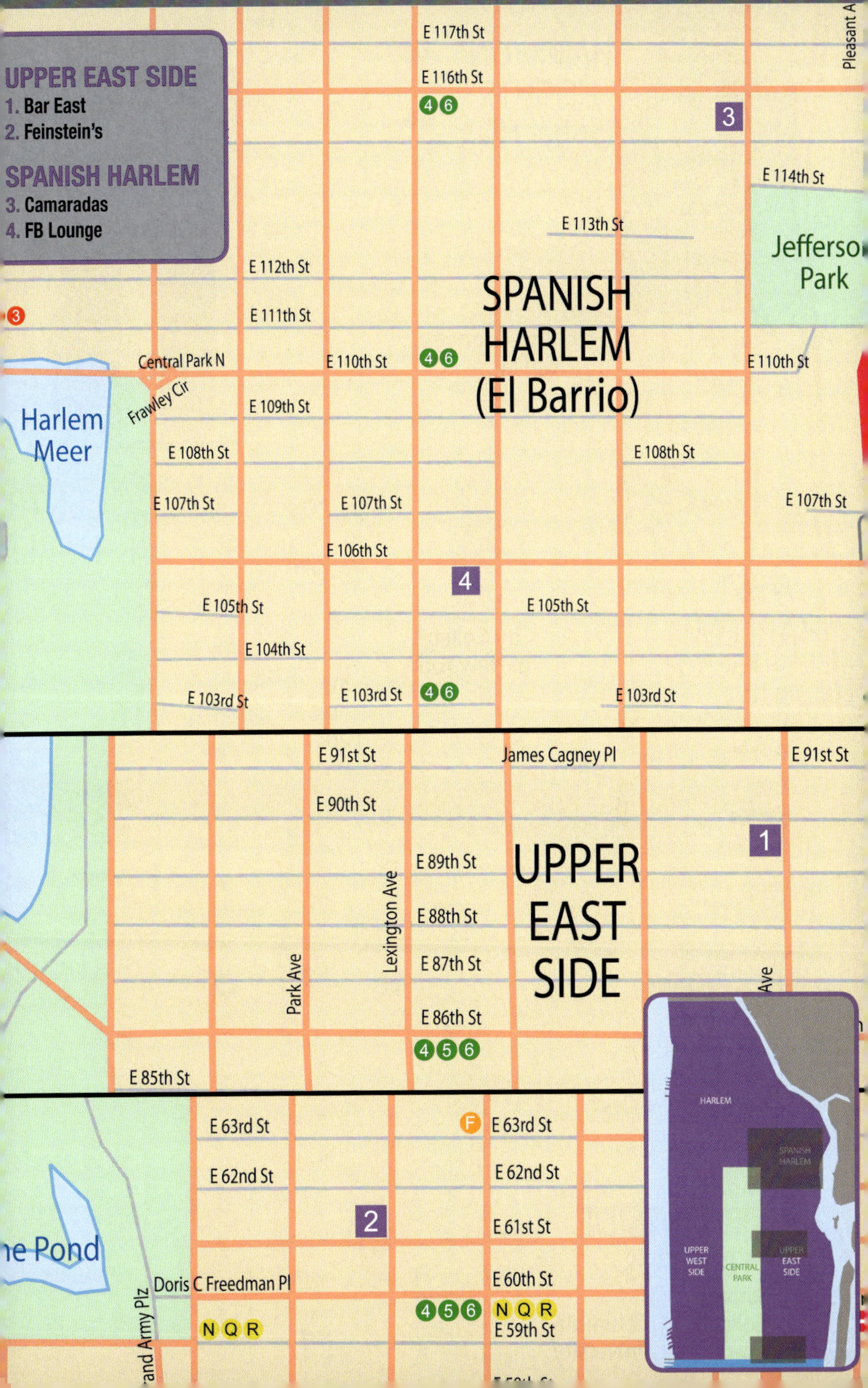

Map 7: Uptown East

UPPER EAST SIDE
1. Bar East
2. Feinstein's

SPANISH HARLEM
3. Camaradas
4. FB Lounge

Map 8: Uptown

HARLEM
1. Apollo
2. Cotton Club
3. Lenox Lounge
4. Showmans
5. Shrine
6. St. Nick's Pub

HAMILTON HEIGHTS (Sugar Hill)

CENTRAL HARLEM

WEST HARLEM

City College of New York

St Nicholas Park

MORNINGSIDE HEIGHTS

Barnard College

Columbia University

Hamilton Grange Natl Mon

Map 9: Brooklyn – Norhside

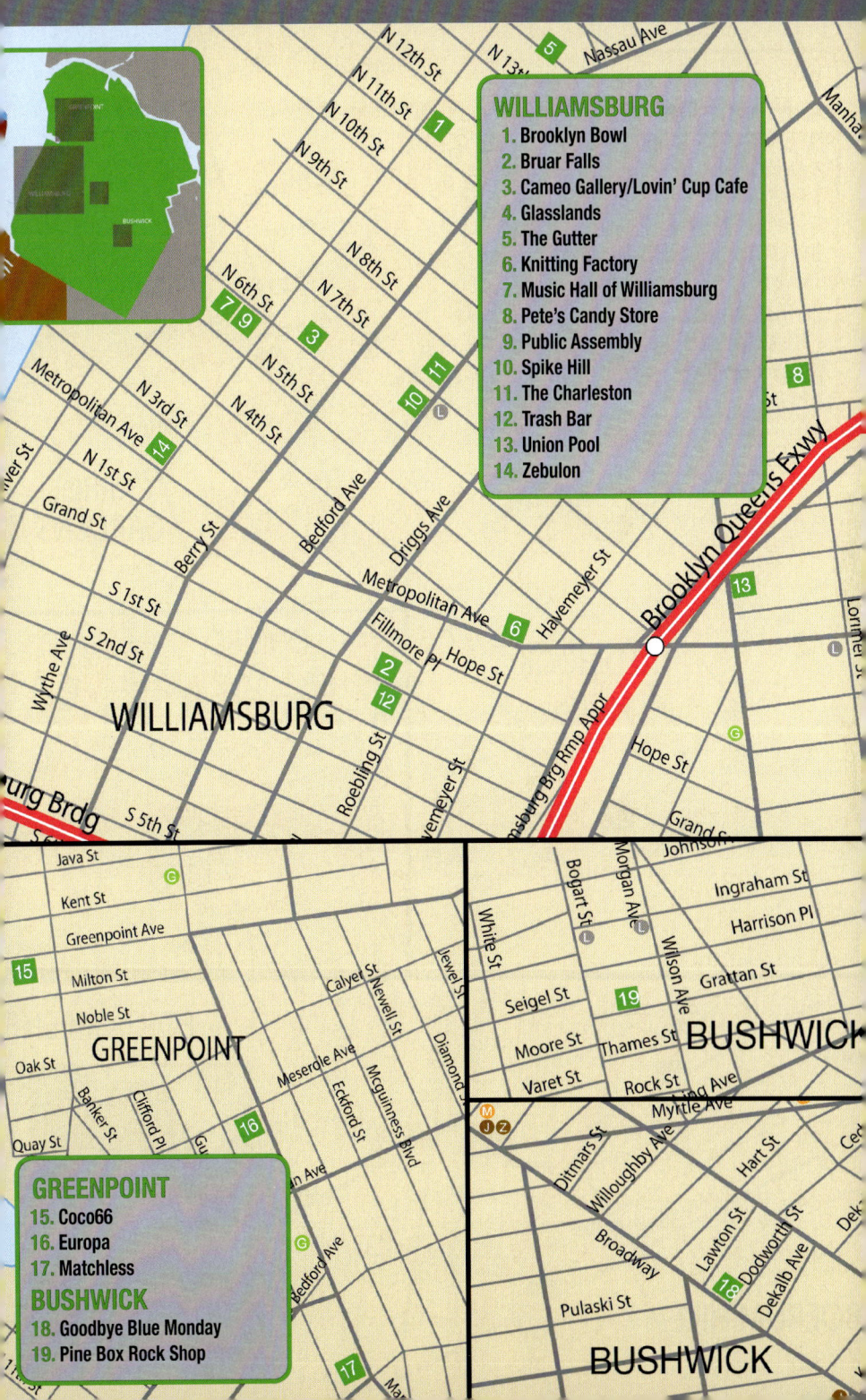

WILLIAMSBURG
1. Brooklyn Bowl
2. Bruar Falls
3. Cameo Gallery/Lovin' Cup Cafe
4. Glasslands
5. The Gutter
6. Knitting Factory
7. Music Hall of Williamsburg
8. Pete's Candy Store
9. Public Assembly
10. Spike Hill
11. The Charleston
12. Trash Bar
13. Union Pool
14. Zebulon

GREENPOINT
15. Coco66
16. Europa
17. Matchless

BUSHWICK
18. Goodbye Blue Monday
19. Pine Box Rock Shop

MAP 10: Brooklyn – Central

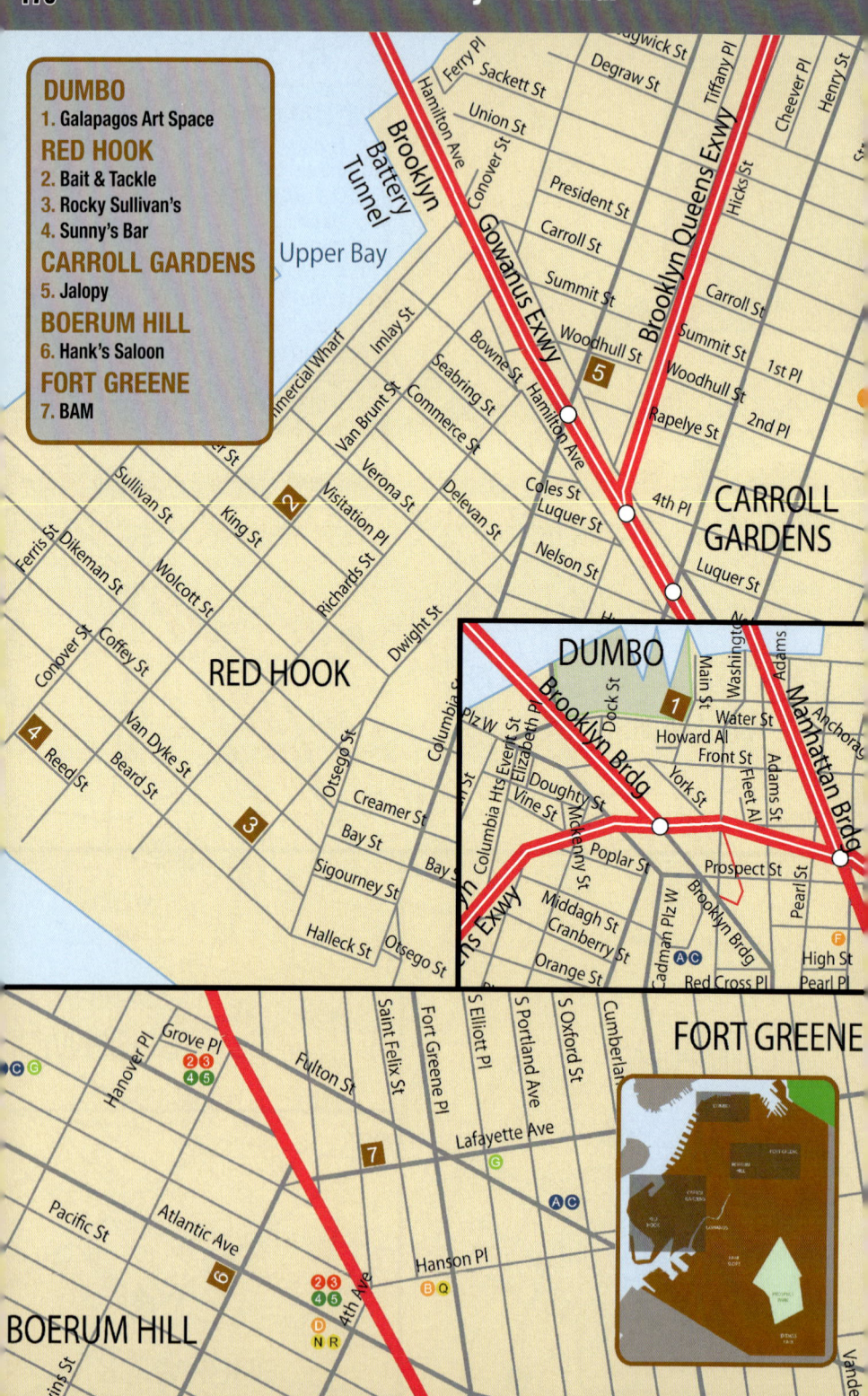

DUMBO
1. Galapagos Art Space

RED HOOK
2. Bait & Tackle
3. Rocky Sullivan's
4. Sunny's Bar

CARROLL GARDENS
5. Jalopy

BOERUM HILL
6. Hank's Saloon

FORT GREENE
7. BAM

MAP 11: Brooklyn – Central

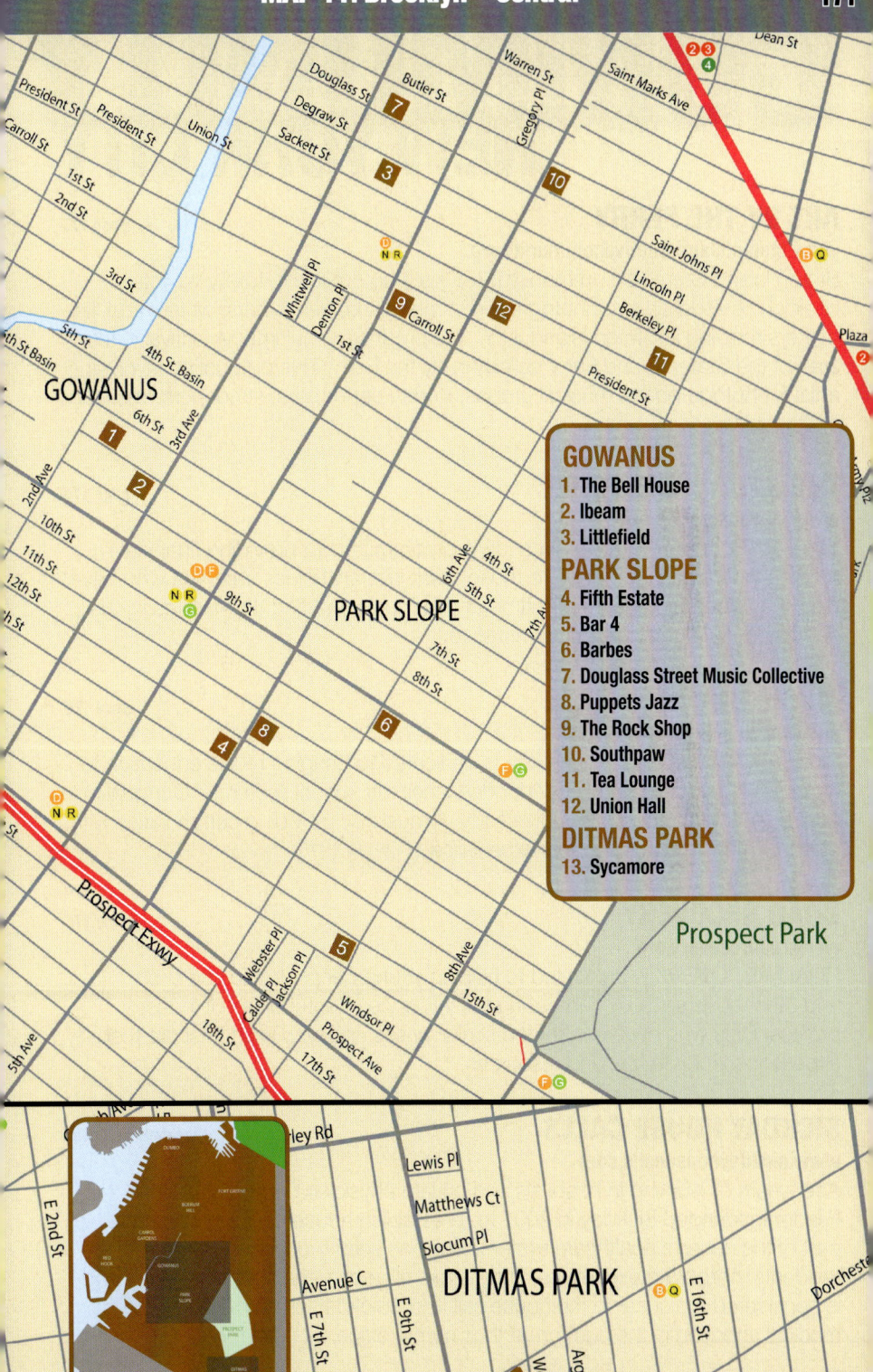

GOWANUS
1. The Bell House
2. Ibeam
3. Littlefield

PARK SLOPE
4. Fifth Estate
5. Bar 4
6. Barbes
7. Douglass Street Music Collective
8. Puppets Jazz
9. The Rock Shop
10. Southpaw
11. Tea Lounge
12. Union Hall

DITMAS PARK
13. Sycamore

COMMUNITY
NEW YORK CITY

ART BY THE FERRY
page 173
www.statenislandcreativecommunity.org
Staten Island Creative Community [SICC] is a not for profit, totally volunteer coalition of visual artists; photographers; musicians; performers; writers and film makers residing in Staten Island, N.Y. We produce a multimedia festival in the area of the Staten Island Ferry called Art by the Ferry. This production involves artists; photographers; musical groups; literary performers; street performers and crafts tables.

THE JAZZ FOUNDATION
page 174
www.jazzfoundation.org
The Jazz Foundation of America (JFA) is committed to providing financial, medical and legal assistance to those great jazz and blues veterans who have paid their dues by making a lifetime of this music and find themselves in crisis due to illness, age and/or circumstance.

MUSIC UNITES
page 175
www.musicunites.org
Music Unites, a 501(c)3 non-profit, is dedicated to bringing music education to underprivileged children in underfunded inner city school systems. Our goal is to connect people through the universality of music by providing communities with opportunities for a rich musical experience.

ROAD RECOVERY
page 176
www.roadrecovery.org
ROAD RECOVERY is dedicated to helping young people battle addiction and other adversities by harnessing the influence of entertainment industry professionals who have confronted similar crises and now wish to share their experience, knowledge, and resources.

SICKDAY HOUSE CALLS
Inside Back Cover
www.sickdayhousecalls.com
After years of working in hospitals and private physician practices, Naomi Friedman founded Sickday in 2001 to re-establish house calls as an integral part of the nation's healthcare system. She has seen thousands of New York's residents, corporate executives, and visitors alike over the past nine years, and is considered a pioneer in the house call field. Sickday clients receive prompt medical attention in the comfort of their home, office, or hotel room.

THE ARTISTS ARE COMING!

MUSICIANS • PERFORMING ARTISTS VISUAL ARTISTS

All Part of The

ART BY THE FERRY FESTIVAL

May 21 and 22, 2011 • 12 – 8 pm

at the Surrounding Area of the Staten Island Ferry Terminal in St. George, Staten Island

ART BY THE
ART MUSIC DANCE SPOKEN WORD CRAFTS PERFORMANCE

A Wonderful Time for All!
Admission is **FREE**

For info please visit:
www.statenislandcreativecommunity.org

scc
STATEN ISLAND CREATIVE COMMUNITY

JAZZ FOUNDATION OF AMERICA

SAVING JAZZ AND BLUES...ONE MUSICIAN AT A TIME.

"When I had congestive heart failure and couldn't work, the Jazz Foundation paid my mortgage for several months and saved my home. Thank God for those people!"
– Freddie Hubbard

"The Jazz Foundation helps us to Live."
– Abbey Lincoln

"When I broke my hip, the Jazz Foundation saved my home, made mortgage payments when I had to cancel my tours, and even visited me in the hospital. I don't know what I would have done without them."
– Odetta

For 22 years the JAZZ FOUNDATION OF AMERICA has been dedicated to saving the homes and lives of elder jazz and blues musicians in crisis. We assist in over 1,600 emergency cases a year including hundreds of New Orleans musicians and their children still recovering from Katrina.

Whatever the need is, we don't just fix the problem, we heal it with love.

www.jazzfoundation.org

MUSIC EMPOWERS
MUSIC INSPIRES
M**US**IC UNITES

WITH MUSIC A CHILD CAN DO ANYTHING.

Music Unites is a 501(c)3 non-profit organization dedicated to supporting emerging and established artists and bringing music education to students in underfunded inner city school systems. Visit www.musicunites.org to learn more about how you can help inspire the next generation of musicians.

ROAD RECOVERY®

HELPING YOUNG PEOPLE BATTLE ADDICTION AND OTHER ADVERSITIES,
by harnessing the influence of entertainment industry professionals who have confronted similar crises and now wish to share their experience, resources and knowledge with a community of like-minded young people.

MUSIC WITHOUT DRUGS...

PERFORMANCE WORKSHOPS PROGRAM

Servicing at-risk youth in recovery and/or adolescents facing adversities who are receiving services from independent treatment providers or attending residential educational treatment facilities.

Road Recovery's program empowers young people to face their struggles collectively as a group, and helps them develop comprehensive life skills by creating, planning, and presenting live-concert events.

for More Info:
Contact@RoadRecovery.org

www.RoadRecovery.org

Road Recovery is a New York City based 501(c)3 non-profit organization established in 1998.
**Road Recovery is NOT a substance abuse / mental health / medical treatment provider.

Partners & Friends

BMI
www.bmi.com   Inside Front Cover

17TH STREET PHOTO
www.17photo.com
AUDIO-TECHNICA   **178**
SKULLCANDY   **179**

ARCADIA MEDIA
www.arcadiamedia.com   **180**

ARLENE'S GROCERY
www.arlenesgrocery.net   **181**

BROOKLYN BOWL
www.brooklynbowl.com   **182**

PINE BOX ROCK SHOP
www.pineboxrockshop.com   **183**

TC ELECTRONIC & TC HELICON
www.tcelectronic.com   **184**
www.tc-helicon.com   **185**

GERM MUSIC
www.germmusic.com   **186**

audio-technica

available at:
17th Street Photo
33 West 17th Street
New York, NY 10011
www.17photo.com
800-664-1971 | 212-366-9870

EXPERIENCE MORE
.: FLEXIBILITY :.

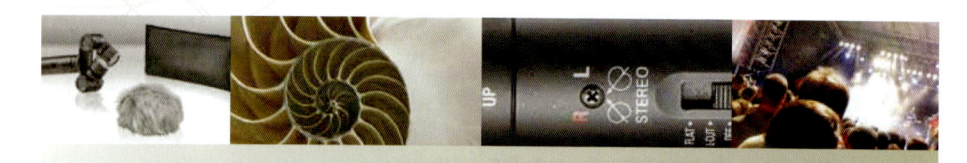

Audio-Technica makes life-like audio acquisition easy with the remarkable AT2022 X/Y Stereo Microphone. Two unidirectional condenser capsules pivot to allow for narrow (90°) or wide (120°) stereo operation. The capsules also fold flat for easy storage. The AT2022 delivers more realism, more flexibility, more for your investment. Wherever your passion for audio takes you, experience more. audio-technica.com

FEATURES
- X/Y stereo microphone with unique pivoting electret condenser capsules for ultimate flexibility
- Battery operation allows use with most recording devices
- Switchable low-frequency roll-off minimizes pickup of unwanted low-frequency noise
- User-selectable 90° or 120° stereo operation for narrow or wide pickup patterns
- Ideal for general stereo recording and field sound capture
- Included fuzzy windscreen offers excellent wind protection

audio-technica
always listening

Skullcandy

available at:
17th Street Photo
33 West 17th Street
New York, NY 10011
www.17photo.com
800-664-1971 | 212-366-9870

Roc Nation Aviator w/Mic (Brown/Gold)
S6AVCM-090

Skullcrushers DJ Subwoofer Stereo Headphones (Rasta)
S6SKCZ058

Hesh Full Size Headphones Shattered Blue
S6HECZ079

Lowrider SC Headphones (Blue)
S5LWCZ-035

Lowrider SC Headphones (Purple/Black)
S5LWCZ-043

Full Metal Jacket Ear Bud Headphones w/Mic (Chrome)
S2FMCY015

Ink'd Ear Bud Stereo Headphones - Blue
S2INCZ035

50/50 Ear Bud Stereo Headphones W/Mic/Volume/Track Control - Black
S2FFCM003

179

ARCADIA
NEW MEDIA SERVICES

ARCADIAMEDIA.COM   973.338.0575

ARLENE'S GROCERY

YOUR Quality PLACE SINCE 1995!

95 STANTON STREET NYC

ROCK • ALT • INDIE • OLD SCHOOL • NEW SCHOOL • LOWER EAST SIDE • NEW YORK CITY

95 STANTON ST. L.E.S., NYC
1 BLOCK SOUTH OF HOUSTON

LOOK! AT THESE AMAZING SPECIALS!

CLIP & SAVE

DON'T FORGET! the BUTCHER BAR
FREE ADMISSION 5 NIGHTS A WEEK!

EVERY SINGLE MONDAY NIGHT at 10 PM!
ROCK AND ROLL **KARAOKE**
FREE FEATURING A LIVE BAND!
May cause feelings of awesomeness. Use as directed

with AMAZING! LIVE MUSIC
7 NIGHTS A WEEK!
See details below for admission prices

SOCIAL MEDIA BLOWOUT!
25¢ WORTH OF FUN! JOIN US ON
facebook
www.facebook.com/arlenesgrocery

GIVE US YOUR 2 cents!
twitter
twitter.com/arlenesgrocery

WHILE SUPPLIES LAST!
myspace a place for friends
www.myspace.com/arlenesgrocery

21+ ALWAYS!
MONDAY: FREE ENTRY! • TUESDAY–THURSDAY $8 • FRIDAY & SATURDAY $10 • SUNDAY $8

95 STANTON ST., NY, NY 10002 • 212.358.1633 • WWW.ARLENESGROCERY.NET

DESIGN: WWW.JOHNBERGDAHL.COM

ZAGAT®

BEST
NYC MUSIC VENUE

BEST
NYC BOWLING ALLEY

BEST
BROOKLYN VENUE

New York City
Nightlife
2010/11

61 WYTHE AVE • BROOKLYN, NY 11211
718.963.3369 • BROOKLYNBOWL.COM

BROOKLYN BOWL

PINE BOX ROCK SHOP

12 Grattan St.
Brooklyn, NY 11206
718-366-6311
www.pineboxrockshop.com

live local music

art exhibits

weekly karaoke

pub trivia

Happy Hour 7 days a week 'til 8pm:
$1 OFF all Drafts and $3 Wells

DIRECTIONS: L to Morgan Ave, walk 1 block South **HOURS:** Open at 4pm Mon-Fri, 2pm Sat-Sun

Large Selection of Craft Ales and Lagers

Kick Ass Bloody Mary's, Pickle Backs, Seasonal Cocktails

183

toneprint

Our awesome new line of stompbox beauties don't only look and sound the part, they also sport a super cool new technology called TonePrint. TonePrint allows you to download custom tunings made by your favourite guitarists, easy, fast and free using a simple USB connection. A veritable who's who in guitar are on board and ready to give you their custom TonePrints. Forget emulation, let's talk collaboration!

Corona	Hall of Fame	Shaker	Flashback	Vortex	Dark Matter	MojoMojo
Chorus	Reverb	Vibrato	Delay	Flanger	Distortion	Overdrive

*Currently, five pedals support TonePrints: Flashback Delay, Hall of Fame Reverb, Corona Chorus, Vortex Flanger and Shaker Vibrato.

tcelectronic.com/toneprint-the-concept

tc electronic

184

You're only a step away from **perfect vocal tone**

With your talent and TC-Helicon vocal effects, you can take complete control of your vocal sound with ease. Simply plug in your mic and get those chart-topping vocal sounds you listen to everyday – live – with our VoiceTone Singles line of affordable effect pedals for singers.

It's your voice. Use it.

www.voicetonesingles.com

TC·HELICON

EQ & Dynamics | HardTune | Doubling | Reverb

Germ Music is the exclusive multimedia content provider for FirstLive.

PAST & PRESENT CLIENTS:
LES SAVY FAV (SOUND ENGINEER)
ANGELIQUE KIDJO (SOUND ENGINEER)
BRAZILIAN GIRLS (TOUR MANAGER)
ELIZABETH & THE CATAPULT
　(SOUND ENGINEER)
MLB.com
GIBSON
AMNESTY INTERNATIONAL
NPR
HIGHLINE BALLROOM
LEVI'S/SUBROSA
AIDS FOR AIDS
iCLIPS
COOPER SQUARE HOTEL
ARLENES GROCERY STUDIO
SONG DIVISION
FRENCH AMERICAN
　CULTURAL EXCHANGE
THE BROOK
LIVESTREAM
STRIKE 3 FOUNDATION
ARTS BY THE FERRY
ARCADIA
FRAMEWORKS MEDIA
BERMAN ARTS
HELEN MILLS THEATER
CULTURE CATCH
JOHN LENNON EDUCATION TOUR BUS
MOVEON.ORG
DIGITAL CLUB NETWORK
BUDWEISER TRUE MUSIC
MIXED BAG RADIO
AT&T BLUEROOM

CLIENT RECORDINGS (LIVE):
Duncan Sheik (Culture Catch)
Vanessa Carlton (Culture Catch)
Bob Weir & Ratdog (Culture Catch)
Sheryl Crow (MLB.com)
Peter Frampton (MLB.com)
Train (MLB.com)
Hoobastank (MLB.com)
Five for Fighting (MLB.com)
Dierks Bently (MLB.com)
Derek Trucks (MLB.com)
Jason Lytle (NPR/Epitaph)
Tragedy (Bowery Ballroom)
Little Death (Mercury Lounge)
Pool Parties 2008 & 2008
(TV on the Radio, MGMT,
Ghostland Observatory, Oakley
Hall, Band of Horses, Man, Man,
Super Chunk, many more)
CMJ Gibson Showcase 2007-09:
(Deer Hunter, Ben Lee, Tim
Easton, Earl Greyhound,
Locksley, The Hold Steady,
Ted Leo, Toby Lightman, Wes
Hutchinson, XX, Peter Bjorn and
John, many more)
SXSW Gibson Showcase 2006:
(Girl in a Coma, Dengue Fever,
Red Walls, Joan Jett, many more)
Mixed Bag Radio Sessions:
(New York Dolls, Katie Melua,
Goat, Janove Ottesen, Amy
Speace, Rhett Miller, Everclear)
Lonestar (AT&T Blue Room)

GERM RECORDINGS (LIVE):
SOULIVE
THE STROKES
THE PLEASURE UNIT
(JALEEL OF TV ON THE RADIO/
TORBITT OF CHIN CHIN)
THE EL CONQUISTADORES
(SAM ENDICOTT OF THE BRAVERY)
SUGARMAN 3
CHRIS BARRON
CROWN JEWELS
(STEVE CONTE OF NEW YORK DOLLS)
SATANICIDE
LOS AMIGOS INVISIBLES
LES SANS CULOTTES
DAREDIABLO
MARK GEARY
LESION
THE PIT BROTHERS BAND
SEX SLAVES
STAND
JULIA DARLING
MICHAEL BRUNNOCK
ANDREW VLADECK
TADANOTION
AKIM FUNK BUDDHA
THE ROOFTOP
MARTIN LUTHER
DANA FUCHS
DIGITAL CLUB NETWORK:
THE WORLD INFERNO FRIENDSHIP
SOCIETY, SAM BISBEE, CANYON,
JOHN STEPHENS (JOHN LEGEND),
WANDA JACKSON, CORDERO

We specialize in live sound, live recording, audio and video production services for live events and online media. AND, we are artist-friendly, nonprofit friendly, and will always work with your budget!

GERM MUSIC

www.germmusic.com
germ music | danny@germmusic.com | 347-531-6372

REFERENCES

92YTribeca
Thompson, Michele. Director, 92YTribeca. In discussion with the author and FirstLive. August & October 2010. • "92YTribeca." 92YTribeca. Accessed October 30, 2010. 92YTribeca.org.

Canal Room
Linial, Marcus. Co-owner, Canal Room. In interview by Danny Garcia. Digital recording, April 2010. • "Canal Room." Canal Room. Accessed October 30, 2010. http://www.canalroom.com.

City Winery
Dorf, Michael. Owner, City Winery. In interview by Emily Niewendorp and Danny Garcia. Digital recording, July 2010. • "One On 1: Michael Dorf Headlines Personal Venue." NY1. Accessed July 27, 2010. http://www.ny1.com.

Don Hill's
Hill, Don. Owner, Don Hill's. In interview by Emily Niewendorp and Danny Garcia. Digital recording, May 2010. • Camp, Nicki. Previous Booker & Co-owner, Don Hill's. In interview by Emily Niewendorp. Digital recording, May 2010. • "Don Hill's – NYC." Don Hill's. Accessed July 2010. http://www.donhills.com. • Slenske, Michael. "Nur Khan's New Don Hill's." Interview Magazine. August 5, 2010. http://www.interviewmagazine.com.

Jazz Gallery
Steinglass, Deborah. Executive Director, The Jazz Gallery. In discussion with the author. September 2010. • "Jazz Gallery." The Jazz Gallery. Accessed October 30, 2010. http://jazzgallery.org.

SOB's
Gold, Larry. Owner, SOB's. In discussion with the author. April 2010. • "SOB's Home of Universal Music." SOB's. Accessed October 30, 2010. http://www.sobs.com.

Ace of Clubs
"Ace of Clubs." Ace of Clubs. Accessed October 30, 2010. http://www.aceofclubsnyc.com.

Bowery Poetry Club
O'Keeffe Aptowicz, Cristin. Words in Your Face: A Guided Tour Through Twenty Years of the New York City Poetry Slam. New York: Soft Skull Press, 2008. • Lucero, Eliel. Production Manager, Bowery Poetry Club. In interview by Emily Niewendorp. Digital recording, June 2010. • Holman, Bob. Owner, Bowery Poetry Club. In discussion with Bill Nevins. September 2010. • "Bowery Poetry Club." Bowery Poetry Club. Accessed July, 2010. http://www.bowerypoetry.com.

Fontana's
Fowler, Deannie. Co-owner, Fontana's. In e-mail message to the author. May 13, 2010. • "Fontana's New York City." Fontana's. Accessed October 30, 2010. http://www.fontanasnyc.com.

Santos Party House
W.K., Andrew. Co-owner, Santos Party House. In discussion with the author. May 2010. • "Santos Party House." Santos Party House. Accessed October 30, 2010. http://www.santospartyhouse.com.

Arlene's Grocery
Burke, Dermot. Co-owner, Arlene's Grocery. Interview by Emily Niewendorp and Danny Garcia. Digital recording, February 2010. • Comasky, Owen. Previous Booking Agent, Arlene's Grocery. In interview by Emily Niewendorp and Danny Garcia. Digital recording, February 2010. • "Arlene's Grocery." Arlene's Grocery. Accessed November 2009. http://www.arlenesgrocery.net.

The Bowery Ballroom
Bango, Frank. General Manager, The Bowery Ballroom. In discussion with the author. July 2010. • Benson, Kyle. Patron, The Bowery Ballroom. In email message to Emily Niewendorp. October 2010. • "The Bowery Ballroom—Live music in New York, NY." Bowery Presents. Accessed July 2010. http://www.boweryballroom.com.

Cakeshop
"Cakeshop." Cakeshop. Accessed June 2010. http://cake-shop.com.

The Delancey
Marco. Sound Engineer, The Delancey. In discussion with the author. July 2010. • "The Delancey Bar & Nightclub." The Delancey. Accessed August 2010. http://www.thedelancey.com.

Fat Baby
Rob. Owner, Fat Baby. Interview by Emily Niewendorp. Digital recording, March, 2010. • "Fat Baby." Fat Baby. Accessed May 2010. http://www.fatbabynyc.com.

The Living Room
"The Living Room." The Living Room. Accessed May 2010. www.livingroomny.com.

The Local 269
Jules. Bartender, The Local 269. In discussion with the author. October 2010. • "The Local 269." The Local 269. Accessed October 2010. http://thelocal269.com.

Mehanata
Martinez, Rachel. Previous Booking Agent, Mehanata. In discussion with the author. April 2010. • "Mehanata—The Bulgarian Bar." Mehanata Bulgarian Bar. Assessed October 2010. http://www.mehanata.com.

Mercury Lounge
"The Mercury Lounge, Live Music in NYC." The Mercury Lounge. Accessed October www.mercuryloungenyc.com. • "Mercury Lounge." Wikipedia, The Free Dictionary. Accessed November 5, 2010. http://en.wikipedia.org.

National Underground
"The National Underground." National Underground. Accessed November 2010. http://www.thenationalunderground.com.

Parkside Lounge
Lee, Christopher. Co-owner, Parkside Lounge. In discussion with the author. May 2010. • MacCarthy, Andrew. Musician, Band of Outsiders. In discussion with the author. May 2010. • "Parkside Lounge." Parkside Lounge. Accessed August 2010. http://www.parksidelounge.net.

Pianos
Carlo. General Manager, Pianos. Interview by Emily Niewendorp. Digital recording, May 2010. • "Pianos NYC." Pianos. Accessed July 2010. http://www.pianosnyc.com.

Rockwood Music Hall
"Rockwood Music Hall." Rockwood Music Hall. Accessed September 2010. http://www.rockwoodmusichall.com.

Banjo Jim's
Bell, Bill. Bartender, Banjo Jim's. In discussion with the author. August, 2010. • Zwier-Croce, Lisa. Owner, Banjo Jim's. In discussion with the author. August 2010. • "Banjo Jim's." Banjo Jim's. Accessed August 2010. http://www.banjojims.com.

The Bowery Electric
Malin, Jesse. Co-owner, The Bowery Electric. Interview by Emily Niewendorp and Danny Garcia. Digital recording, May 2010. • "The Bowery Electric." The Bowery Electric. Accessed June 2010. http://www.theboweryelectric.com.

Dominion
Ogden, Sam. Sound Engineer, Dominion. In discussion with the author. February 2011. • "Dominion NY." Dominion NY Theater & Lounge. Accessed February 2011. http://www.dominionny.com.

Lakeside Lounge
Amble, Eric. Co-owner, Lakeside. In discussion with the author. May 2010. • "Lakeside Lounge." Lakeside Lounge. Accessed August 2010. www.lakesidelounge.com.

Lit Lounge
"Lit Lounge." Lit Lounge. Accessed August 2010. http://www.litloungenyc.com.

Joe's Pub
Thake, Shanta. Director, Joe's Pub. Interview by Emily Niewendorp. Digital recording, November 2009. • "The Public Theater." Wikipedia, The Free Encyclopedia. Accessed March 30, 2010. http://en.wikipedia.org. • "Joseph Papp." Wikipedia, The Free Encyclopedia. Accessed March 30, 2010. http://en.wikipedia.org. • "Joe's Pub." Joe's Pub. Accessed November 2009. http://www.joespub.com.

Jules
Jerome. Bartender, Jules. In discussion with the author. July 2010.• Ryan, Patrick. Musician, Jules. In discussion with the author. July 2010. • Schumer, Fran. "Jules's Caesar." New York Magazine. 26, no. 18 (1993): 81. http://books.google.com. • "Jules Bistro." Forgeois-Group. Accessed July 18, 2010. http://forgeois-group.com.

Nublu
Ersahin, Ilhan. Owner, Nublu. In discussion with the author. June 2010. • "Nublu." Nublu. Accessed November 1, 2010. http://www.nublu.net.

Nuyorican Poets Cafe
Gallant, Daniel. Executive Director, Nuyorican Poets Cafe. In discussion with the author. August 2010. • "Nuyorican Poets Cafe." Nuyorican Poets Cafe. Accessed September 2010. http://www.nuyorican.org.

Sidewalk Cafe
Krieger, Ben. Booking Agent, Sidewalk Cafe. In discussion with the author. May 2010. • "Lach." Wikipedia, The Free Encyclopedia. Accessed October 2010. http://en.wikipedia.org. • "Music at the Sidewalk Cafe." Sidewalk Cafe. Accessed August 2010. http://www.sidewalkmusic.net.

Webster Hall/The Studio at Webster Hall
Silmser, Trevor. Co-founder, The Studio. In discussion with the author. July 2010. • Trevor Morello, Trevor. Marketing Director, Webster Hall. In discussion with the author. October 2010. • Lane, Rawb. Bartender, Webster Hall. In discussion with the author. October 2010. • "Webster Hall New York City." Webster Hall. Accessed November 1, 2010. http://www.websterhall.com.

Bar Next Door
Mazza, Peter. Booking Agent, Bar Next Door. In e-mail correspondence with FirstLive. October 2010. • "La Lanterna Caffe." Bar Next Door. Accessed October 2010. http://lalanternacaffe.com.

The Bitter End
Block, Emma. Musician, Bitter End. In discussion with the author. June 2010. • Rizzo, Paul. Owner and Manager, Bitter End. In discussion with the author. June 2010. • "The Bitter End." Sonic Bids. Accessed June, 2010. http://www.sonicbids.com. • "The Bitter End." The Bitter End. Accessed June 2010. http://www.bitterend.com.

Blue Note
Bensusan, Steve. Owner, Blue Note. Interview by Emily Niewendorp. Digital recording, November 2009. • "Blue Note Jazz Club." Blue Note. Accessed June 2010. http://www.bluenote.net.

Cafe Wha?
"Cafe Wha?." Cafe Wha?. Accessed August 2010. http://cafewha.com.

Groove
"Club Groove NYC." Groove. Accessed August 2010. http://www.clubgroovenyc.com.

Kenny's Castaways
Kenny, Maria. Owner, Kenny's Castaways. In discussion with the author. August 2010. • "Friday Night Fever, The Slide / Kenny's Castaways." The Bowery Boys, New York City History. Accessed September 2010. http://theboweryboys.blogspot.com. • "Kenny's Castaways." Kenny's Castaways. Accessed October 2010. http://www.kennyscastaways.com.

Le Poisson Rouge
Handler, David. Owner, Le Poisson Rouge. Interview by Jason Siegel. Digital recording, April 2010. • "Le Poisson Rouge." Le Poisson Rouge. Accessed July 2010. http://lepoissonrouge.com.

Sullivan Hall
Schnee, Howie. Co-owner, Sullivan Hall. Interview by Emily Niewendorp. Digital recording, March 2010. • "CEG." Creative Entertainment Group. Accessed April 2010. http://cegmusic.com. • "Sullivan Hall." Sullivan Hall. Accessed April 2010. http://www.sullivanhallnyc.com.

Red Lion
Ann. Manager, Red Lion. In discussion with the author. July 2010. • "The Red Lion." The Red Lion. Accessed June 2010. http://www.redlionnyc.com.

Terra Blues
Powers, Michael. Musician, Terra Blues. In discussion with the author. July 2010. • Aldort, Gabriel. Bartender, Terra Blues. In discussion with the author. July 2010. • "Terra Blues." Terra Blues. Accessed June 2010. http://www.terrablues.com.

Village Underground
"Folk music." Wikipedia, The Free Encyclopedia. Accessed August 2010. http://en.wikipedia.org. • "Gerde's Folk City." Wikipedia, The Free Encyclopedia. Accessed August 2010. http://en.wikipedia.org. • "Village Underground." Village Underground. Accessed June 2010. www.thevillageunderground.com.

Village Vanguard
"The Village Vanguard." Village Vanguard. Accessed February 2011. http://www.villagevanguard.com. • "The Village Vanguard: A Hallowed Basement." NPR Music. http://www.npr.org. • "After 70 Years, The Village Vanguard Is Still in the Jazz Swing." The Wall Street Journal Online. Accessed February 2011. http://online.wsj.com. • Eisenman, Jed. Musician, Village Vanguard. Interview by Danny Garcia. Digital recording, February 2011. • Cuadrado, Alexis. Musician, Village Vanguard. In discussion with the author. February 2011.

Zinc Bar
K, Alex. Co-owner, Zinc Bar. In discussion with the author. August 2010. • K, Kristina. Co-owner, Zinc Bar. In email message to FirstLive. October 2010. • "Zinc Bar." Zinc Bar. Accessed August 2010. http://www.zincbar.com.

55 Bar
Kirby, Mark. Manager, 55 Bar. In discussion with the author. August 2010. • "The 55 Bar." 55 Bar. Accessed July 2010. http://www.55bar.com.

Caffe Vivaldi
Ansari, Ishrat. Owner, Caffe Vivaldi. Interview by author and FirstLive. February 2011. • "Caffe Vivaldi." Caffe Vivaldi. Accessed February 2011. www.caffevivaldi.com.

Cornelia Street Cafe
Hirsch, Robin. Co-owner, Cornelia Street Cafe. In discussion with the author. July 2010. • Chang, Tom. Jazz Booking Agent, Cornelia Street Cafe. In e-mail correspondence with the author. July 2010. • "The Cornelia Street Cafe—2010." The Cornelia Street Cafe. Accessed July 2010. http://www.corneliastreetcafe.com.

Fat Cat
Yellowhair, Sheldon. Sound Engineer, Fat Cat. In discussion with the author. July 2010. • Lapore, Joseph. Musician, Fat Cat. In discussion with the author. July 2010. • Ben. Manager, Fat Cat. In discussion with the author. July 2010. • Brown, Charlie. Doorman, Fat Cat. In discussion with the author. July 2010. • "Fat Cat NYC." Fat Cat. Accessed July 2010. http://www.fatcatmusic.org.

Garage
Briones, Juan Carlos. Manager, Garage. In discussion with the author. July 2010. • "Garage Restaurant." Garage Restaurant & Cafe. Accessed July 2010. http://www.garagerest.com.

Smalls
Wilner, Spike. Owner, Smalls. Interview by Rachel Antonio. Digital recording, August 2010. • "Smalls Jazz Club." Smalls. Accessed August 2010. http://www.smallsjazzclub.com.

169 Bar
"169 Bar NYC." 169 Bar. Accessed October 2010. http://www.169barnyc.com.

ABC No Rio
"ABC No Rio." ABC No Rio. Accessed October 2010. http://www.abcnorio.org

Arthur's Tavern
"Arthur's Tavern New York City." Arthur's Tavern. Accessed October 2010. http://www.arthurstavernnyc.com.

B Flat
"Authentic Bar B Flat." B Flat. Accessed October 2010. http://www.bflat.info.

Crash Mansion
"Crash Mansion." Crash Mansion. Accessed October 2010. http://www.crashmansion.com.

Duplex
"Duplex." Duplex. Accessed October 2010. http://www.theduplex.com.

Marie's Crisis
"How to Sing at Marie's Crisis in New York City." Tripwolf, Worldwide Travel Guide. Accessed October 21, 2010. http://www.tripwolf.com. • "A Paine in the…" Forgotten NY Street Scenes. Accessed October 21, 2010. http://www.forgotten-ny.com. • "Marie's Crisis: Piano Bar with History." Newbie NYC. Accessed October 21, 2010. http://newbienyc.blogspot.com.

Otto's Shrunken Head
"Otto's Shrunken Head." Otto's Shrunken Head. Accessed October 2010. http://www.ottosshrunkenhead.com.

R Bar
"R Bar New York." R Bar. Accessed October 2010. http://www.rbarnyc.com.

Tammany Hall
"Tammany Hall." Tammany Hall. Accessed February 2011. http://www.tammanyhalllive.com.

Jazz Standard
Abramson, Seth. Booking Agent, Jazz Standard. Interview by Emily Niewendorp. Digital recording, July 2010. • "Welcome to Blue Smoke and Jazz Standard." Jazz Standard. Accessed July 2010. http://www.jazzstandard.com.

Rodeo Bar
Pollak, Mitch. Owner, Rodeo Bar. Interview by Emily Niewendorp. Digital recording, April 2010. • Grace, Jack. Booking Agent, Rodeo Bar. Interview by Emily Niewendorp. Digital recording, March 2010. • "Rodeo Bar." Rodeo Bar. Accessed April 2010. http://www.rodeobar.com.

The Kitano
Moratti, Gino. Manager, Kitano Hotel. In discussion with the author. October 2010. • "The Kitano." The Kitano. Accessed October 2010. http://kitano.com.

Highline Ballroom
"Highline Ballroom." Highline Ballroom. Accessed July 2010. http://www.highlineballroom.com.

Hill Country
Glosserman, Mark. Founder & CEO, Hill Country. Interview by Emily Niewendorp. Digital recording, March 2010. • Grace, Jack. Booking Agent, Hill Country. Interview by Emily Niewendorp. Digital recording, March 2010. • "Hill Country—Texas Barbecue, Market—Music to your mouth." Hill Country. Accessed April 2010. http://www.hillcountryny.com.

Madison Square Garden
"Madison Square Garden." Wikipedia, The Free Encyclopedia. Accessed October 2010. http://en.wikipedia.org. • "Stage Theatre." Wikipedia, The Free Encyclopedia. Accessed October 2010. http://en.wikipedia.org. • "MSG." Madison Square Garden. Accessed October 2010. http://www.msg.com.

Manhattan Center
Bennison, Sarah-Jane. Director of Sales & Marketing, Manhattan Center. In discussion with the author, Emily Niewendorp and Danny Garcia. October 2010. • "Welcome to Manhattan Center." Manhattan Center. Accessed November 1, 2010. http://www.mcstudios.com.

Carnegie Hall
"Carnegie Hall." Carnegie Hall. Accessed November 2010. http://www.carnegiehall.org.

Miles' Cafe
Hoshikawa, Ayumi. Co-owner, Miles' Cafe. In discussion with the author. February 2011. • "Miles' Cafe Jazz Club New York." Miles' Cafe. Accessed February 2011. www.milescafe.com/ny.

Radio City Music Hall
"Radio City Music Hall." Radio City Music Hall. Accessed August 2010. http://www.radiocity.com.

Terminal 5
"Terminal 5 NYC." The Bowery Presents. Accessed November 1, 2010. http://terminal5nyc.com.

Tutuma Social Club
Matwey, Santina. Owner, Tutuma Social Club. In discussion with the author. February 2011. • "Tutuma Social Club." Tututuma Social Club. Accessed February 2011. http://www.tutumasocialclub.com.

B.B. King
"B.B. King Blue Club & Grill." B.B. King. Accessed November 1, 2010. http://www.bbkingblues.com.

Best Buy Theater
Young, Jeff. Production Manager, Best Buy Theater. Interview by Daniel Morrow. Digital recording, August 2010. • "Best Buy Theater." Best Buy Theater. Accessed September 2010. http://bestbuytheater.com.

Don't Tell Mama
Pace, Jennifer. Bartender, Don't Tell Mama. In discussion with the author. February 2011. Myer, Sydney. Booking Director, Don't Tell Mama. In discussion with the author. February 2011. • "Don't Tell Mama." Don't Tell Mama. Accessed February 2011. http://www.donttellmamanyc.com.

Iridium
Sturm, Ron. General Manager, Iridium. In discussion with the author. August 2010. • "Iridium Jazz Club New York City." Iridium. Accessed September 2010. http://www.iridiumjazzclub.com.

Swing 46
"Swing 46 Jazz and Supper Club." Swing 46. Accessed November 1, 2010. http://www.swing46.com.

Birdland
"Birdland, The Jazz Corner of the World!" Birdland. Accessed November 2010. http://birdlandjazz.com.

Guantanamera
"Guantanamera." Guantanamera. Accessed October 2010. http://guantanameranyc.com.

Hard Rock Cafe
"Hard Rock." Hard Rock Cafe. Accessed October 2010. http://www.hardrock.com.

Hiro Ballroom
"Hiro Ballroom at the Maritime Hotel." Hiro Ballroom. Accessed October 2010. http://www.hiroballroom.com.

Gramercy Theater
"Gramercy Theater." Wikipedia, The Free Dictionary. Accessed October 2010. http://en.wikipedia.org.

Irving Plaza
"Rethinking, Irving Plaza Keeps Its Maiden Name." The New York Times. May 31, 2010. http://www.nytimes.com. • "Union Square Loses Its Old Residencies." The New York Times. June 18, 1916. http://query.nytimes.com.

Roseland Ballroom
"Roseland Ballroom." Roseland Ballroom. Accessed February 2011. http://www.roselandballroom.com.

Beacon Theater
"New Beacon Shines Brightly." Traditional Building. Accessed October 19, 2010. http://www.traditional-building.com. • "Beacon Theatre (New York City)." Wikipedia, The Free Encyclopedia. Accessed October 19, 2010. http://en.wikipedia.org. • "Beacon Theater New York City." Beacon Theater. Accessed October 2010. http://www.beacontheatre.com.

Dizzy's Club Coca Cola
"Dizzy's Club Coca-Cola." Jazz at Lincoln Center Accessed September 2010. http://www.jalc.org. Chassagne, Roland. Manager, Dizzy's Club Coca-Cola. Interview by Robbie Gonzalez. Transcription of digital recording, August 2010.

P&G Bar
Chahalis, Steve. Owner, P&G. In discussion with author and Danny Garcia. July 2010. • "New York P&G Bar." P&G Cafe. Accessed July 2010. http://pandgbar.com.

Smoke
"Smoke Jazz & Supper Club-Lounge." Smoke Jazz & Supper Club-Lounge. Accessed November 2, 2010. http://www.smokejazz.com.

Bar East
Wilson, Paul. Owner, Bar East. Interview by Emily Niewendorp. Digital recording, February 2010. • "Bar East Ale House." Bar East. Accessed March 2001. http://bareast.com.

Camaradas
Plaza, Orlando. Co-owner, Camaradas el Barrio. Interview by Emily Niewendorp and Danny Garcia. Digital recording, October 2009. • "Camaradas el Barrio." Camaradas el Barrio. Accessed November 2010. http://www.camaradaselbarrio.com.

FB Lounge
Ayala, Roberto. Co-owner, FB Lounge. In discussion with the author. February 2011. • "FB Lounge - LA FONDA BORICUA." FB Lounge. Accessed February 2011. http://www.fondaboricua.com/NS_lounge.php.

Showmans
Mona. Co-owner, Showmans. In discussion with the author. February 2011.

Shrine
Abdel. Owner, Shrine. In discussion with the author. August 2010. • "Shrine Bar & Restaurant." Shrine. Accessed November 2, 2010. http://www.shrinenyc.com.

St. Nicks Jazz Pub
"St. Nick's Jazz Pub NYC." St. Nick's Jazz Pub. Accessed August 24, 2010. http://www.stnicksjazzpub.net. • "New York City Nightlife, St. Nick's Pub." The New York Times. Accessed August 20, 2010. http://travel.nytimes.com.

Apollo
"The Apollo Theater." The Apollo Theater. Accessed October 2010. http://www.apollotheater.org.

Cleopatra's Needle
"Cleopatra's Needle." Cleopatra's Needle. Accessed October 2010. http://www.cleopatrasneedleny.com. • "Cleopatra's Needle." All About Jazz. Accessed October 2010. http://www.allaboutjazz.com.

Cotton Club
"Cotton Club." Cotton Club. Accessed October 2010. http://www.cottonclub-newyork.com.

Feinstein's
"Feinstein's at Loews Regency." Feinstein's. Accessed October 2010. http://feinsteinsattheregency.com.

Lenox Lounge
"Lenox Lounge, Historic Harlem Jazz Club." Lenox Lounge. Accessed October 2010. http://www.lenoxlounge.com.

Brooklyn Bowl
Shapiro, Peter. Co-owner, Brooklyn Bowl. Interview by Emily Niewendorp. Digital recording, July 2010. • "Brooklyn Bowl." Brooklyn Bowl. Accessed July 2010. http://www.brooklynbowl.com.

Bruar Falls
Bodor, Andy. Owner, Bruar Falls. In e-mail correspondence with the author. April 2010. • "Bruar Falls." Bruar Falls. Accessed May 2010. http://bruarfalls.com. • "Fall of Bruar." Wikipedia, The Free Encyclopedia. Accessed June 2010. http://en.wikipedia.org. • "Fall of Bruar." Undiscovered Scotland, the Ultimate Online Guide. Accessed October 2010. http://www.undiscoveredscotland.co.uk.

Glasslands
Rosenthal, Jake. Booker, Glasslands. In e-mail message to the author. July 2010. • "Glasslands Gallery." The Glasslands Gallery. Accessed July 2010. http://glasslands.blogspot.com. • Galeani, Theresa. Patron, Glasslands. In discussion with FirstLive. October 2010. • Ley, Abbey. Assistant, Glasslands. In e-mail correspondence with FirstLive. November 2010.

Knitting Factory
Vishawadia, Shay. Previous Vice President of East Coast Operations, Knitting Factory. Interview by Emily Niewendorp. Digital recording, October 2010. • "Knitting Factory—Brooklyn." Knitting Factory Entertainment. Accessed October 2010. http://bk.knittingfactory.com.

Music Hall of Williamsburg
"Northsix." Wikipedia, The Free Encyclopeida. Accessed October 22, 2010. http://en.wikipedia.org. • "The Bowery Presents." Bowery Presents. Accessed October 22, 2010. http://www.bowerypresents.com. • "Neither Arenas Nor Dives, New Clubs Hope to Succeed With More Style." The New York Times. Accessed July 9, 2010. http://www.nytimes.com.

Lovin Cup Cafe & Cameo Gallery
Sampson, Nicolette. Co-owner, Lovin' Cup Cafe and Cameo Gallery. In e-mail correspondence with the author. April 2010.

Pete's Candy Store
Andy. Owner, Pete's Candy Store. Interview by Emily Niewendorp. Digital recording, May 2010. • "Pete's Candy Store." Pete's Candy Store. Accessed May 2010. http://www.petescandystore.com.

Public Assembly
Hsu, Lisa. Employee, Public Assembly. In discussion with the author. July 2010. • "Public Assembly NYC." Public Assembly. Accessed July 2010. http://www.publicassemblynyc.com.

Spike Hill
Schmitz, Joe. Co-owner, Spike Hill. In discussion with the author. July 2010. • "Spike Hill." Spike Hill. Accessed July 2010. http://www.spikehill.com.

The Trash Bar
Pierce, Aaron. Owner, Trash Bar. Interview by Emily Niewendorp. Digital recording, May 2010. • "Welcome to The Trash Bar." The Trash Bar. Accessed June 2010. http://www.thetrashbar.com.

Union Pool
Sage. Manager, Union Pool. Interview by Emily Niewendorp. Digital recording, May 2010. • "Union Pool." Union Pool. Accessed May 2010. http://unionpool.blogspot.com.

Zebulon
Soubiran, Jef. Co-owner, Zebulon. In discussion with the author, June 2010. • "Zebulon Cafe Concert." Zebulon. Accessed June 2010. http://www.zebuloncafeconcert.com.

Matchless
"Bar Matchless." Bar Matchless. Accessed September 2010. http://www.barmatchless.com.

Goodbye Blue Monday
Trimboli, Steve. Owner, Goodbye Blue Monday. Interview by Sarah Oramas. Digital recording, May 2010. • "Goodbye Blue Monday." Goodbye Blue Monday. Accessed September 2010. http://www.goodbyeblue.com/wordpress.

Pine Box Rock Shop
Rush, Jeff & Heather. Owners, Pine Box Rock Shop. Interview by Emily Niewendorp. Digital Recording, January 2011. • "Welcome to Pine Box Rock Shop." Pine Box Rock Shop. Accessed January 2011. http://www.pineboxrockshop.com.

The Charleston
"The Charleston." Free Williamsburg. Accessed October 2010. http://www.freewilliamsburg.com.

Coco66
"Coco66." Coco66. Accessed October 2010. http://www.coco66.com.

Europa
"Europa Night Club." Europa Night Club. Accessed October 2010. http://www.europaclub.com.

Tommy's Tavern
"Tommy's Tavern." Tommy's Tavern. Accessed October 2010. http://www.tommystavern.com.

The Gutter
"The Gutter — Brooklyn, NY." The Gutter. Accessed February 2011. http://www.thegutterbrooklyn.com.

Barbes
Olivier. Owner, Barbés. Interview by Emily Niewendorp. Digital recording, October 2010. • "Barbes." Barbes. Accessed June 2010. http://www.barbesbrooklyn.com.

Puppets Jazz Bar
Fagin, Martin. Co-owner, Puppets Jazz. In discussion with Emily Niewendorp. October 2010. • "Puppets Jazz Bar." Puppets Jazz Bar. Accessed July 2010. http://www.puppetsjazz.com.

The Rock Shop
Hakenrider, Brian. General Manager, The Rock Shop. In discussion with the author. September 2010. • "The Rock Shop NY." The Rock Shop. Accessed October 2010. http://therockshopny.com.

Southpaw
Palms, Michael. Co-owner, Southpaw. Interview by Emily Niewendorp. Digital recording, October 2009. • "Southpaw Music & Entertainment." Southpaw. Accessed November 2009. http://spsounds.com.

Union Hall
Avanzato, Kevin. General Manager, Union Hall. Interview by Emily Niewendorp. Digital recording, June 2010. • "Union Hall." Union Hall. Accessed July 2010. www.unionhallny.com.

The Bell House
Dunsmoor, Heather. Booking Agent, The Bell House. In e-mail correspondence with the author. October 2010. • Orozco, Julio. Manager, The Bell House. In discussion with FirstLive. September 2010. • "The Bell House." The Bell House. Accessed October 2010. http://www.thebellhouseny.com.

Littlefield
Julie. Co-owner, Littlefield. Interview by Emily Niewendorp. Digital recording, June 2010. • "Littlefield NYC." Littlefield. Accessed June 2010. http://www.littlefieldnyc.com.

Bait & Tackle
Erin. Former Bartender, Bait & Tackle. In discussion with the author. October 2010. • "Red Hook Bait & Tackle." Bait & Tackle. Accessed October 2010. http://www.redhookbaitandtackle.com.

Jalopy
Wiley, Lynette. Co-owner, Jalopy. In discussion with the author. October 2010. • Steve. Student, Jalopy. In discussion with the author. October 2010. • "Jalopy Theater and School of Music." Jalopy. Accessed October 2010. http://www.jalopy.biz.

Rocky Sullivan's
"Rocky Sullivan's of Red Hook." Rocky Sullivan's. Accessed October 2010. http://www.rockysullivans.com.

Sunny's Bar
Sultan, Tim. Bartender, Sunny's. In discussion with the author, October 2010. • Balzano, Tone. Co-owner, Sunny's. In discussion with the author, October 2010. • "Sunny's Bar." Sunny's. Accessed October 2010. http://www.sunnysredhook.com.

Galapagos Art Space
Elmes, Robert. Director, Galapagos Art Space. Interview by Emily Niewendorp. Digital recording, October 21. 2010. • "Galapagos Art Space." Galapagos Art Space. Accessed October 2010. http://www.galapagosartspace.com. • "Black Monday." Wikipedia, The Free Encyclopedia. Accessed October 25, 2010. http://en.wikipedia.org.

BAM
"BAM." Brooklyn Academy of Music. Accessed February 2011. http://www.bam.org.

Douglass Street Music Collective
"Douglass Street Music Collective." Douglass Street Music Collective. Accessed February 2011. http://295douglass.org.

Fifth Estate
"The Fifth Estate open where Royale was in Brooklyn." Brooklyn Vegan. Accessed February 2011. http://www.brooklynvegan.com.

Hank's Saloon
John. Owner, Hank's Saloon. In discussion with the author. October 2010. • "Hank's Rootin' Tootin' Saloon." Hank's Saloon. Accessed October 2010. http://www.hankssaloon.com.

Ibeam
"Ibeam." Ibeam. Accessed February 2011. http://ibeambrooklyn.com.

Sycamore
"Sycamore Bar & Flowershop." Sycamore. Accessed February 2011. http://www.sycamorebrooklyn.com.

Tea Lounge
"Tea Lounge." Tea Lounge. Accessed February 2011. http://www.tealoungeny.com.

INTERVIEW QUOTES

There is a type of physical energy that's generated when lots of people are in a space together. It's a feeling of electricity—you can sense it in your bones and brain. When all those people focus that energy on something like music, dancing, or any shared pleasure, there is truly enough power generated to change the world.
Andrew W.K. (Musician & Co-owner of Santos Partyhouse)

I love feeling connected to musicians. There is something very intimate about that and it's very personal. You can be in a room of 1,000 people, but if you feel connected to the music, that's an amazing feeling.
Julie (Co-owner of Littlefield)

To see talented musicians up on stage just doing their thing and being in the zone is one of the best things…I'm not into the singer with backing tracks and it's all clean and crisp. It's just like sitting at home and closing your eyes and listening to a record. Boring. Boring as hell. You want to be there and compare the live sound to their record sound, see how they interact with the crowd. It's such a powerful experience.
Shay Vishawadia (Former Vice President at Knitting Factory)

"The live setting is the most primitive, dynamic pull that I have to music. I've been passionate about music my whole life, but I think to see music live, and to see it realized in a live setting, right before your very eyes, is something that's particularly captivating. You really don't know what's going to happen next… I mean, it's like life.
David Handler (Co-owner of Le Poisson Rouge)

The purpose of this place is to have an open stage. I've seen people develop in the years I've been here and it's really great to see that happen.
Steve Trimboli (Owner of Goodbye Blue Monday)

A lot of times you hear a record…you can tell there is some production going on. And when you hear the live music, fresh, coming at you—the musicians are just playing and its a super practiced song or maybe its not, maybe they are improvising and you get all that fresh, good stuff at a moment's notice…I like that raw sound.
Kevin Avanzato (Manager of Union Hall)

Personally, it [music] is the most beautiful form of expression. What I like is that it is very immediate and it just appears. It goes from [the musician] to the listener… it is very direct. It's unique.
Carlo Vutera (Singer & Co-owner of former venue Rose Live Music)

It's an experience you can't duplicate anywhere else. Music is the universal language. We all feel beats, we all dance; it brings us all together on a universal level. I love that about it. It's crazy. If you think about it, the old saying, 'sex, drugs and rock 'n' roll,' those are the three things that affect all human beings know matter where you are from. I think that's why they all go hand in hand. The Three Musketeers, you know.
Paul Wilson (Owner of Bar East)

Music brings people together. It's sorta like church.
Christopher Lee (Co-owner of Parkside)

I saw my first Grateful Dead concert when I was 11 so I was just hooked on live music. I saw 30 Dead shows before I even got to college. In college I saw a ton of Dead shows. A lot of people actually in the music business got interested in it because of the Grateful Dead and the whole mystique of the live experience.
Howie Schnee (Co-owner of Sullivan Hall)

Live music has been my whole life. I played in bands, I promoted clubs, I booked bands…It goes on and on, it never stops, you know. It's the one thing that is constant. It might change, the style, what's popular, what's big, but there will always be live music. Music is good. It's good for the soul.
Nicki Camp (Former Co-Owner and Booker of Don Hills)

There is a completely different way people engage with music when they are listening to it live… there is different appreciation for the musicians themselves and the stage presence and the charisma and the lighting…a much more vibrant experience…
Mark Glosserman (Founder & CEO of Hill Country)

"The FirstLive Guide is a musician's and fan's best resource for finding the best music venues in New York! It answers all your questions and gives honest and thorough reviews."
Jean Shepherd, Navegante

"First Live Guide is a sorely needed resource for people at all ends of the music table…from bands, to fans, to industry folks and beyond. Everything you need to know about any music venue in NYC is right at your fingertips…pretty damn cool and very handy!!!
Al Risi, ARMM

special thanks to

all **firstlive contributors**, especially the following for going the extra mile—daniel morrow, mark osborne, john bergdahl, monica garcia, bill nevins, rachel martinez, heather mccown, erika omundson, eric reichbaum, stephanie summerville, theresa galeani, jason siegel, benjamin ramos, jasmine-lovell-smith, jasna boudard; **all venues**—owners, bookers, sound engineers, and staff for allowing us into your home; **our advertisers**, without you this print would not be available—allan strand, kevin alexander, tobias weltzer, andrew witte, laura davidson, all at tc electronic and tc helicon; paul ghamar at 17th street photo, audio technica microphones and skullcandy; dan and jan at arcadia; jeff and heather at pine box rock shop, samantha cox at bmi; kate dussault, naomi friedman, al risi with sickday house calls; peter and charlie at brooklyn bowl for your extraordinary hospitality; **community organizations** for allowing us to help; joyce and ira goldstein, wendy oxenhorn and joe petrucelli at jazz foundation, michelle at music unites, jack at road recovery; **also,** an enormous thanks to arlenes grocery—dermot burke, tony caffrey, julia darling, germ music studio engineers—ariel temptidaz, soo youn lee, simone janae, lenny bernardez, and all at arlenes; mike mullin, jim felber, shanon chaiken, dino virella, tyler barth, john maier, and all at blue microphones; navegante, dave brooks, jon darling, the greyrace, night fevers, didi gutman, la realit, mark unthank, justin hosek, greg godon, tara gore, eric milliken, ron wolf and all at pro audio star, jinsoo kim, dave pit, naj, april, meridith, vintage fillings, david vadim, jesse carbone; frank and don at corporate forms and printing; karl at neko printing, david weiss at sonic scoop; darren & all at livestream, andres levin, our friends who have pre-purchased the guide and **lastly,** we thank the local, regional, interntional booksellers, music and retail stores who choose to carry the guide; all the folks who purchase a copy of FirstLive.

FIRSTLIVE

www.firstliveguide.com